Lecture Notes in Computer Science 13490

The series Lecture Notes in Computer Science (LNCS), including its subseries Lecture Notes in Artificial Intelligence (LNAI) and Lecture Notes in Bioinformatics (LNBI), has established itself as a medium for the publication of new developments in computer science and information technology research, teaching, and education.

LNCS enjoys close cooperation with the computer science R & D community, the series counts many renowned academics among its volume editors and paper authors, and collaborates with prestigious societies. Its mission is to serve this international community by providing an invaluable service, mainly focused on the publication of conference and workshop proceedings and postproceedings. LNCS commenced publication in 1973.

Antonio Cerone

Editor

Formal Methods for an Informal World

ICTAC 2021 Summer School
Virtual Event, Astana, Kazakhstan, September 1–7, 2021
Tutorial Lectures

 Springer

Editor
Antonio Cerone (iD)
Nazarbayev University
Astana, Kazakhstan

ISSN 0302-9743   ISSN 1611-3349 (electronic)
Lecture Notes in Computer Science
ISBN 978-3-031-43677-2   ISBN 978-3-031-43678-9 (eBook)
https://doi.org/10.1007/978-3-031-43678-9

This Springer imprint is published by the registered company Springer Nature Switzerland AG
The registered company address is: Gewerbestrasse 11, 6330 Cham, Switzerland

Paper in this product is recyclable.

*To the memories of Alimzhan Khairullin,
Nurdaulet Nauryzbay, Mark Sterling, Abylay
Toktassyn and Kuanishbek Toktassyn.*

Preface

This volume includes the articles that were written following the ICTAC School 2021 on "Formal Methods for an Informal World", which was held on 1–7 September 2021, before the 18th International Colloquium on Theoretical Aspects of Computing (ICTAC 2021). The school was supposed to be held in Astana (at the time called Nur-Sultan), Kazakhstan, organized by Nazarbayev University. However, due to the persisting pandemic situation, it was a fully virtual event.

The school addressed the use of formal methods at various levels of rigour in various application domains: human-computer interaction, cognitive science, business process management, robotics and healthcare. The emphasis of the school was on practical applications in which formal methods provide unambiguous descriptions of the real world that facilitate understanding and formal and informal analysis.

The target audience consisted of graduate students, young researchers and industrial practitioners, from both computer science and other fields that make use of computational methods. In fact, in addition to a number of computer scientists and roboticists, the audience also included social scientists from cognitive science and business and practitioners from the healthcare and automotive industries.

This volume comprises six articles. Alan Dix (Swansea University) provides an introduction to the use of formal methods in human-computer interaction, with a special focus on the specification and analysis of physical and digital aspects. Antonio Cerone (Nazarbayev University) completes the introduction to the use of formal methods in human-computer interaction by focusing on cognitive aspects and their impact on human thinking and behaviour. Wil van der Aalst (RWTH Aachen University) uses formal methods as a descriptive tool to carry out process mining, moving the focus of process mining towards a holistic setting that involves objects of multiple types interacting through shared activities. Ana Cavalcanti et al. (University of York) introduce a robotic technology that supports a model-based approach to development with domain-specific notations in line with those accepted by roboticists and that can be used for verification by model checking or theorem proving. Finally, the two contributions on Research and Industry are by Benjamin Tyler (Nazarbayev University), who presents his experiences in the development and promotion of formal methods tools for public and government agencies while working for a small business before joining Nazarbayev University, and Padmanabhan Krishnan (Oracle Labs, Brisbane), who presents the key features of some of the security analysis tools developed at Oracle Labs and shows how these tools can be integrated at different phases of the software development life-cycle. Each of the six contributions was reviewed by at least one reviewer.

The school featured two further lectures that are not accompanied by contributions in this volume. Peter Csalba Ölveczky (University of Oslo) presented "A Tutorial to

Maude" and Juliana Küster Filipe Bowles (University of St Andrews) presented "Applying Formal Methods in Healthcare". School materials, including the videos of some lectures, are available at the ICTAC 2021 website: http://ictac2021.github.io.

We would like to thank the school lecturers for accepting our invitations and all the attendees, including several Professors and Master and PhD students from NU School of Engineering and Digital Sciences, for their active participation in the school. We are also grateful to the reviewers of the contributions included in this volume for their professional work. Finally, we would like to thank Martin Leucker and the other members of the ICTAC Steering Committee for their encouragement and support, the regional publicity chairs for their excellent job in advertising the event, and the members of the local organizing committee, Benjamin Tyler and Adnan Yazici.

Unfortunately, 2021 was a tragic year for Nazarbayev University, especially for the Department of Computer Science. In May, three NU senior students, Alimzhan Khairullin, Nurdaulet Nauryzbay and Abylay Toktassyn, along with Abylay's younger brother Kuanyshbek, lost their lives in a hiking accident. In December, Computer Science Professor Mark Sterling passed away after a long illness. This volume is dedicated to their memories.

March 2023   Antonio Cerone

Organization

Local Organizers

Antonio Cerone (Editor)	Nazarbayev University, Kazakhstan
Benjamin Tyler	Nazarbayev University, Kazakhstan
Adnan Yazici	Nazarbayev University, Kazakhstan

Volume Contributors

Wil van der Aalst	RWTH Aachen University, Germany
Ziggy Attala	University of York, UK
James Baxter	University of York, UK
Ana Cavalcanti	University of York, UK
Antonio Cerone	Nazarbayev University, Kazakhstan
Alan Dix	Swansea University, UK
Padmanabhan Krishnan	Oracle Labs, Brisbane, Australia
Alvaro Miyazawa	University of York, UK
Pedro Ribeiro	University of York, UK
Benjamin Tyler	Nazarbayev University, Kazakhstan

Reviewers

Antonio Cerone	Nazarbayev University, Kazakhstan
Emmanuel Helm	Upper Austria University of Applied Sciences, Austria
Padmanabhan Krishnan	Oracle Labs, Brisbane, Australia
Graham Pluck	Chulalongkorn University, Thailand
Sanjiva Prasad	Indian Institute of Technology, India
Augusto Sampaio	Federal University of Pernambuco, Brazil
Benjamin Tyler	Nazarbayev University, Kazakhstan
Olzhas Zhangeldinov	Nazarbayev University, Kazakhstan

Other Lecturers

Juliana Küster Filipe Bowles   University of St Andrews, UK
Peter Csalba Ölveczky   University of Oslo, Norway

ICTAC Steering Committee

Frank de Boer   CWI, The Netherlands
Martin Leucker (Chair)   University of Lübeck, Germany
Zhiming Liu   Southwest University, China
Tobias Nipkow   Technical University of Munich, Germany
Augusto Sampaio   Federal University of Pernambuco, Brazil
Natarajan Shankar   SRI International, USA
Tarmo Uustalu   Tallinn University of Technology, Estonia

Regional Publicity Chairs

Stefan Gruner   University of Pretoria, South Africa
Kazuhiro Ogata   Japan Advanced Institute of Science and
                                   Technology, Japan
Elaine Pimentel   Federal University of Rio Grande do Norte, Brazil
Riadh Robbana   INSAT, Carthage University, Tunisia
Nikolay Shilov   Innopolis University, Russia

Sponsor

School of Engineering and Digital Science (SEDS), Nazarbayev University, Astana, Kazakhstan

Contents

Contents

Modelling Interactions: Digital and Physical

Alan Dix[1,2(✉)] [iD]

[1] The Computational Foundry/Ffowndri Gyfrifiadol, Swansea University, Wales, UK
alan@hcibook.com
[2] Cardiff Metropolitan University, Wales, UK
https://alandix.com/academic/papers/LNCS-modellinginteractions-2023/

Abstract. The first part of this chapter gives a lightening introduction to the use of formal methods in human–computer interaction. This includes an overview of the kinds of models, and typical domains where techniques are currently applied. It then outlines some of the potential future directions for the field. The second part focuses on a specific area, the formal specification and analysis of systems that have both physical and digital aspects. This includes the use of physigrams, an extension of finite state networks for describing interactions with physical devices such as hand-held controllers. It also describes how formal analysis contributed to the design of an internet-enabled 'café open' sign – IoT in action!.

Keywords: human-computer interaction · formal methods · formal models · physigrams · IoT · physical-digital design

1 Introduction

This chapter offers an overview of formal modelling of human computer interaction, focused particularly on techniques to deal with the physical aspects of digital devices and when systems are deployed using IoT devices in the environment such as smart homes. The chapter is based on a tutorial the author delivered at the ICTAC summer school in September 2021 and draws on several chapters of "The Handbook of Formal Methods in Human-Computer Interaction" [30], which is the most recent definitive state-of-the art collection in the area.

The chapter falls into two main parts each comprising several sections.

The first part offers a lightening tour of formal modelling of interactive systems. This will include looking at different kinds of model and also gaps and challenges ahead. Section 2 will consider different kinds of model that can be used for interactive systems and examples of a few. Then in Sect. 3 we look forward towards the gaps and challenges in current knowledge, creating a road map for the way that modelling can proceed in this area.

A. Cerone (Ed.): ICTAC 2021, LNCS 13490, pp. 1–29, 2023.
https://doi.org/10.1007/978-3-031-43678-9_1

The second part delves into two areas in greater detail, both of which are about the nature of physical interaction with interactive systems. Classic desktop applications have been modelled for many years and while the issues are not fully solved, they are well studied. Systems that involve physical interactions create additional challenges, but are essential given the way computation is becoming embedded into everyday objects and environments.

The first model in Sect. 5 uses physigrams, which offer a way to model the physical aspects of digital devices. The second model in Sect. 6 is focused more on IoT applications where we need to model a higher level of human activities within a sensor-rich environment.

2   Where We Are – Modelling Interactions

This section will present a brief overview of past and current state of formal modelling of user interactions, before we take a peek into what the future may hold in Sect. 3. For a more comprehensive view of the history and state of the art in the area see Chaps. 1 and 2 of "The Handbook of Formal Methods in Human-Computer Interaction" [30].

2.1   What to Model

When modelling human–computer interaction, the first question to ask is "what do we want to model?" There are obviously the *users* of the system, sometimes a single person, sometimes multiple people working together; then there is the *computer system* or application itself, and this is all set in the *wider context* in which they are operating, maybe an office environment, maybe at home, maybe in an urban environment, Let's look at these in turn:.

users – There are different aspects we can model of people using a system. We can look inside their heads and try and have some sort of *cognitive model* as they think about the task they are doing and the system they are using. Alternatively, we can look more at their external behaviour, using *task models* that capture the steps they take to do a job, whether this is a simple task such as making yourself a cup of coffee, or more complex, such as using the dictation facility in a word processor to write a book chapter.

computer system – We can look at the outside or the inside of the computer system too. From the outside, we can model its *behaviour*, the way in which it creates outputs in response to user inputs and possibly sometimes prompts the user through notifications. Alternatively we might want to create *architectural models* of the internal structure of the system. User interactions are actually hard to code well and so special abstractions and architectures have been developed over the years in order to help create effective user interfaces.

world or wider context – Furthermore, we may create a *domain model* of an office environment (documents, desks, workflows), transport system (cars, roads, traffic lights) or domestic environment (cooking, entertainment, family life). Modelling these contexts can help in the development or evaluation of systems to work within them.

In this chapter we are going to focus largely on models of the *computer system behaviour*, that is the external observable actions as it responds to or affects the user, although in Sect. 6 this will also include models of human behaviour.

Focusing on models of the systems external behaviour, there are three main kinds of model:

Dialogue models – Which consider the main states or modes, often represented by some form of network linked by user actions. The user actions could include a mouse click or keypress, or spoken instructions.

Full state specifications – Which build a model of the internal state of the system and how user actions change this. This is a little like computer code, but at a higher level, often expressed using sets and functions.

Abstract interaction models – Which use mathematical techniques to reason about generic properties of interactive systems.

The first two are used primarily to model a *specific system* under design, whereas the last is used to reason generally about a *whole class of systems*.

We will see a form of dialogue model in Sect. 5, when we discuss Physigrams, so in the rest of this section we'll look at examples of the second two kinds of model.

Fig. 1. Clock controls

2.2   Modelling of System State

The internal state of an application may be complex. For example, within a word processor, there will be some representation of the text itself, the cursor location, style definitions, the current state of search/replace, and much more. As a simpler example, we will consider an automobile car clock (Fig. 1), however the basic elements of the specification are similar:

– a specification of the **facets/variables** representing the state – for example, the text, cursor, current scroll location, etc.;
– any **constraints** on the possible values of the state, for example, that the cursor position must lie within the document;
– the **initial state** when the system is first started/installed, for example, an empty document;

- the way any externally visible **display** (or audible outputs) relate to the system state, for example, the text being displayed;
- the way each **user action** updates the system state, for example, typing a key inserts a character at the cursor location.

We'll see each of these in turn for the alarm clock.

As we can see in Fig. 1, the fascia of the car clock consists of:

- a time display at the top;
- a mode button below that is to used to cycle between setting hours, minutes and seconds;
- plus and minus buttons, which are used to increment or decrement the selected item.

---

state ────────────────────────────

hours: Nat, mins: Nat, secs: Nat   – all just numbers

selected: { 'NONE', 'HRS', 'MINS', 'SECS' }

hours < 24 ∧ mins < 60 ∧ secs < 60

initial state ────────────────────────

hours = 0, mins = 0, secs= 0

selected = 'NONE'

display ────────────────────────────

hours ":" mins ":" secs   *(with selected flashing)*

Fig. 2. Clock state

We first define the clock state variables (Fig. 2, top). This is expressed in a simplified variant of the Z notation [27]. We can see three facets for the hours, minutes and seconds respectively. Note this is an abstract representation; for example, in the code these might be represented as a single count of seconds since midnight. The purpose of the specification is not to mirror the code exactly, but to represent it in ways that are easiest to understand and reason about. The fourth facet of the state is labelled 'selected' and represents whether we are in editing mode for hours, minutes or seconds ('HRS', 'MIN', 'SECS' respectively), or simple time display ('NONE'). In the specification this is represented as a set of possible values, but in the code it may be a numeric code: 0, 1, 2, 3.

Below the state facets, separated by a thin line, we can see state constraints, which state that each of the time facets must lie within a legal range. One of the things one might choose to verify about the system is to prove that from any legal start state of the system each action results in a state that still satisfies the constraints.

In the middle of Fig. 2 we see the initial state of the system. In this case the time starts at zero, and the clock starts in time display mode.

So far, these are things you would have in any formal specification of a computer system. The last portion (Fig. 2, bottom), labelled 'display', is related specifically to the fact that it is a device for user interaction. This describes what is shown on the display of the clock depending on the current internal state. This allows one to discuss usability issues. For example, if there is no way to know what mode it is in, perhaps we should change the specification so that parts of the display to flash to show this.

```
increment (+) ─────────────────────────
│ if ( selected = 'NONE' )  do nothing
│
│ if ( selected = 'HRS' )
│     if ( hours < 23 )        hours' = hours+1
│     if ( hours = 23 )        hours' = 0
│
│ if ( selected = 'MINS' )
│     if ( mins< 59 )          mins' = mins+1
│     if ( mins= 59 )          mins' = 0
│
│ ...
```

Fig. 3. Clock actions

Having defined the state, we need to say how the possible user actions affect it. Recall there were three buttons: 'mode', '+' and '−'. We'll just look at one of these, the increment action '+'.

Figure 3 shows part of the specification of this. The first line says that if you press the plus button in the time display mode it does nothing. In some modelling notations this is not explicitly stated, but where possible it is worth explicitly saying when things do nothing, as these are often times when you want to give the user an indication that something is wrong. The rest of the specification is fairly obvious: if the current mode is 'HRS' then it will increment the hours, if it is 'MINS' it will increment the minutes, etc.

You may notice that when the hours hit the maximum, 23, it cycles round to zero. You could imagine specifying something different, perhaps a clock that maxed out at 23 rather than cycling. One of the reasons for writing a formal specification is that it allows you to have those discussions within the design team, or perhaps with a client or with users. You won't necessarily show them the formal specification itself, but it allows you to be clear about what the system is going to do. By carrying this over into discussions with others, there will be fewer surprises when the software is eventually built. Part of the value of modelling is it forces you to be precise. For example, when you increment at 59 min and it cycles back to zero, do the hours increment or not? In this specification the answer is no, but is that right? You are forced to *think about these decisions* at design time.

2.3   Abstract Interaction Models

Recall the third kind of system model, sometimes called abstract interaction models, deals with generic properties of a whole class of specific systems. Rather than modelling a particular word processor or a particular clock, you model an abstraction, for example, to analyse general issues of cursor behaviour in a paginated document, or how search 'next' should work at the end of a document. Because these models are more abstract it may be possible to produce a rigorous proof of something that is true for a large range of systems.

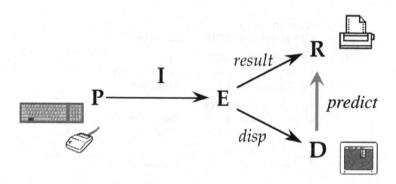

Fig. 4. PIE model and predictability

One of the earliest examples of an abstract interaction model is the PIE model (Fig. 4), which the author worked on extensively early in his career [4, 16]. The reason for the acronym is buried in history (!), but in brief terms:

P (*program*) is a set of possible user input sequences to system;
E (*effect*) is roughly the state (although slightly more abstract);
I (*interpretation*) is the function that says how any sequence of user inputs (P) gives rise to an effect (E).

In addition, in Fig. 4 we can see a function *result* that yields the eventual outcome, for example a printed document from a word processor; and a function *display*, that represents what the user can see on the screen or other perceived aspects of the system. As is evident, this could be applied to a wide range of office information systems.

One of the classes of issue that were of interest were related to the notion of WYSIWYG (what you see is what you get), and different forms of *predictability* property attempt to capture aspects of this. In the figure we can see a function *predict* from the display to the result. One of the simplest ways to capture a predictability property is to ask that the diagram commutes, that is:

$$\exists \, predict \in (D \rightarrow R) \; s.t. \; predict \circ display \; = \; result$$

Another class of property that is of interest are reachability properties; these relate to how you can get from one state to another. A particular example of this is *undo*, which happily has rather simple algebraic properties. The idea of undo is simple: if you do *any command* and then hit 'undo', you expect the system to revert to the state before the first command. In mathematical terms undo acts as a form of universal right inverse:

$$\forall c \in Commands: \ c \frown undo \ \sim \ null$$

Because this can be formulated this way it is possible to reason about undo algebraically. One of the questions about early undo systems was whether undo should be able to undo itself. That is whether the 'any command' includes undo itself. Some systems attempted to do this, that is to have undo undo undo! Each worked to some extent, but always had boundary cases where things were not perfect. The question was whether they didn't quite work right because they hadn't been implemented well or whether there was a more fundamental reason. In fact we were able to prove that it is *impossible* for undo to undo itself in this way, and the proof is actually quite simple. Indeed, if you think of it in terms of inverses and you know a little semi-group theory, you may already start to see why.

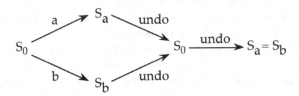

Fig. 5. Undo simple proof

Figure 5 is a diagrammatic representation of the proof. Imagine you start in state S_0 and then execute command a (perhaps press the 'a' key). This puts you into a new state, call it S_a. You then execute undo, which should take you back to exactly the same state you started in S_0. You now do undo again, which undoes the first undo taking you back into state S_a.

So far, so good. However, now lets imagine doing the same for a different command b. This is shown in the bottom arc of the diagram. Doing b puts into state S_b, undo takes us back to S_0 and then a second undo undoes the first undo giving state S_b.

This means that doing undo starting in state S_0 gives both S_a and S_b, so they must be identical. However, a and b were *arbitrary commands* and this was true for *any starting state* S_0, which means that the effect of every command must be identical. If we want undo to apply perfectly to itself, the system can have *at most two states*. Either there are precisely two states and every command (including undo) toggles between the two states, or just a single state were every command (including undo) does nothing.

That is we proved that for *any system* with a modicum of complexity (more than two states), it is *impossible* to have undo apply to itself in a uniform manner. In a system of more than two states, no matter how cleverly coded, there will always be cases when undo of undo is not quite the same as doing nothing. So, you don't have to keep on searching for something that satisfies this impossible property. If you want undo to be universal you have to regard it (and sometimes other commands such as redo) as belonging to a separate class of command.

This realisation led to the study of more complex types of undo, where there are special undoing commands, possible including redo. There are two main classes of undo you may encounter.

Flip undo where the system simply keeps track of one past state and 'undo' toggles between the current and previous state.

Stack undo (most common now) where you also have a redo button. Undo/redo navigate forward and backward through a stack of past states, but any normal command effectively throws away any actions beyond the current location.

In her PhD thesis [20], Roberta Mancini showed that if you want some fairly basic properties of undo/redo then these two are the *only* forms of undo that are possible. The proof used category theory and an abstraction called the 'cube' (Fig. 6) that described in formal terms the way that when you add undo commands to a system, the original system is in some way still 'there' inside [15]. This construction itself took inspiration from Sannella's early work on the semantics of extending modules with additional functionality [23].

The proof itself is quite complex. Category theory is fairly heavy maths, but also meant that the proof could make use of theorems relating to the uniqueness of initial and final categories. However, having once done this proof, we can say with certainty that these are the only sensible forms of undo, and that when implemented properly they will satisfy some strong but simple rules.

This is the strength of abstract models, and indeed mathematics in general. You may have to do a lot of work to establish a fundamental property, but once proved the result can be applied again and again.

Would that everything were that simple! Predictability properties tend to be far more complex. It is possible to write simple properties, such as the simple commutativity equation we saw earlier:

$$\exists\ predict \in (D \to R)\ s.t.\ predict \circ display\ =\ result$$

However, when you look at it in more detail, it does not say what you really want it to. There are two main problems:

Information – Functions that have similar mathematical properties may be very different for a human, for example, a function that shows a screen mirror image is equivalent from an information theoretic perspective, to one the right way round ... but not very readable.

Observation – The display of a device typically only shows a portion of the internal state. Demanding that the ultimate result is a function of the display means we cannot edit a document longer than a single short page!

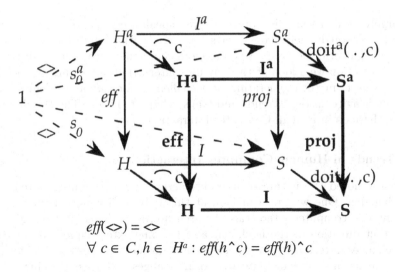

Fig. 6. Modelling more complex undo – the cube

In practice, we know that there is document above and below the portion we can see and what matters is (a) that we *can see it* when we want to through scrolling and (b) when we do changes the *impact of those changes* is evident in the current display. It is possible to create variants of the predictability properties that more faithfully capture these real-world requirements, but the resulting formulation becomes increasingly complex and hard to reason about.

2.4   Common Application Domains for Formal Methods

As is evident, there is a trade-off between the amount of effort creating and analysing a model and the results you get. It's not surprising therefore that the majority of areas where formal methods are currently used are safety critical domains such as aerospace and the nuclear industry.

There are other areas where formal methods would be valuable, but the costs cannot be justified. If you are writing, you do care if you accidentally lose the work you've been doing all afternoon, but no-one will die because of it. Similarly, if you misprogramme your central heating, you might be cold for a while when you get home, but that is all. If formal models could help prevent these things it would be good, but the cost-benefit ratio has to be radically different.

In the next section we will see a variety of challenges, but crucially we need ways of using formal methods that require *less expertise* and *less effort*.

3   Gaps and Challenges – The Future Is Formal!

The models we've looked at so far are largely about systems with buttons, pointers and screens – the traditional elements of a WIMP interface. The models are also largely user driven: click/press/or even speak a command and the system responds. Although there have always been applications and domains that do not fit this pattern, they are becoming more common or even the norm.

In this section we'll look at the way user-interactions are changing and then see how this is in turn generating new challenges for formal modelling. This will draw heavily on the "Trends and Gaps" chapter [17] of "The Handbook of Formal Methods in Human–Computer Interaction".

3.1 Trends in Human–Computer Interaction

As already noted the nature of user interactions with computer systems has been changing. One way we can look at this is by reviewing emerging topics in the human computer interaction literature. This offers insight into the current direction of the field, but also to some extent simply responds to recent changes in technology and society. In addition, if we wish to look forward further, we also need to look outwards, to the changes that are happening around us, and then ask how these will shape the needs for emerging human-computer interaction.

Changing User Interaction. In the early days of computers and indeed still in many work environments, it is the employer who chooses what computer systems should be used. This led to a focus of productivity and efficiency in HCI. As computation became domestic or personal this choice became an individual one: you decide what you do on your own phone, tablet or laptop. However, now this very ubiquity of computation means that many essential services assume access to computers: banking, air travel, even government health services. This has been a trend over many years, but accelerated by Covid. Digital access and digital literacy are no longer a matter of personal choice, but *essential* to be a fully active citizen in 21st century society.

Inclusive design has been a long standing goal of HCI, but the emerging digital citizenry means that dealing with a diversity of people takes centre stage: different ages, different social demographics, different physical, perceptual and mental abilities.

The rise of domestic and entertainment computing led the growth of user experience and personal values as a core part of HCI [21]. However, the embedding of computation in society means we are also needing to consider the larger ethical and social values implicitly embedded in the systems we use [31].

We are also seeing a greater variety of devices from smart phones to IoT (Internet of Things) devices in smart cities smart homes. Often these have some form of physical embodiment beyond a screen and a keyboard, but they may also be embedded in the environment. The term 'invisible computer' was used for many years as a term for various forms of ubiquitous computing research, but has now become a day-to-day reality. In a smart city you may simply be driving down the road or relaxing in a city square, but your presence is sensed and used to change aspects of the environment from traffic signals to digital signage.

Our personal systems also rely increasingly on notification-based interaction – instead of the system responding to your 'commands', you are expected to do what the system says. This may be a strong demand if you are a gig-worker, or may be more subtle as with social media, but the general trend is that the system is taking more of the initiative in human–computer interactions [13]. There have been worries for many years that these changes may have an impact on cognitive development [8] and more than ten years ago Gardner and Davies [19] described how different styles of app could either enable creativity or stifle it. Over more recent years it has become clear that 'digital natives' brought up on simplistic apps may in fact have problems when faced with workplace digital technology [2].

Of course, despite all of these changes, when you upload a photo to social media, or respond to a job request, the basics of HCI are still essential.

Changing Technology. In parallel, and often driving these changes in the use of technology, are changes in the nature of technology itself. Indeed many feel they are on a roller-coaster of technology change. We are now dealing not just with one device at a time, but often vast assemblies' devices, hundreds of embedded computers in a train carriage or new car, dozens of smart devices in the home, and many more embedded in urban environments. Reasoning about large numbers of simple devices is precisely something we struggle with as humans, but where formal methods excel.

Big data and associated AI is rarely out of the news. To some extent this is about data centres and back-end processing, but of course impacts users, whether it is used for recommendations on shopping sites or to guide diagnosis in health systems. As well as creating complexity and the need for explainable AI [5,11], this inevitable means that computer systems have more autonomy, from self-driving cars to notification-based systems described above. This is leading to substantial growth in the level of HCI research dedicated to human-AI interactions [12,22,24,25].

Changing Design and Development. Finally the nature of design and development is changing. The growth of maker/hacker culture and digital fabrication has made it possible to create rapid one-off prototypes of physical devices, with associated challenges for prototyping that combine physical and digital aspects [14,29]. It also opens up the potential for mass-customization of consumer devices whether by large-scale industry or by digital artisans [10]. However, if every device is unique, how can we ensure effective usability and enjoyable user experience? Traditional design is about a single uniform product, or small range of product variants – mass customisation requires that some aspects of design have to be embodied in rules that can be applied automatically during the generation of bespoke devices and interfaces.

Software production has also changed, with far greater reliance on agile methods and test-driven development. In some ways agile development reflects iterative methods of user experience and user interface design. However, it can also lead to quick fixes, that solve immediate problems but lack overall design integrity. This suggests an opportunity for formal models that can be executed as part of the automatic test suites that are an integral part of agile methods. Note these do not need to be perfect, but could be configured to produce warnings or red/amber/green indicators that can allow dedicated UX designers to prioritise human evaluation effort.

3.2 Challenges for Formal Models of Interaction

As we've looked at these trends for HCI, we have already noted ways in which formal models could contribute. In general, these trends and changes in user interaction generate research challenges for formalisation.

What Is Being Modelled. Who and what are the actors and entities involved in the systems we model? There are of course *people* and we can apply existing cognitive and task modelling techniques; however, the increasing diversity of people and settings may require modifications or enhancements. We have also seen that *physical objects and environments* are increasingly important so our models need to be able to take into account that you are holding your mobile phone in your hand, or sitting inside a semi–autonomous car. *Space and movement* are also important to model, maybe while driving the semi autonomous car through the traffic system, or as a smart house adjusts the temperature as its occupants move from room to room. Finally, *information* is clearly critical when considering areas such as privacy, big data or social media. We need to be able to explicitly reason about the ways users interact with or are the subjects of data capture, flows, and processing, if nothing else to ensure legal compliance [1,3,18].

What Level of Abstraction. We need to think about different levels of *granularity*, not just click-response models, but also the fine-grain interaction as you swipe, drag or experience haptic feedback, and the course-grain interaction as you use and reuse a social-media system over days, weeks and years. Both fine-grained interactions and also the passing of time remind us that we need to think about *continuity and temporal behaviour* beyond alternating action-response models. The semi-autonomous car moves continuously not in discrete steps, when you adjust the volume of music you *experience* continuity, even if the underlying system is digital. We may also need to consider *levels of generality* that lie between specific systems and totally abstract models, for example, the use of domain specific notations [28].

Who Is Doing the Modelling – When and Why. We can also ask questions about who is doing the modelling. Can we reduce the level of formal expertise needed so that UX designers without mathematical tools can use forms of prepackaged model in a similar way to structural models used by engineers. This is important in traditional safety-critical domains for formal methods such as aerospace where those with dual expertise in mathematical techniques and human-centred design are rare. However, as end-users configure and connect IoT devices in smart home they need to be able to understand the implications of the HCI design choices they are effectively making. In general, we need to be able to have formal models that require *less expertise*, and *less effort* to obtain *greater benefit*!

How. This all sounds pretty demanding. We need formal models for new kinds of system, but we also need to make our models easier to use and more accessible. This may require different *types of reasoning* ranging from hard mathematics to more check-box and audit algorithms. This is likely to include more *knowledge-rich reasoning*: formalism typically involves a small set of axioms however semi-automated reasoning can combine this with large data sets and world knowledge. This will undoubtedly require us to deal with *flexible levels of detail*, reasoning about fine details when we need to, but at other times taking a broader view. We will need to combine *multiple notations* to deal with different levels of granularity and abstraction: not simply choosing between generic or domain specific models, but being able to connect them. Looking forward to much more bespoke or consumer-configured systems, these models of good user-interaction need to be embodied in *generic systems or standards* so that highly expert knowledge can be effectively prepackaged and then applied by those without sophisticated levels of knowledge about HCI or formalism.

3.3 Focus for This Chapter

So having thought about where formal modelling of interactive systems is now and is changing, in the rest of this chapter we will dabble our toes in some of the outer edges. We will look at practical applications beyond the classic safety-critical domains such as the nuclear industry. They are going to be physical as well as digital and embody both varying levels of granularity and flexibility of level of detail. Crucially, we will consider methods where the users of the models do not need a mathematics degree.

4   Try It Yourself – Model Something Physical

Before moving on and looking at methods and models for physical systems, try for yourself a small exercise. This will help you to appreciate the complexity and to understand better the proposed solutions. Try not to peak forward in their chapter until you have finished for yourself!

4.1 The Exercise

For the exercise do the following:

1. Choose something with physical form. This could be a book, phone or even a pair of scissors or a rock.

2. If the device is digital or electronic turn it off or remove the battery (or imagine doing so). You need to look at the *physical* aspects of the device.
3. Try to produce a formal(ish) model of the physical thing. Don't overthink it, do whatever works whether it is diagrams, bullet points, or equations.

Your model can explore different things.

What it is like? How it looks and feels, visual features, heavy or light, smooth or rough.

What can you do with it? Press buttons, open/close a lid, see yourself reflected on a (blank) screen.

If the device is digital, try to write about the physical actions themselves, not what you would expect them to do when it is working. For a phone there may be a small button that goes in and bounces out – describe this, try to forget that it is the power button. Perhaps imagine the device has been transported back in time and you are a cave-person looking at it for the first time.

You may find you need to think about other things in the environment as you describe the object. For example, for a pair of scissors as well as opening and shutting the scissors, you might want to talk about what happens if there is a sheet of paper as well.

After you have read further in the chapter, you might want to revisit this exercise, but for now just use whatever sketching, design or analysis tools you know ... or invent what you need!

4.2 Reflect

How did the exercise go? Was it hard or easy? If you come from a computing domain you might have found it quite hard to think about modelling physical things. If you come from, say, a design domain, you might find it easier to talk or sketch the physical aspects, but maybe harder to specify the behaviours.

Did you need to include how the device or object fitted into its environment, like the scissors with paper, or were you able to describe it largely in isolation?

In the following two sections we will look at two different scales of description, but both focused on physical things. Section 5 will deal with physigrams which model the device 'unplugged' like the example of the phone without its battery, first describing the physical interactions and only then connecting these to digital functions. Section 6 looks at a larger scale of physical setting, the behaviour of people in a café and the design of an internet-connected open/closed sign.

5 Physigrams – Modelling the Device 'Unplugged'

Effective feedback is one of the earliest lessons in HCI. Often this is thought of in terms of semantic response: you are writing an email press the 'X' key, and the letter 'x' appears on the screen. However, this is just one of several levels of description and one of several kinds of feedback all of which are important.

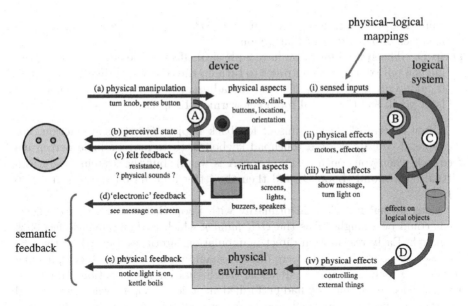

Fig. 7. Multiple feedback loops

Figure 7 attempts to capture some of the many feedback loops that happen when you interact with a digital device that has a physical element ... and of course every digital device has some sort of physical aspect to it even if it is just a keyboard you press or a microphone that you speak into. The whole diagram is quite complicated but we'll go through the four loops (A–D) one by one.

Loop A – This is the basic contact you feel or hear from the physical interaction with the device. When you press a button you feel the resistance, perhaps hear the sound it makes as it makes contact. When you slide your finger across a touchscreen, you can feel you are in contact, perhaps hear the squeak of your finger across the screen. If you are using an audio mixing desk you may not only feel the movement of the sliders, but also see their position as you move them.

Loop B – The system might also produce immediate feedback. For instance many computer keyboards don't make a click sound physically and so they generate a simulated click, which tries to be as closely synchronised as possible to pressing the key. Some versions of the BMW iDrive controller included a small haptic device within the knob so that you felt resistance and 'stops' even though the actual control was continuous. The aim of all of these is to emulate Loop A, that is to be as if the feedback were physical. However, if there are even small delays, this illusion is lost.

Loop C – The actions you perform have some sort of impact on the system state. For example, the 'x' being inserted into the email text. This semantic effect is then reflected in the screen display, providing semantic feedback. Note that Loops B and C both act through the digital aspects of the device; however, while Loop B gives feedback that you *performed* an action, Loop C gives feedback on the *effect* of that action.

Loop D – The system may also have a physical effect in the environment. Imagine you tell your house controller to turn up the central heating. Immediately it may reply to say that it made the adjustment (Loop C), but some time later you'll feel the actual room get warmer (Loop D).

Often several of these forms of feedback happen for the same action. For example, if you are using a touchpad keyboard, there may be little perceptual feedback when you touch a key (Loop A is weak), but the system produces a virtual click sound (Loop B) and then the letter appears on the screen (Loop C).

Many formal models deal primarily with Loop C, but this in part reflects what could be thought of as the *GUI fallacy*, which is that semantic feedback is enough. Early research on direct manipulation interfaces focused on the way the user felt as though they were directly manipulating virtual objects, leading to a strong focus on rapid feedback of the virtual impact of actions (Loop C). Excessive feedback that you had performed an action (Loop B) was down-graded in order to avoid a more mediated experience where you ask the computer to perform a command and then the computer does it. This is of course good when the effect really is instant, but if computational or network delays introduce any sort of lag the experience degrades rapidly. In addition, of course, many audio systems are based precisely on mediated models of interaction.

Physigrams focus primarily on Loop A, identifying the interaction potential of the physical controller 'unplugged', without power or digital effect. This feedback and interaction is guaranteed, even if there are delays or complications with the software, it is still a physical device. Furthermore, we have experience of physical manipulation from being the smallest child as well as aeons of development as a species in a physical world.

Of course, this is not the end of the story! The physical device is connected to digital or electronic functionality, but, by understanding the physical interactions first, we are in a better place to ensure that the connection between physical manipulation and digital action is appropriate and intuitive.

Unplugged – Switches. As a first example of a device unplugged, imagine tearing a light switch from the wall. The switch is in your hands, the wires broken and ineffective (maybe safest not to try this in reality!). However, you can still play with the light switch, flick it up and down. The details vary a little, but typically there are two visible and tactile states, you can both feel the switch move and see what position it is in. This is represented in the simple physigram in Fig. 8. This is a variant of a state transition network with a state for each physical configuration of the device and transitions between those states.

Of course, while it is useful to think about the light switch unplugged, the eponymous importance of the light switch is that it controls a light! We do care about the digital or electronic behaviour. On the right of Fig. 9 is a model of the light itself. It has two states, on or off. The ease of use of the light switch is due

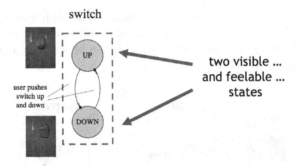

Fig. 8. The light switch 'unplugged'

to the fact that the switch state on the device and the state of the controlled system are in one to one correspondence.

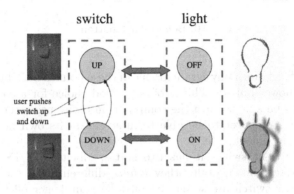

Fig. 9. Exposed state – one to one mapping between switch and light states

One of the good things about the visible switch is that you can tell if it is on even if you can't see the light, it has *exposed state*. This does not matter so much if you can see the switch and the light turns instantly on, semantic feedback is sufficient. However imagine you are controlling a security light outside the house, or if the lights have a short start-up delay as is common with neon lighting.

The light switch is not the only form of exposed state device, for example, the audio controls on speakers often have marked settings. Of course, this only works for relatively simple devices where the internal state has few settings and fixed values, however, where it is possible exposed state is very powerful.

5.1   Hidden State – Bounce-Back Buttons

Some light switches are simply a button you press: once to turn the light on and once more to turn it off again. Sometimes this is used because of the physical environment (plastic covered buttons in dirty environments), sometimes for aesthetic reasons or simply because the designer didn't think clearly about the purpose of the button. However, there are also times when you do not want the one-to-one correspondence, for example, if the lights have a timer to turn themselves off after an hour.

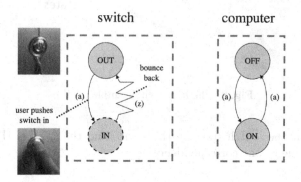

Fig. 10. Bounce-back button

Figure 10(left) shows a physigram for one of these bounce-back buttons acting as a computer power button. This is often a good choice for a computer – we want the user to be able to turn the computer on easily using the button, but would prefer the computer to be able to intervene in its own power-down to allow it to save documents, etc.

Just like the light switch it has two states, albeit OUT/IN rather than UP/DOWN. More fundamentally, they *behave* differently. In the light switch both states of the switch are stable: if you take your finger off the switch, it stays in the last position you pushed it into. In contrast, for the bounce-back switch the IN state is *transient* (shown by a dashed outline), as soon as you let go it bounces back to the OUT state. This bounce-back is shown by the 'lightening' arrow from IN to OUT.

Like the light switch the internal logical state of the computer power has two states, on and off (Fig. 10, right). However here instead of there being in one-to-one mapping between button state and power state, the transition of the button as it is pressed from OUT to IN (an *event*) is connected to the transition of the computer power. This is represented in the physigram by labelling the critical transition (a).

Responding to Pressure – Levels of Granularity. We can use physigrams to dig a little deeper into physical interactions.

We'll return to the simple light switch (Fig. 8). We described this in terms of simply pressing the switch up and down between two binary states. However, in reality you feel slight resistance as you press down, the button moves a little, and then suddenly snaps into the downward position. Similarly, as you push it back up you get that initial resistance, slight movement and then snap back to the up position.

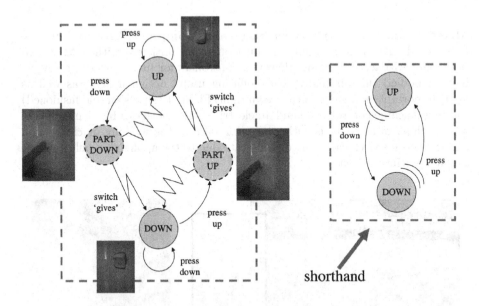

Fig. 11. pressure.

Figure 11 (left) shows a slightly more detailed version of this interaction with a 'PART DOWN' and a 'PART UP' state as well as the fully up and down states. The transition between 'UP' and 'PART DOWN' is modelled as a bounce back, as in Fig. 10. This captures the fact that if you start to press down a little and then release, the switch reverts back to the up position. However, in addition there is a lightening arrow from the 'PART DOWN' to the 'DOWN' state representing the give point when it snaps down.

This type of switch is common and if every time we wanted this behaviour we drew the diagram like this it would be very hard to see the larger picture. As this behaviour is so common physigrams have a shorthand notation. The small arcs decorating the transitions in the two-state diagram on the right of Fig. 11 represent this 'slight give' behaviour.

Formalisms have to tread the line between detail and readability. Most often we simply want to say 'there is transition with slight give', in which case the version on the right is best. However, occasionally we may need to think in more detail and then the left-hand version would be needed. Even this may not be sufficient, there is not simply one 'PART DOWN' position, but a continuous movement until the give point. Some researchers have modelled this in even more detail, including continuous models of pressure and movement [32], and this would be important, for example, if designing a haptic feedback device that wanted to mimic natural physical feedback.

There is no single correct level of representation, but we choose the level of granularity depending on the issues we wish to focus on. A good notation supports this fluidity.

Mixed Initiative – Controlled State and Compliant Interaction. We have noted that there is a shift in autonomy and initiative with notification-based and AI-backed systems. However, controllers for many consumer devices have embodied this for many years, offering useful design insight, as well as being important appliances in their own right. Figure 12 shows an (old fashioned) washing machine control knob and an electric kettle. Both exhibit elements that we can think of as controls with *controlled state* as the washing machine knob and the kettle switch can change their state due to the appliance's behaviour as well as user interaction.

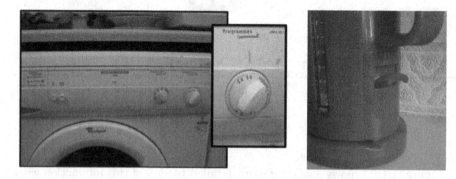

Fig. 12. Controlled state devices

You turn the washing machine knob to set the washing programme. However, in addition, as the washing machine works through the programme the knob also turns acting as a visible indicator of progress. The reason for this is that in the earliest washing machines the movement of the knob actually controlled the programme step by step. However, the accidental impact of this was a very visible indicator of state that could also be manipulated by the user. An expert washing-machine user might say "I'll just move it on to drain" in order, for example, to have a shorter washing cycle for lightly soiled clothes. Not all manipulations are possible – turning the dial back does not unwash the clothes – but there is a close correspondence between the user's actions, the system's actions and the knob position. This parity of user and system action is called *compliant interaction*.

Electric kettles often also exhibit this compliant interaction. You push the switch up to turn on the kettle and down if you want to turn it off before the kettle boils. However, if the kettle boils it flicks the switch to the off position automatically. Figure 13 shows this with a physigram of the switch on the left (notice the little 'give' arcs on the switch) and the kettle state on the right.

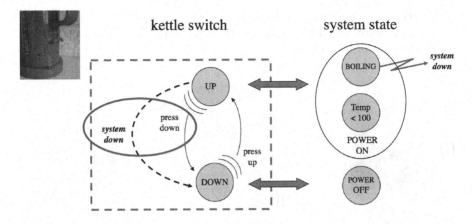

Fig. 13. Compliant interaction

However in addition the switch has an additional arrow from UP to DOWN driven by the system.

As with the washing machine not all the changes are driven equally by user and system, the kettle turns itself off, but never turns itself on. However, the parity of compliant interaction makes the behaviour self-evident.

As an added example to see why compliant interaction is so helpful, think about electric toasters you have used. There is a handle on the side that you push down to lower the toast and turn on the toaster. When the toast is ready the toast and handle pop. Imagine you start to smell burning. For some toasters you can simply lift the handle and the toast pops up, but for others you need to press a special cancel button. For the latter it is common to see people pulling helplessly on the handle even if they have used the toaster for years. In stress we revert to simple physical properties of devices, the opposite of pushing down is pulling up, so we instinctively try that first.

5.2   In Designer's Hands

If you are from a computer science background, the physigram notation will look similar to other state diagrams you have seen. An advantage of this form of notation is that they are also relatively comprehensible to those without a technical training, indeed you sometimes see forms of state transition diagram in end-user documentation for consumer devices, or even social media memes.

A document describing the physigram notation with a small number of examples was given to a group of industrial designers, who then used it to produce the diagrams in Fig. 14. On the left are three early designs of an experimental media controller they were working on at the time. The images you can see are 3D printed prototypes. The first (i) has a small knob that turns and has noticeable click stops. The second (ii) has a dial that has no tangible stops, but simply spins. The third (iii) has a trackpad style control. They were being used to drive the same menu-based software, turning or moving one's finger around the relevant control moved up and down the menu and pressing the control down selected the current menu item.

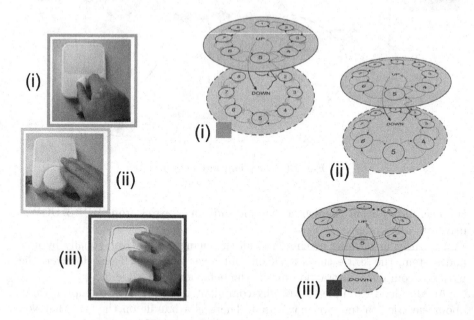

Fig. 14. Designer physigrams.

The diagrams on the right are the physigrams. The two top diagrams (i) & (ii) look fairly similar, whereas the one on the bottom (iii), the trackpad, is very different. This is because the track pad has no 'memory' of its position once pressed. In fact, the upper diagrams also look different when viewed more closely (Fig. 15). In the device with the stops (i), there are 'slight give' state transitions back and forward corresponding to the user moving back or forward a stop and no transitions between the last and first state, you have to rotate the dial all the way back when it gets to the end. In contrast the middle diagram (ii) has a simple transition between the menu states corresponding to the way the dial has a tangible location, but nothing to give a sense of when changes make a difference. Finally the lowest diagram (iii) has no tangible transitions at all, which has been represented as a single transition arc sweeping through all the menu states, as the only real feedback is virtual.

Perhaps most interesting is the way the designers used a 3D-like representation of the physigram to give a sense of the way that the controllers can be depressed, and how in the top two controllers the knob/dial retains its physical position. The 3D image makes it very easy to distinguish visually the pressed state of the controller. The semantics of a state transition diagram does not depend on the precise location of the states, only the network structure of the

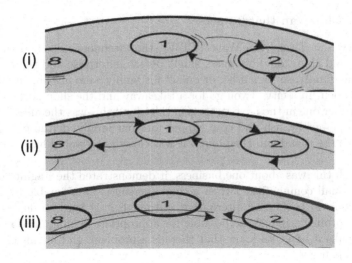

Fig. 15. Detail of physigrams in Fig. 14

links between them. It is tempting when designing a new notation to make every aspect mean something. However, by leaving aspects of the notation uninterpreted, users of the notation have freedom to add human interpretable side-notations or simply lay the diagram out in a way that is more readable; that is a form of appropriation [7].

6 The Internet Café Open Sign – Formal Models in Practice

Finally, we'll look the way formal models can help in the design of IoT devices. The example is a community display for the Isle of Tiree, a small island off the west coast of Scotland.

Twice a year an event on the island, Tiree Tech Wave[1], brought makers, designers technologists, artists and the occasional philosopher to meet, make and talk. In particular this often involved ideas and projects for technology in remote rural settings. This gave rise to a number of formal and informal projects including Frasan, a mobile app for An Iodhlann, the island heritage centre [9]; and OnSupply, a co-design project focused on renewable energy awareness [26].

Several projects were connected with island communications. It is often assumed that communication is easy in a rural settings, and indeed it is hard to keep a secret! However, when a small number of people are spread over a large area (Tiree has a population of 650 in an area larger than Manhattan) it can be hard to deliberately let people know about events and news.

---

[1] https://tireetechwave.org/.

6.1   The Chip Van that Tweets

At the very first Tiree Tech Wave (TTW), the attendees talked to the owner of the fish and chip van. This was a single person enterprise and the proprietor had a young family, so that if he, or one of his family were unwell, the chip van might not open. In a city, if you go for a takeaway and the shop is closed, there will be another one in the next street. On the island this was the only takeaway. If you had planned a fish and chip supper for your family, driven on the small roads across the island and then found it was closed, you would have nothing to eat.

Although this was about one business, it demonstrated the fragility of many aspects of small communities, when a single person is ill or unable to do a job there is often no backup or alternative. Although it is hard to deal with the underlying problem, it may be possible for appropriate communication mechanisms to make it easier to know that there is a problem, and in this case avoid the wasted journey.

As a fun envisionment of a possible solution the TTW participants created a near full-size cardboard model of the fish and chip van frontage. There was a large hatch-door on the front that would be opened to reveal the serving area. Onto this they attached a small Arduino board with a tilt sensor. When the hatch-door was opened the Arduino detected the movement and communicated with an attached to a phone to send an SMS text message to Twitter "#tireechip-vanopen". When it closed this was also detected and the Arduino sent the text "#tireechipvanclosed". Elsewhere a computer was attached to the Twitter API and would get a notification when either of the hash tags was detected. This then sent a message to another Arduino which was placed inside a small toy model of the van. This second Arduino controlled a motor that could open or close the toy's serving hatch. The idea was that the toy could sit on your mantelpiece mirroring the real fish and chip van, so that you would always know when the van was open.

This was a light-hearted envisionment and was never deployed on the actual chip van, but, as noted, it did address a very real problem. Note that the choice of the flap was critical from a design perspective. We did not want to ask the van owner to explicitly send a message to say that the van was open as this would add another task at an already busy time, and hence likely to be forgotten. Instead the hatch was used as the van could only be open when the hatch was open. It was a *reliable indicator* that sensed an action that the van owner would do anyway; that is an example of *incidental interaction* [6].

6.2   The Internet Connected Open Sign

Some years later, at another TTW, there was a small café in the same location as the event. The café had issues rather similar to the van. It was a small family-run business and if a family member was ill, or supplies were needed from the local shop the café might open late some days. If you decided to go there for

Fig. 16. Open-sign.

breakfast (they did good breakfasts) and drove across the island, but then found it closed you would be very disappointed.

It was not practical to add sensors to the café doors, so an exact parallel of the chip van was not possible, but the café did have an electric open sign (see Fig. 16, left). So an IoT sensor was added to this which detected when the power was on (Fig. 16, right). This was then used to drive a view of the sign on a web page which could be used to tell remotely whether the café was open or not. The sign is something the owners were using anyway, so by augmenting it, we are again creating a form of incidental interaction, using their day-to-day activities in order to drive the web page rather than asking them to explicitly tell an application when they are open or not.

The crucial question is whether this was a *reliable* way of knowing whether the café was open or not? If the web indicator is not reliable, then customers will ignore it and it will not be useful. This is where the formal model comes in.

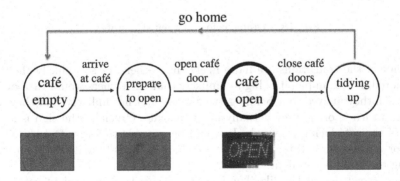

Fig. 17. Ideal café and open sign states

Figure 17 shows a simple model of the states of the café. It is empty and closed overnight, then when the owners arrive in the morning they go in and prepare the café for opening. When it is time they unlock the doors and are open for business. At the end of the day they close the doors, but spend some time tidying up before leaving to go home.

Below the states of the shop in Fig. 17, the ideal state of the open sign is shown: on precisely when the café is open. Of course in practice things may deviate from this ideal, if the owners forget to turn it on or off at the right times.

How can we assess how close the actual sensed behaviour is to this ideal?

Figure 18 shows a more detailed model of the café activities including whether the sign is on or off. There are four possible states of the café and two states of the sign yielding eight states in total. The transitions include those related to turning the sign on and off as well as opening and closing the café itself. The states with solid outlines are the ones which correspond to the ideal situation and those with dashed outlines states we would prefer not to happen.

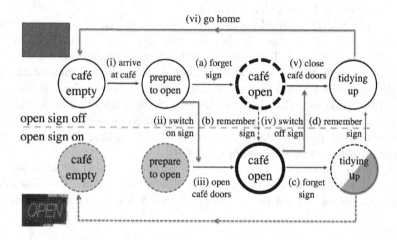

Fig. 18. Possible café and open sign states

Some of the transitions are more likely than others, or so unlikely they can be ignored. For example, it is highly unlikely that the owners would turn on the sign when they arrived, but before getting ready, but not unlikely that they may forget to turn it on as they actually open the café. Crucially the sign is at the front of the café facing outwards. It would be possible to forget to turn off the sign for a while while tidying up, but very hard to miss that it is still on when leaving the building at night.

This knowledge of the likelihood of transitions is then used to colour the states depending on how likely they are to occur, with white states being likely, grey states very unlikely and the half-and-half grey state possible, but not highly likely.

This can then be used to make an assessment of the likelihood of each state and the severity of the problem if it is wrong. The states that would be most problematic are if the sign is on before the café is open as this would mean customers would come when they can't be served. Having the sign off when the café is open is not good, as they might lose customers, but that is less severe than having disappointed customers. Similarly, if the sign is left on a little during the tidying up period it is not so bad as most potential customers know the normal closing time.

Notice how there are states where the reliability of the sensor (sign power) is highly critical, and those where it either does not matter at all or is less severe. These less severe or indifferent states are critical as they give us leeway in using sensor data to drive interventions, especially when combined with information about the approximate likelihood of different states.

Note too how this combines models of human activity, probabilistic estimates, and more formal reasoning.

7 Takeaways

We've covered a lot of ground in this chapter from a bird's eye view of the future of formal modelling of interactive systems, to specific examples of formal modelling in use.

In summary:

- Formal modelling of interactive systems sounds hard as it involves people as well as computers but yes, we can model aspects of them.
- We can model aspects of traditional mouse and screen systems but also ones that involve physical interactions and space.
- We need models that encompass: physical interactions, digital interactions and the rich external contexts, physical and social, in which they are set.
- In order to model humans and physical things we need to embrace and model uncertainty as we can rarely have 100% accuracy in every user action or sensed data point, but do need to be able to deliver robust solutions despite this.

This chapter has shown some of the exciting developments in the modelling of interactions, but also many open challenges and research opportunities.

References

1. Crabtree, A., Urquhart, L., Chen, J.: Right to an explanation considered harmful. Edinburgh School of Law Research Paper Forthcoming (2019). https://doi.org/10.2139/ssrn.3384790
2. Demopoulos, A.: 'Scanners are complicated': why Gen Z faces workplace 'tech shame'. BBC News, 28 February 2023. https://www.theguardian.com/technology/2023/feb/27/gen-z-tech-shame-office-technology-printers
3. Dix, A.: Information processing, context and privacy. In: Human-Computer Interaction, INTERACT 1990, pp. 15–20. IFIP, North-Holland (1990). https://alandix.com/academic/papers/int90/

4. Dix, A.: Formal Methods for Interactive Systems. Academic Press (1991). https://alandix.com/books/formal/

5. Dix, A.: Human issues in the use of pattern recognition techniques. In: Beale, R., Finlay, J. (eds.) Neural Networks and Pattern Recognition in Human Computer Interaction, pp. 429–451. Ellis Horwood (1992). https://alandix.com/academic/papers/neuro92/

6. Dix, A.: Beyond intention - pushing boundaries with incidental interaction. In: Proceedings of Building Bridges: Interdisciplinary Context-Sensitive Computing, Glasgow University, 9 September 2002 (2002). https://alandix.com/academic/papers/beyond-intention-2002/

7. Dix, A.: Designing for appropriation. In: Proceedings of the 21st British HCI Group Annual Conference University of Lancaster, HCI 2007, UK, pp. 1–4 (2007). https://doi.org/10.14236/ewic/HCI2007.53. https://alandix.com/academic/papers/HCI2007-appropriation/

8. Dix, A.: A shifting boundary: the dynamics of internal cognition and the web as external representation. In: Proceedings of the 3rd International Web Science Conference, pp. 9:1–9:8 (2011). https://doi.org/10.1145/2527031.2527056

9. Dix, A.: Mental geography, wonky maps and a long way ahead. In: GeoHCI, Workshop on Geography and HCI, CHI 2013 (2013). http://alandix.com/academic/papers/GeoHCI2013/

10. Dix, A.: Deep digitality: fate, fiat, and foundry. Interactions **26**(1), 20–21 (2018). https://doi.org/10.1145/3289427

11. Dix, A.: Sufficient reason. Keynote at HCD for Intelligent Environments, BHCI, Belfast, 3 July 2018. https://alandix.com/academic/talks/sufficient-reason-2018/

12. Dix, A.: Artificial Intelligence for Human-Computer Interaction. CRC/Taylor&Francis (2024). https://alandix.com/ai4hci/

13. Dix, A., Gill, S.: Physical computing | When digital systems meet the real world. In: Filimowicz, M., Tzankova, V. (eds.) New Directions in Third Wave Human-Computer Interaction: Volume 1 - Technologies. HIS, pp. 123–144. Springer, Cham (2018). https://doi.org/10.1007/978-3-319-73356-2_8

14. Dix, A., Gill, S., Hare, J., Ramduny Ellis, D.: TouchIT: Understanding Design in a Physical-Digital World. Oxford University Press (2022). https://physicality.org/TouchIT/

15. Dix, A., Mancini, R., Levialdi, S.: The cube – extending systems for undo. In: Proceedings of DSVIS 1997, pp. 473–495. Eurographics (1997). https://alandix.com/academic/papers/dsvis97/§

16. Dix, A., Runciman, C.: Abstract models of interactive systems. In: Johnson, P., Cook, S. (eds.) People and Computers: Designing the Interface, pp. 13–22. Cambridge University Press (1985). https://alandix.com/academic/papers/PIE85/

17. Dix, A., Weyers, B., Bowen, J., Palanque, P.: Trends and gaps. In: Weyers, B., Bowen, J., Dix, A., Palanque, P. (eds.) The Handbook of Formal Methods in Human-Computer Interaction. HIS, pp. 65–88. Springer, Cham (2017). https://doi.org/10.1007/978-3-319-51838-1_3

18. European Parliament and of the Council of Europe: Regulation (EU) 2016/679 of the European Parliament and of the Council of 27 April 2016 on the protection of natural persons with regard to the processing of personal data and on the free movement of such data, and repealing Directive (General Data Protection Regulation), 27 April 2016. http://data.europa.eu/eli/reg/2016/679/oj

19. Gardner, H., Davis, K.: The App Generation: How Today's Youth Navigate Identity, Intimacy, and Imagination in a Digital World. Yale University Press (2014)

20. Mancini, R.: Modelling interactive computing by exploiting the undo. Ph.D. thesis, Università degli Studi di Roma "La Sapienza" (1997). dottorato di Ricerca in Informatica, IX-97-5

21. Norman, D.A.: The Design of Everyday Things. Basic Books, Inc., USA (2002)

22. Palanque, P.: Ten objectives and ten rules for designing automations in interaction techniques, user interfaces and interactive systems. In: Proceedings of the International Conference on Advanced Visual Interfaces. Association for Computing Machinery, New York (2020). https://doi.org/10.1145/3399715.3400872

23. Sannella, D.: Semantics, Implementation and pragmatics of clear, a program specification language. Ph.D. thesis, Department of Computer Science, University of Edinburgh (1982). Report CST-17-82

24. Schmidt, A.: Interactive human centered artificial intelligence: a definition and research challenges. In: Proceedings of the International Conference on Advanced Visual Interfaces. Association for Computing Machinery, New York (2020). https://doi.org/10.1145/3399715.3400873

25. Shneiderman, B.: Human-centered artificial intelligence: reliable, safe and trustworthy. Int. J. Hum. Comput. Interact. **36**(6), 495–504 (2020). https://doi.org/10.1080/10447318.2020.1741118

26. Simm, W., et al.: Tiree energy pulse: exploring renewable energy forecasts on the edge of the grid. In: Proceedings of the 33rd Annual ACM Conference on Human Factors in Computing Systems, CHI 2015, pp. 1965–1974. Association for Computing Machinery, New York (2015). https://doi.org/10.1145/2702123.2702285

27. Spivey, J.M.: The Z Notation: A Reference Manual. Prentice-Hall, Inc., USA (1989)

28. Van Mierlo, S., Van Tendeloo, Y., Meyers, B., Vangheluwe, H.: Domain-specific modelling for human-computer interaction. In: Weyers, B., Bowen, J., Dix, A., Palanque, P. (eds.) The Handbook of Formal Methods in Human-Computer Interaction. HIS, pp. 435–463. Springer, Cham (2017). https://doi.org/10.1007/978-3-319-51838-1_16

29. Weichel, C., Hardy, J., Alexander, J., Gellersen, H.: ReForm: integrating physical and digital design through bidirectional fabrication. In: Proceedings of the 28th Annual ACM Symposium on User Interface Software and Technology, UIST 2015, November 2015, pp. 93–102. ACM (2015). https://doi.org/10.1145/2807442.2807451

30. Weyers, B., Bowen, J., Dix, A., Palanque, P. (eds.): The Handbook of Formal Methods in Human-Computer Interaction. HIS, 1st edn. Springer, Cham (2017). https://doi.org/10.1007/978-3-319-51838-1

31. Winter, E., Forshaw, S., Ferrario, M.A.: Measuring human values in software engineering. In: Proceedings of the 12th ACM/IEEE International Symposium on Empirical Software Engineering and Measurement, ESEM 2018, Association for Computing Machinery, New York (2018). https://doi.org/10.1145/3239235.3267427

32. Zhou, W., Reisinger, J., Peer, A., Hirche, S.: Interaction-based dynamic measurement of haptic characteristics of control elements. In: Auvray, M., Duriez, C. (eds.) EUROHAPTICS 2014. LNCS, vol. 8618, pp. 177–184. Springer, Heidelberg (2014). https://doi.org/10.1007/978-3-662-44193-0_23

Modelling and Analysing Cognition and Interaction

Antonio Cerone$^{(\boxtimes)}$ (iD)

Department of Computer Science, School of Engineering and Digital Sciences,
Nazarbayev University, Astana, Kazakhstan
antonio.cerone@nu.edu.kz

Abstract. In this chapter we investigate how to formally model human cognition and how cognition drives the way people think and behave, thus linking people's external behaviour, described in terms of their tasks, with people's internal cognitive processing. This complements the physical and digital aspects of human-computer interaction considered in Chap. 1. Human memory is the basis of cognitive processing. The chapter starts presenting conceptual models of memory and the way they can be represented to best facilitate human understanding as well as to provide a formal, linear notation that can be used computationally but still does not prevent human understanding. Such a notation, the Behaviour and Reasoning Description Language (BRDL), is then used to illustrate how to model both factual and behavioural knowledge and how to use these two types of knowledge in cognitive processing and human activities. The last part of the chapter provides a light introduction to informal and formal approaches to the analysis of cognition and interaction.

Keywords: Cognitive Science · Human-Computer Interaction · Behaviour and Reasoning Description Language · Formal Methods

1 Conceptual Models of Human Memory

Our entire way of living heavily counts on our memory. Human memory involves long-term storage of both factual knowledge of the world, which we incrementally acquire throughout our lives, and the remembrance of episodes of our lives, which includes associated specific time and place information. It is also the main resource driving all our activities. In fact, knowledge also needs to be retrieved and processed to produce further information, which needs to be temporarily stored in order to be used to drive our activities, which involve *thinking* and *behaviour*. In Sect. 2.1, we consider a model of memory that describes how knowledge is stored and, in Sect. 2.2, we introduce a more machine-oriented representation of that model to illustrate how knowledge is retrieved and used.

Work partly funded by Project SEDS2020004 "Analysis of cognitive properties of interactive systems using model checking", Nazarbayev University, Kazakhstan (Award number: 240919FD3916).

A. Cerone (Ed.): ICTAC 2021, LNCS 13490, pp. 30–72, 2023.
https://doi.org/10.1007/978-3-031-43678-9_2

Thinking may carry out *reasoning* or may aim at *problem solving*. Reasoning involves using long-term stored rules that support our reasoning processes as well as temporarily storing the current information on which such rules are applied and the results of their application. The temporarily stored current information on which rules are applied may be taken either from perceptions from the external environment or from long-term stored knowledge. We illustrate various forms of reasoning in Sects. 2.3–2.7. Problem solving, in addition, involves goals that define plans and drive a thinking process that possibly makes assumptions on the external environment and mentally simulates our behaviour. We illustrate simple planning in Sect. 2.8 and actual problem solving in Sect. 3.2.

Behaviour is also driven by long-term stored rules, which may be controlled by goals or through the thinking process, thus determining deliberate activities, or may also be triggered by perceptions from the external environment, thus resulting in automatic skilled activities.

In the former case, the behaviour rules can be grouped together to make a plan, which involves a number of deliberate, conscious decisions, and then take action. For example, when we plan our holidays in an exotic place we need to go through a number of steps in order to select and book the flights, the accommodation, possible packages and tours. Each of these steps requires decisions which depend on our goals and/or the outcome of our thinking process. We illustrate deliberate behaviour in Sect. 3.1.

In the latter case, the behaviour rules can be grouped together to make a procedure, which is 'wired' in our mind and consists of alternative steps in which we automatically, mostly unconsciously react to what we perceive in the external environment. Such a procedure is what we normally call a skilled behaviour. Examples of skilled behaviour are: tying a shoe lace, walking, riding a bike, playing a sport and driving a car. There is a large variability in the apparent complexity of such skilled behaviours, from basic ones such as tying a shoe lace to very articulated ones such as driving a car. We illustrate automatic behaviour in Sect. 4.4.

Finally, we need to make sense of the large amount of information present in the external environment and available to our perception, and select only what is needed to achieve our goal or, more in general, what is beneficial to our activities. For example, if we are at a party, in a very noisy environment in which several conversations are going on simultaneously within several groups of people, we only need to select what people in our group are saying, their gestures and facial expression, and ignore all other groups. This important process of our mind is called *selective attention*, and is also controlled by rules that we may consider as somehow associated with our memory. As in the case of human behaviour, such rules may be controlled by goals or through the thinking process, thus determining an *explicit*, conscious form of attention, or may be also triggered by perceptions from the external environment, thus determining an *implicit*, mostly unconscious form of attention. For example, listening to what people say in our group at the party may be driven by our goal of being involved in the conversation and/or by our thinking about what has been said previously. It is thus a form of explicit attention. However, if someone from another group mentions our name, our attention is suddenly captured. This is thus a form of implicit attention. This example motivated *cocktail party effect* as an alternative name for selective attention or, more specifically for *selective hearing*, since the effect involves auditory perceptions. We illustrate deliberate attention in Sect. 4.1.

In general, our behaviour/attention tends to switch between deliberate/explicit and automatic/implicit and vice versa, depending on the need. Although, planning a holiday is a deliberate behaviour, when we browse the Internet looking for airfares, accommodations, packages, etc., we often react to the information shown on web pages in an automatic way. In fact, we may even be carried away from our goal and automatically and unconsciously switch to browse information that does not have anything to do with our original goal of planning a holiday. Similarly, the cocktail party effect shows that our attention may switch from explicit to implicit when we hear our name. The switch between automatic/implicit and deliberate/explicit behaviour/attention may have a large variety of distinct causes: need to make a decision, realisation of a danger, emerging interest, etc. For example, although for an expert driver driving is a fairly automatic activity, we may switch to deliberate behaviour if we find ourselves in a traffic jam and we need to decide an alternative way (decision making), or if we realise that the car in front of ours keeps breaking continuously with no appearent reason (realised danger), or if we see a road signal to an interesting destination that was not in our original plans (emerging interest).

From these considerations, it appears that

1. there is a large variability in the information stored in human memory: factual information, episodes of our living, thinking rules (for reasoning and problem solving) and attentional rules;
2. some of this information needs to be stored long term whereas other information only needs to be stored temporarily;
3. not all information we perceive needs to be processed, but we need to use attention and select only what is relevant and ignore the other information;
4. relevant information has to be transferred to a temporary store where it can be processed and some information has to be transferred to a permanent store to produce knowledge.
5. our behaviour and attention may be controlled either deliberately/explicitly by our goals and thinking processes or automatically/implicitly by our perceptions.

These five points suggest that human memory can be described as consisting of distinct functions that reflect (1) the kind of stored information, (2) the persistence of the information (short-term versus long-term storage), (3) the selection of the information to be processed, (4) the information flow, and (5) the way, deliberate or automatic, stored rules control human activities. Such distinct functions can be seen as supported by logically distinct memory components. Moreover, information needs to move among memory components in order to be selected for processing or to be stored for a long term.

It is generally agreed by psychologists and cognitive scientists that human memory features three distinct main functions, which are described by the *multistore model* proposed Atkinson and Shiffrin [1]. This model, which is the most well-known but not the only way to conceptualise memory, is characterised by three stores between which various forms of information flow: *sensory memory*, where information perceived through the senses persists for a very short time, *short-term memory (STM)*, which has a limited capacity and where the information that is needed for processing activities is temporarily stored with rapid access and rapid decay, and *long-term memory (LTM)*, which has a virtually unlimited capacity and where information is organised in structured ways, with slow access but little or no decay.

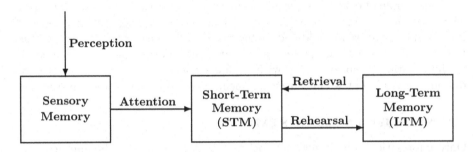

Fig. 1. Atkinson and Shiffrin's multistore model of human memory

As we can see in Fig. 1 perceptions from the external environment enter through sensory memory, then the information moves from sensory memory to STM through attention and from STM to LTM through rehearsal. Moreover, the retrieval process is the selection of the long-term stored knowledge that is needed for processing. We discuss retrieval in Sect. 2.2 and rehearsal in Sects. 4.2 and 4.3. We describe the three main memory components in details in Sects. 1.1–1.3.

1.1 Sensory Memory

All the information that we can perceive though our senses from the environment where we live may be stored in sensory memory. Although it is not clear how much information can be stored in sensory memory, there is strong evidence that information persists for a very short time (*rapid decay*). Moreover, we should more properly speak about sensory memories, since a distinct storage register correspond to each sense: the *iconic, echoic, haptic, olfactory, gustatory* sensory registers.

Although all the sensory registers present large capacity and rapid decay, the actual information decay times vary. For instance, for young adults, it has been estimated to be 150–500 ms (milliseconds) for iconic memory and a few seconds for echoic memory. We can have some obvious evidence about the existence of the sensory registers and their decay times. For example, our perception of fireworks consists of colourful lines in the sky, which are, in fact, produced by roundish particles shot at high speed by the explosion, and the lines we perceive are nothing else than their trajectories. These lines are perceived for less than one second, the time the visual perception of the different positions of the corresponding moving particles persists in the iconic register, and then disappears. This could be confirmed by a simple home experiment. In a dark room with a mirror, switch on your smartphone torch and move the smartphone rapidly in a circle projecting the light on the mirror. You will really see a circle of light (maybe more circles, depending on the rotation speed) projected in the mirror. Obviously, the circles do not exist in reality, since the light does not leave traces on the mirror, but they are the result of the many persistent perceptions of light points that are generated in a time sequence and stored in your iconic memory.

An example of evidence of echoic memory and its decay time is the fact that when someone speaks to us while we are engaged in another activity, we may not listen to what we are told and we have to ask the speaker to repeat, but just to realise that we actually had already heard that information. This happens if the information is repeated to us within a few seconds, because what we actually did not listen to (but we unconsciously heard) is still in our echoic register.

1.2 Short-Term Memory (STM)

Only information that is relevant for the ongoing or planned human activity, which we select through the process of attention, moves to STM before it disappears from sensory memory. In fact, STM has a limited capacity, which has been measured using experiments in which the subjects had to recall items presented in sequence. By presenting sequences of digits, Miller [23] found that the average person can remember 7 ± 2 digits. However, when digits are grouped in *chunks*, as it happens, for example, when we memorise phone numbers, it is actually possible to remember larger numbers of digits. In fact, it is easier to memorize a sequence of ten digit when they are chunked in three groups, such as 279–854–3916, rather than when they are taken separately: 2–7–9–8–5–4–3–9–1–6.

Therefore, Miller's 7 ± 2 rule applies to chunks of information and the ability to form chunks can increase people's actual STM capacity. That is the way chess masters are able to remember complex chessboard configurations and expert card player can memorise long sequences of cards. Further experiments have shown that chunking is facilitated by similarities that result in associations between different pieces of information and, even more, by the meaning of the information with respect to the subject's knowledge. For example, a chess master is able to easily remember a chessboard configuration from a real game, because that configuration has a logical meaning according to the master knowledge and, therefore, the entire configuration can be made into a single chunk. However, with a random chessboard configuration, which would probably never occur in a game, and thus is somehow illogical for the master, the master is as bad as a beginner in chunking.

The estimation of the STM decay time is still a contentious issue. Although there is a general agreement that information may passively persists in STM for a time in the order of seconds, it is not easy to get a precise estimation. There is a general agreement that the decay time is less than 30 sec. Mueller and Krawitz suggest that it should be between 4 and 10 sec [24] and there are recent suggestions that the time is actually less than 3 sec, with Campoy proposing an average estimate of 2,700 msec [6].

An important point is the form in which the information is stored in STM. Experimental evidence shows that information that may be verbalised is actually stored acoustically rather than visually. This kind of information makes up an acoustic-based STM, known as the *phonological loop*. Further experiments have been conducted to understand how purely visuospatial information may be stored in STM to make up the so-called *visuospatial sketchpad*. However, such experiments tend to contain confounds, due to the entanglement and interference of the various visual components considered. A number of experiments, including those using the American Sign Language, seem to show that visual STM can hold approximately 4 items. In the rest of this chapter, we consider only acoustic-based STM and we call it simply STM.

1.3   Long-Term Memory (LTM)

LTM is the permanent repository of our knowledge of the world, the procedures underlying our skills, both at the motor and mental level, and the important episodes of our life. It is sometime likened to a 'library'. When people informally talk about 'memory', they are usually talking about LTM.

Consistently with our previous considerations, LTM may be decomposed into:

- **Declarative Memory**, which refers to our knowledge of the world ("knowing what") and consists of *events, facts, associations, inferential rules* that allow us to think about the world and *plans* that allow us to deliberately act upon the world. It may be further decomposed into:
  - **Episodic Memory**, which refers to our experiences and life events, each being associated with a specific time and place;
  - **Semantic Memory**, which refers to a structured record of facts, meanings, concepts and knowledge about the world and ways to deliberately act upon it, which we have acquired and organised through association and abstraction.
- **Procedural Memory**, which refers to our skills ("knowing how") and consists of rules organised to form *procedures* that allow us to automatically act upon the world.

LTM has huge capacity, maybe unlimited capacity, and retains information for a very long time, possibly indefinitely, which means that it has little or no decay.

Declarative memory is also called *explicit memory*, since, normally, the information it contains is consciously retrieved in an explicit way, and procedural memory is also called *implicit memory*, since, normally, procedures underlying our skills are used unconsciously, in an implicit way.

Although it is true that events and facts are consciously retrieved from LTM, formally speaking, this is arguable for free associations. If we consider the question "which animals fly?" then we consciously use the two facts that "birds are animals" and "birds fly" and explicitly retrieve them from LTM to give the answer "birds" to the question. If, instead, we play a word association game, we may answer to the prompted word "dog" by saying the word "cat". Although we consciously say the word "cat", the way we retrieve the concept "cat" and its association with the concept "dog" from LTM is pretty unconscious and occurs in an implicit way, namely without our explicit control. In fact, free associations are used in psychotherapy to gain access to unconscious processes. Thus, although there is an association between "dog" and "cat" in our semantic memory, we are qualitatively but not quantitatively aware of the semantic distance between the notions of "dog" and "cat". However, it is the higher closeness that makes us choose "cat" rather than "eagle". Moreover, we do not consciously decide to choose "cat" rather then "wolf", although we could argue that "cat" and "wolf" are both equally close to "dog".

A more subtle issue is which facts are retrieved from semantic memory to answer questions such as "can a bird breathe?" and "can a bird fly?" and whether their retrieval is conscious or unconscious. In order to explore these issues, we need to move from the conceptual model of memory we considered in this section, which is based on Atkinson and Shiffrin's *multistore model*, toward a more rigorous model that includes some formality in representing memory. In fact, as we see in Sect. 2, the use of some formality in the representation of semantic memory is needed in order to be able to analyse, though still informally, how semantic memory is navigated to retrieve information.

2   Modelling and Processing Factual Knowledge

The information stored in semantic memory consists of a variety of *factual knowledge*. The most basic information of this kind is a *fact*, such as "a bird is an animal", "a bird has two legs", "a dog is an animal", "a dog has four legs", "an animal can breathe", "a bird can breathe" and "a dog can breathe".

2.1   Semantic Networks and Facts

An important issue is how facts are represented and stored in semantic memory. If we consider the facts above, we note that "a bird can breathe" can be inferred from "a bird is an animal" and "an animal can breathe". Therefore, we expect that semantic memory optimises the way information is stored.

A possible hypothesis is then that only "a bird is an animal" and "an animal can breathe" are in some way represented in semantic memory, whereas "a bird can breathe" is inferred from them. In 1969 Collins and Quillian [17] carried out experiments to verify this hypothesis. They asked questions of the kind "can a bird breathe?" and "can a bird fly?" and they measured the time taken by the experimental subject to answer the questions. They found out that it takes longer to answer the question "can a bird breathe?" than answering the question "can a bird fly?" This experimental outcome led to the development of a model of semantic memory as a semantic network, as shown in Fig. 2, where we use words in bold for categories such as 'animal', 'bird', 'duck', and normal fonts for their attributes.

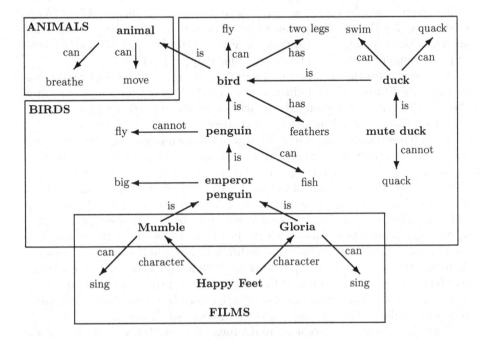

Fig. 2. Example of Semantic Network.

Associations are described using unlabelled or labelled arrows. The label 'is' denotes a *generalisation*. For example, the '**bird**' category is generalised as the more generic category '**animal**' at a higher level. Simple attributes are described using unlabelled arrows. For example, an emperor penguin is 'big'. The other labels denote complex attributes. For example, a bird has complex attributes 'can fly', 'has two legs' and 'has feathers'.

Categories at the lower level inherit the attributes of the categories at the upper level. For example, category '**bird**' inherits attribute 'can breathe', from '**animal**'. That is why we can answer the question "can a bird breathe?" although there is no attribute 'breathe' associated with '**bird**', that is, there is no explicit representation of the fact "a bird can breathe".

We also consider 'cannot'-labelled attributes, although these are not part of Collins and Quillian's model. Category '**penguin**' has the 'cannot fly' attribute, which redefines the 'can fly' attribute of the '**bird**' category. In fact, a penguin is a bird, but cannot fly. Analogously, category '**mute duck**' has the 'cannot quack' attribute, which redefines the 'can quack' attribute of the '**duck**' category. In fact, a mute duck is a duck, but cannot quack.

Note that the attributes 'fly' and 'quack' are duplicated only for better readability of the semantic network. In fact, single 'fly' and 'quack attribute should occur each as the target of two arrows, labelled by 'can' and labelled by 'cannot'.

Information is also organised in *knowledge domains*, for which we use words in bold uppercase. In Fig. 2, we have three knowledge domains: **ANIMALS**, **BIRDS** and **FILMS**. Note that some categories may belong to more than one knowledge domain. For example, in Fig. 2, **Mumble** and **Gloria** are both emperor penguins and characters in the film **Happy Feet**.

Semantic networks are a useful descriptive model, with a visual representation that facilitates understanding, also in a holistic way as a full picture. It is also a very intuitive notation, which facilitates communication within teams of scientists, who may be from different expertise domains.

We can use semantic networks to carry out some informal analysis. It is easy to see that the path from '**penguin**' to 'breathe' is longer than the path from '**animal**' to 'breathe'. That explains why it takes longer to answer to "can a bird breathe?' than to "can an animal breathe?" In fact, Collins and Quillian concluded that the deeper the information in semantic memory the longer it will take time to retrieve it. Obviously, this works under the assumption that it takes an equal amount of time to get the fact from a single node regardless of its level. In fact, there is no explicit time indication shown in the semantic network. Although the network model provided by Collins and Quillian was envisaged over 50 years ago, it has remained the most influential theory of semantic representation and underpins contemporary thinking on the organisation of semantic memory, which continues to use the network approach [7].

If we wish to carry out some more rigorous analysis, then we need to define a representation that is more amenable to mathematical manipulation, and translate the semantic network into. However, we expect that in such a process we lose, together with the visual features, the intuitive aspects and the immediacy of understanding the model as a whole. In fact, we are moving from a human-oriented to a machine-oriented representation. Nevertheless, we aim at a representation that is still understandable for humans.

In Sect. 2.2 we translate semantic networks in a more mathematical model, which evolves throughout the rest of the chapter as an increasingly more formal model. The final outcome of this evolution process is the presentation of the core part of the Behaviour and Reasoning Description Language (BRDL), a modelling language for *cognitive systems*, which was defined in our previous work [10]. We then show how to use BRDL for the informal and formal analysis not only of cognitive systems but also *interactive systems*, in which the cognitive component that models human thinking and behaviour is composed with a system component, which models the physical/computer environment with which the human interacts.

2.2 Fact Representation, Retrieval and Reconstruction

Although a network representation provides a full picture of the model, in order to have a representation that can be manipulated mathematically, we need to convert the network representation into some form of linear representation. Therefore we represent individual facts as the basic entities in semantic memory. We can see a fact as a labelled association of a category with another category or an attribute. The label denotes the type of association. For example, in the knowledge domain of animals, fact "a bird is an animal" associates category '**bird**' with category '**animal**'. The label 'is' denotes that the association is a generalisation. Similarly, in the knowledge domain of birds, fact "a bird can fly" associates category '**bird**' with attribute 'fly'. In this case the label 'can' denotes that the association describes an ability of the category. We introduce the following notation to represent, in the knowledge domain d, the association of category c to category or attribute e with label l:

$$d : c \mid\!\longrightarrow\!\mid l(e)$$

Thus "a bird is an animal" is represented by

$$\text{animals} : \text{bird} \mid\!\longrightarrow\!\mid \text{is(animal)}$$

and "a bird can fly" is represented by

$$\text{birds} : \text{bird} \mid\!\longrightarrow\!\mid \text{can(fly)}$$

We call these associations *fact representations*.

We can therefore give a full representation of the semantic network given in Fig. 2 by the following 22 fact representations:

1. animals : animal $\mid\!\longrightarrow\!\mid$ can(breathe)
2. animals : animal $\mid\!\longrightarrow\!\mid$ can(move)
3. birds : bird $\mid\!\longrightarrow\!\mid$ is(animal)
4. birds : bird $\mid\!\longrightarrow\!\mid$ can(fly)
5. birds : bird $\mid\!\longrightarrow\!\mid$ has(two legs)
6. birds : bird $\mid\!\longrightarrow\!\mid$ has(feathers)
7. birds : penguin $\mid\!\longrightarrow\!\mid$ is(bird)
8. birds : penguin $\mid\!\longrightarrow\!\mid$ can(fish)
9. birds : penguin $\mid\!\longrightarrow\!\mid$ cannot(fly)
10. birds : emperor penguin $\mid\!\longrightarrow\!\mid$ is(penguin)
11. birds : emperor penguin $\mid\!\longrightarrow\!\mid$ big
12. birds : Mumble $\mid\!\longrightarrow\!\mid$ is(emperor penguin)
13. birds : Gloria $\mid\!\longrightarrow\!\mid$ is(emperor penguin)
14. birds : duck $\mid\!\longrightarrow\!\mid$ is(bird)
15. birds : duck $\mid\!\longrightarrow\!\mid$ can(swim)
16. birds : duck $\mid\!\longrightarrow\!\mid$ can(quack)
17. birds : mute duck $\mid\!\longrightarrow\!\mid$ is(duck)
18. birds : mute duck $\mid\!\longrightarrow\!\mid$ cannot(quack)

19. films : Happy Feet |——→| character(Mumble)
20. films : Happy Feet |——→| character(Gloria)
21. films : Mumble |——→| can(sing)
22. films : Gloria |——→| can(sing)

If we are asked a question, for example "can a penguin fish?", this information is somehow temporarily stored in our STM. We see in this section that, under certain conditions, this causes a search in semantic memory for some fact representation with category 'penguin', label 'can' and attribute 'fish'. Fact representation 8 perfectly matches the question, thus an affirmative answer is stored in STM. In this way we have retrieved fact "a penguin can fish" from semantic memory.

The situation is different if we are asked the question "can a penguin breathe?". In fact we cannot find any fact representation with category 'penguin', label 'can' and attribute 'breathe'. As humans, we can just look at the semantic network in Fig. 2 and give an affirmative answer. But this is possible because the question is quite simple and the semantic network is small. However, given the characterisation of the semantic networks in terms of fact representation, we can define an algorithm to carry out this search and answer the question.

The general algorithm to answer question "can a c e?", where c is a category and e an attribute, is as follows:

1. assign c to c_0;
2. if there is a domain d and a fact representation

$$d : c_0 \; |\!\!-\!\!\!-\!\!\longrightarrow\!| \; can(e)$$

then the algorithm terminates with answer 'yes', otherwise go to step 3;
3. if there is a domain d and a fact representation

$$d : c_0 \; |\!\!-\!\!\!-\!\!\longrightarrow\!| \; cannot(e)$$

then the algorithm terminates with answer 'no', otherwise go to step 4;
4. if there is a a domain d, a category c_1 and a fact representation

$$d : c_0 \; |\!\!-\!\!\!-\!\!\longrightarrow\!| \; is(c_1)$$

then assign c_1 to c_0 and go to step 2, otherwise the algorithm terminates with answer 'no'.

An essential assumption for the correctness of this algorithm is that there is a high confidence concerning the knowledge domain d. However, when we consider a knowledge domain in which we are not very confident, if at step 4 we do not find the fact representation, then our answer should be "I don't know" rather than "no". In fact, in that case, it would be likely that we do not find a matching fact representation simply because our knowledge of the domain is limited. In this respect, our model could be extended by associating a level of confidence to each knowledge domain. Then an appropriate threshold would be used to discriminate between "no" and "I don't know" answer when we do not find the fact representation at step 4.

An important remark is that, unless there is a fact representation that matches the question, we actually reconstruct the fact that gives an affirmative answer to the question. However, this is still a form of retrieval. In fact, human memory is reconstructive and, in general, when we believe to remember some information or event, we normally reconstruct that information from the partial knowledge we have stored in LTM. Thus retrieval normally requires reconstruction.

Furthermore our confidence may not be realistic. For example, we may answer 'no' to the question "can a penguin breathe?" just because we do not have the category penguin in our semantic memory or because for us a penguin is only the Linux logo, which obviously does not breathe. Or we may answer 'no' to the question "can a penguin lay eggs?" because we do not have the attribute 'lay eggs' in any of the supercategories of penguin. This is the case of the semantic networks in Fig. 2, which provides only partial knowledge about birds. In all these cases our reconstruction fails and we provide wrong answers.

Human memory is reconstructive not only when retrieving facts from semantic memory, but also when retrieving events from episodic memory. Although in this chapter we do not consider models of episodic memory, it is important to note that we often believe to have seen things that did not happen or we recall wrong details. This is a serious legal problem regarding eyewitnesses, whose confident but incorrect recall may lead to sentencing of an innocent person.

Another important remark is that we did not include time in our model. Under the assumption mentioned in Sect. 2.1, that it takes an equal amount of time to get the fact from a single node regardless of its level, we can assume that step 1 of the algorithm takes a negligible time and each of the other steps take the same constant time, that is the time needed to check the matching between c_0 and a single fact representation. We could actually associate a specific time with each fact representation. In the original work [10] in which we defined BRDL, fact representations are annotated with time as follows

$$d : c \mid \overset{t}{\longrightarrow} \mid l(e)$$

where t is the time needed to check the matching with the fact representation. In that work, we also provide an algorithm to determine the answer to questions that instantiate the pattern "what can a c do?", where c is a category. Example of such questions are "what can a bird do?" and "what can a penguin do?" This kind of question does not have a yes–no answer, but is answered by providing a list of attributes. Obviously, this kind of question must be considered in the context of specific knowledge domains, which is just '**BIRDS**' in the case of the two questions above, since categories '**bird**' and '**penguin**' belong to this knowledge domain. However, if we ask the question "what can Mumble do?", then we need carry out the search on '**BIRDS**' and '**FILMS**' knowledge domains, since category '**Mumble**' belongs to both knowledge domains.

Moreover, time plays an essential role in answering such questions because the knowledge domain might be quite large and exhaustively searching it would be too long. In fact, nobody would give an exhaustive answer to a question of this kind but, instead, a normal answer would be a short list of attributes. Therefore, in order to model this process, it is necessary to consider a time threshold to the length of the search. And if nothing is found within the time limit, then the answer would be "I do not know".

A final remark is that the process of retrieving a fact from semantic memory is conscious in terms of the outcome but not in terms of the retrieval process we carry out. For example, we are aware that the answer to the question "can a bird breathe?" is "yes", but we are not aware that this outcome is achieved by combining the two facts that "a bird is an animal" and "an animal can breathe". In fact, the process of climbing the hierarchy in the semantic network occurs unconsciously. This is actually a general aspect of thinking. We are self-aware about our thoughts, the outcome of the thinking process, but the process itself may not be identified.

To conclude this section, we can say that the model of semantic memory we introduced is deliberately kept partial. The model is a basic formalisation that is very flexible and leaves many aspects open: the time needed to check the matching of question components with fact representations, the structure of the questions and the managing of the confidence level for knowledge domains, to mention a few of these aspects. This is, in fact, a general approach, as we see in the rest of this chapter, which aims at using BRDL in two ways:

– Consider alternative theories of human memory developed by psychologists, for example concerning the matching time, and provide BRDL with alternative semantics that formally model such theories in order to perform in silico experiments and compare their results with real-world data to understand which theory best reflects the reality.
– Compose the human memory model with models of a physical/computer system and analyse properties of the interaction at various levels of abstraction, for example abstracting from time versus modelling time explicitly.

2.3 Inference

The facts we considered in Sect. 2.2 are very basic but, in general, factual knowledge may be very articulated. For example, "a dog that wags is friendly" is also a fact but its representation in natural language is made of a subordinate sentence ('that wags') nested within the main sentence ('a dog... is friendly'). This complex structure of the sentence encapsulates an inferential process, whereby we infer the consequence 'is friendly' from the premise 'that wags'.

Inference is one of our thinking tools. In order to carry out inference we need to have the premise in our working memory, that is, in our STM, or in some part of our LTM. Basically, the inference will replace the premise with the consequence in STM, or it will use the premise in LTM to produce the consequence in STM.

Here we call *inferential rule* any factual knowledge that incapsulates an inferential process. We represent an inferential rule that infers a *consequence* from a given *premise* as follows:

$$premise \uparrow \implies \downarrow consequence$$

In this notation the '$\implies$' denotes the logical flow, while symbol '$\uparrow$' suggests removal from STM or the access to LTM and symbol '$\downarrow$' suggests storage in STM. We call *enabling* the part of the rule on the left of '$\implies$' and *performing* the part of the rule on the right of '$\implies$'.

With this notation, factual knowledge "a dog that wags is friendly" may be represented as

$$\text{"a dog wags"} \uparrow \implies \downarrow \text{"the dog is friendly"}$$

We have mixed formal notation and informal sentences in natural language. This is another important aspect that contributes to the flexibility of BRDL: the notation provides a structural template, but does not require any specific format for the template components. As in our previous work [12], we could alternatively give an explicit linguistic structure to such components, by distinguishing the main element of the sentence (*head*) from the rest (*argument*). Thus the representation above becomes

$$\text{wags(dog)} \uparrow \implies \downarrow \text{friendly(dog)} \tag{1}$$

where 'wags' and 'friendly' are heads and 'dog' is the argument. Note that we do not represent 'is' as a label here to avoid ambiguity between a hierarchical representation ('is a dog') and an attributive description ('is friendly'). This is consistent with the semantic network representation we have seen in Sect. 2.

If our thinking process refers to an unnamed but specific dog, we might have information 'wags(dog)', that is, "the dog wags", in STM and, as a consequence of the inference, replace it with information 'friendly(dog)', that is, "the dog is friendly". But our thinking may, instead, consider a named dog, let's say Bobby. In this case our STM would contain the two pieces of information '(is(dog))(Bobby)', that is, "Bobby is a dog" and 'wags(Bobby)', that is, "Bobby wags". Information '(is(dog))(Bobby)' consists of head 'is(dog)' and argument 'Bobby', with 'is(dog)' consisting of head 'is' and argument 'dog'. Then '(is(dog))(Bobby)' drives the application of inference rule 1 with 'dog' replaced by 'Bobby'. This results in 'wags(Bobby)' replaced with 'friendly(Bobby)' in STM.

This example also gives us the opportunity to show how fact representations retrieved from semantic memory are represented in STM. In fact, rather than referring to a dog we see for the first time, we might have the information about 'Bobby' in our semantic memory as the following fact representation:

$$\text{dogs : Bobby} \mid\!\longrightarrow\!\mid \text{is(dog)} \tag{2}$$

which refers to the known dog Bobby. In this case the application of inference rule 1 with 'dog' replaced by 'Bobby', which is equivalent to the application of inference rule

$$\text{wags(Bobby)} \uparrow \implies \downarrow \text{friendly(Bobby)} \tag{3}$$

is driven by fact representation 2. In fact, inference rule 3 is stored neither in semantic memory nor in other parts of human memory but we can say that it is virtually applied,

Inference rule allow humans to reason. *Reasoning* is a conscious process that uses inference for drawing a conclusion from existing knowledge and aims at the truth of such a conclusion. It is normally carried out within a specific knowledge domain, but may sometime go across different domains. In Sects. 2.4–2.6 we see how inference is used to carry out three different forms of human reasoning: *deductive reasoning*, *inductive reasoning* and *abductive reasoning*.

2.4 Deductive Reasoning

Deductive reasoning is based on the well-known rule of *modus ponens*

$$\frac{antecedent, \ antecedent \Rightarrow consequent}{consequent}$$

which consists of two *premises*

- the *antecedent* of the *conditional claim*, and
- the *conditional claim* itself,

and the *conclusion*, which is

- the *consequent* of the *conditional claim*.

The rule states that if the two premises are true, then also the conclusion is true. It is pretty obvious that the inferences we have seen in Sect. 2.3 are forms of deductive reasoning. In fact, the first premise of modus ponens may be instantiated as the information in STM or a fact representation in semantic memory and the second premise, the conditional claim, is the inference rule in semantic memory. Thus the application of inference rule 1 can be modelled by the following instantiation of the modus ponens rule:

$$\frac{\text{wags(dog), wags(dog)} \Rightarrow \text{friendly(dog)}}{\text{friendly(dog)}}$$

where 'wags(dog)' is the information in STM and 'wags(dog) $\Rightarrow$ friendly(dog)' is the inference rule in semantic memory.

Analogously, the virtual application of rule 3, can be modelled by the following instantiation of the modus ponens rule:

$$\frac{\text{wags(Bobby), wags(Bobby)} \Rightarrow \text{friendly(Bobby)}}{\text{friendly(Bobby)}}$$

when 'wags(Bobby)' is in STM.

Finally, we observe that also the retrieval of information by climbing the hierarchy in semantic memory could, in principle, be described using modus ponens. For example, the answer to the question "can a bird breathe?" could be obtained by considering the following instantiation of modus ponens:

$$\frac{\text{is(animal)},\ \text{is(animal)} \Rightarrow \text{can(breathe)}}{\text{can(breathe)}}$$

which applied to 'bird' has '(can(breathe))(bird)' as the outcome. However, we mentioned in Sect. 2.2 that this retrieval process occurs unconsciously and only the outcome of the retrieval is conscious, whereas in deductive reasoning the process itself also occurs consciously.

2.5   Inductive Reasoning

Inductive reasoning is not the mathematical form of induction. It is, instead, a form of *generalisation* whereby we generalise from cases that we have experienced and stored in episodic memory to infer information about cases that we have not experienced. For example, if every time we see a dog, we hear the dog barking, then we can generalise that 'all dogs bark', which can also be expressed as 'a dog can bark' and permanently stored in semantic memory as the following fact representation:

$$\text{dogs} : \text{dog} \ |\!\longrightarrow\!| \ \text{can(bark)} \tag{4}$$

This shows that *generalisation* is also a form of *learning*. In the example above we actually learn that 'a dog can bark' and store the representation of this fact in semantic memory. However, inductive reasoning may also occur impromptu. For example, suppose that we are at a bus stop waiting for the bus number 1, which is late. If we recall from our episodic memory that bus number 1 was also late the day before, we may then generalise that bus number 1 is always late. In BRDL this can be expressed by the following inference rule:

"no. 1 was late yesterday" "no. 1 is late today" $\uparrow \implies \downarrow$ "no. 1 is always late"

Obviously, such a specific rule would not exist in human semantic memory. However, an emotional individual might have the following inference rule stored in semantic memory:

"bus late yesterday" "bus late today" $\uparrow \implies \downarrow$ "bus always late"

which using linguistically structured components would be:

$$(\text{yesterday(late)})(\text{bus})\ (\text{today(late)})(\text{bus}) \uparrow \implies \downarrow (\text{always(late)})(\text{bus}) \tag{5}$$

As we saw for inference rules 1–3, the presence of the following fact representation in our semantic memory:

$$\text{buses} : \text{no. 1} \ |\!\longrightarrow\!| \ \text{is(bus)} \tag{6}$$

models our knowledge in the domain 'buses', which enables the application of inference rule 5 with 'bus' replaced by 'no. 1', which is equivalent to the application of inference rule

$$(\text{yesterday(late)})(\text{no. 1}) \ (\text{today(late)})(\text{no. 1}) \uparrow \implies \downarrow (\text{alway(late)})(\text{no. 1}) \quad (7)$$

driven by fact representation 6.

Inference rule 5 appears as an overgeneralisation, since we normally do not generalise from just two cases, but an emotional person might do it. We also have to remark that generalisation is not reliable. And this consideration does not only applies to overgeneralisations as inference rule 5, but also to more realistic generalisations that are based on the experience of many cases. For example, even if fact representation 4 has been permanently stored in our semantic memory following a considerable number of experienced cases, this belief can be proved to be false the first time we find a dog who is unable to bark. And, in fact, there is actually a breed of dogs, called basenji, which cannot bark. Note that even if we encounter a basenji after having learned fact representation 4, this would not disappear from our semantic memory. Instead, the following new fact representation would be produced:

$$\text{dogs : basenji} \ |\!\longrightarrow\!| \ \text{cannot(bark)} \quad (8)$$

In general, humans are not good in using negative evidence. This is strongly supported by 1966s Wason's cards experiments [36]. Thus, even if fact representation 8 logically contradicts fact representation 4, this is not removed from semantic memory and 8 is stored has an exception to the general rule for dogs. In fact, general questions on whether a dog barks or not will still be answered 'yes'.

2.6 Abductive Reasoning

Abductive reasoning goes from a known fact to its possible cause via an observed event. For example, if we know that Bob is always late at classes and today Bob is not present after the class has started, then we may infer that today Bob is late. Using BRDL, if the following fact representations are in our STM

$$\text{mates : Bob} \ |\!\longrightarrow\!| \ \text{always(late)} \quad (9)$$

$$\text{mates : Bob} \ |\!\longrightarrow\!| \ \text{is(mate)} \quad (10)$$

then we can see the abduction 'today(late(Bob))' from the virtual inference rule

$$(\text{always(late)})(\text{Bob}) \ (\text{not(in(class))})(\text{Bob}) \uparrow \implies \downarrow (\text{today(late)})(\text{Bob})$$

which is an instantiation of the inference rule

$$(\text{always(late)})(\text{mate}) \ (\text{not(in(class))})(\text{mate}) \uparrow \implies \downarrow (\text{today(late)})(\text{mate})$$

which is in our semantic memory and expresses that if we know that a mate is always late at classes and today that mate is not present after the class has started, then we may infer that today that mate is late. In fact, fact representation 10 drives the replacement of 'mate' with 'Bob', and fact representation 9, which is actually the representation of fact '(always(late))(Bob)', and the presence of (not(in(class)))(Bob) in STM, which is a consequence of an internalised perception, enable the virtual inference rule, thus determining the replacement of '(not(in(class)))(Bob)' with '(today(late))(Bob)' in STM.

2.7 Feeling and Emotion

As we have seen in our examples, there might be more than one piece of information in the enabling part and in the performing part of an inference rule. In fact, a richer version of inference rule 1 could be

$$\text{wags(dog) small(dog)} \uparrow \implies \downarrow \text{friendly(dog) cute(dog)} \tag{11}$$

if we feel that a small dog that wags is not just friendly but also cute. Note that 'cute(dog)' is a feeling rather than a fact. In fact, BRDL can model the production of *feelings* and *emotions*. For example,

$$\text{barks(dog) big(dog)} \uparrow \implies \downarrow \text{scary(dog)} \tag{12}$$

models that we are scared of big, barking dogs. Thus inference rules 11 and 12 produce our feelings, which are indicators of emotions, 'love' for inference rule 11 and 'fear' for inference rule 12. In previous work [11] we have presented how to use BRDL to model emotions

2.8 Planning

Planning is a process in which we are driven by a goal in manipulating information. This manipulation involves consuming and producing information, with the produced information possibly being further goals and the driving goal being removed only once it is achieved. For example, if our goal is to plan a holiday then we need to produce new goals for planning travel, accommodation and tours.

In BRDL we model a goal as 'goal(*achievement*)', where *achievement* is a set of pieces of information. In the context of factual knowledge, the goal is achieved when at least one of the pieces of information of *achievement* is in STM. The elements of the set are listed in any order, separated by commas. For example, in the context of planning a holiday, possible goals are

- 'goal(purchased(package), planned(components))'
  the holiday is planned once we have purchased a package or we have planned all holiday components (travel, accommodation and tours) separately;
- 'goal(purchased(airfare))'
  the travel is planned once we have purchased the airfare;

- 'goal(booked(room), booked(apartment)))'
  the accommodation is planned once we have booked a hotel room or an apartment;
- 'goal(booked(tours))' tours are planned once we have booked them.

Any planning process consists of a number of stages. The transition from one stage to the next can be modelled by a BRDL planning rule with the following structure:

$$goal : \ current \ stage \uparrow \implies \downarrow next \ stage$$

For example, the first stage in planning a holiday may be given by planning rules

$$goal_1: \text{enough(time)} \uparrow \implies \downarrow goal_2 \ goal_3 \ goal_4 \tag{13}$$

$$goal_1: \text{little(time)} \uparrow \implies \downarrow goal_5 \tag{14}$$

where

- $goal_1$ = goal(purchased(package), planned(components))
- $goal_2$ = goal(purchased(airfare))
- $goal_3$ = goal(booked(room), booked(apartament))
- $goal_4$ = goal(booked(tours))
- $goal_5$ = goal(purchased(package)).

Planning rules 13 and 14 could be in the semantic memory of a person who prefers to plan travel, accommodation and tours if there is enough time to carry out all these planning tasks, but would resort to an all-inclusive package if there is little time.

We normally set the initial goal that drives the planning process with reference to the specific task or tasks we want to model and/or analyse. However, in general, the initial goal may be produced by the application of an inference rule. For example, $goal_1$ may be generated by the following inference rule:

$$\text{approved(leave)} \uparrow \implies \downarrow goal_1 \tag{15}$$

which models the fact that we establish the goal of planning a holiday once we got our leave from work approved.

We have seen that rule 11 produces our feeling that a small dog that wags is not just friendly but also cute. Such a feeling can actually determine our desire to pat the dog, that is, produce our goal of patting the dog. This may be modelled by the following inference rule:

$$\text{wags(dog) small(dog)} \uparrow \implies \downarrow \text{friendly(dog) goal(patted(dog))} \tag{16}$$

Alternatively, we may add inference rule

$$\text{cute(dog)} \uparrow \implies \downarrow \text{goal(patted(dog))} \tag{17}$$

in addition to inference rule 11. An important remark is that inference rule 17 produces a goal from an emotional feeling. This is consistent with the most recent evidence from neuroscience that emotions play an essential role in decision making. In fact, here we decide to pat the dog as a consequence of a love emotion. More on this can be found on our previous work on modelling emotions with BRDL [11].

3   Modelling and Processing Behavioural Knowledge

In Sect. 2 we have presented how to model human thinking in BRDL. Now we present how to model human deliberate actions on the external environment. Obviously the action appears in the performing part of the rule.

Human deliberate actions may be associated with different levels of *will* and *consciousness*. A strong will is characterised by the presence of a goal that drives the behaviour but it may be made even stronger or actually weaker by the current mental state. For example, if we have the will of patting a dog, this will may be strengthened if in our mental state the dog is assessed as friendly and weakened if in our mental state the dog is assessed as unfriendly. A weak will is not driven by a goal, but just by the current mental state. For example, the feeling that the dog is cute may urge us to pat a dog even if we have not established this as our goal.

The presence of the goal is also an indicator of consciousness. Moreover, consciousness is increased if the action has an explicit effect on our mental state, that is, if the next mental state determined by the action performance is different from the current mental state in which the action is performed.

In Sect. 2.8 we said that, in the context of factual knowledge, the achievement of the goal 'goal(*achievement*)' occurs when at least one of the pieces of information of *achievement* is in STM. When action is involved, as in the case of behavioural knowledge, *achievement* may also contain actions and the goal is achieved when one of these is performed. Therefore, in general we can say that goal 'goal(*achievement*)' is achieved when either one of the actions of *achievement* is performed or at least one of the pieces of information of *achievement* is in STM.

In Sect. 3.1 we introduce templates of behaviour rules, which are stored in semantic memory, and in Sect. 3.2 we discuss problem solving.

3.1   Deliberate Behaviour

Deliberate behaviour can be of three types corresponding to different levels of will and consciousness: fully deliberate, strongly deliberate and weakly deliberate.

Fully Deliberate Behaviour. We say that the behaviour is *fully deliberate* when it is totally driven by the goal, with no influence from the current mental state. For example, driven exclusively by our goal, we might pat the dog although our current mental state assesses the dog as unfriendly. In this case the mental state is totally ignored, thus it does not appear in the behaviour rule. Therefore a *fully deliberate behaviour rule* may have one of the following two forms:

$$goal : \uparrow \implies action \downarrow$$

or

$$goal : \uparrow \implies action \downarrow next\ mental\ state$$

The presence of the *next mental state* in the second form denotes a higher consciousness.

The fully deliberate behaviour in patting the dog is modelled by one of the following two forms:

$$goal(\text{pat}(\text{dog})) : \uparrow \implies \text{pat}(\text{dog}) \downarrow$$

or

$$goal(\text{pat}(\text{dog})) : \uparrow \implies \text{pat}(\text{dog}) \downarrow \text{happy}(\text{dog})$$

when there is a higher consciousness about the effect of our action on the dog.

Strongly Deliberate Behaviour. We say that the behaviour is *strongly deliberate* when it is driven by the goal but also influenced by the current mental state. For example, our goal to pat the dog might be pursued only if there is the additional assessment, in our current mental state, that the dog is friendly. In this case the mental state must appear in the behaviour rule in addition to the goal. Therefore a *strongly deliberate behaviour rule* may have one of the following two forms:

$$goal : \; current \; mental \; state \uparrow \implies action \downarrow$$

or

$$goal : \; current \; mental \; state \uparrow \implies action \downarrow next \; mental \; state$$

The presence of the *next mental state* in the second form denotes a higher consciousness.

The strongly deliberate behaviour in patting the dog is modelled by one of the following two forms:

$$goal(\text{pat}(\text{dog})) : \; \text{friendly}(\text{dog}) \uparrow \implies \text{pat}(\text{dog}) \downarrow$$

or

$$goal(\text{pat}(\text{dog})) : \; \text{friendly}(\text{dog}) \uparrow \implies \text{pat}(\text{dog}) \downarrow \text{happy}(\text{dog})$$

when there is a higher consciousness about the effect of our action on the dog.

In Sect. 2.8 we have seen the template of a question-answer rule. Similarly, a strongly deliberate behaviour rule may have *factual knowledge* rather than *current mental state* in the enabling part. Thus the application of the rule involves a further retrieval from semantic memory.

Weakly Deliberate Behaviour. We say that the behaviour is *weakly deliberate* when it is totally driven by the current mental state with no actual goal. For example, we might be driven in patting the dog by the assessment, in our current mental state, that the dog is friendly, but without any explicit goal. In this case the mental state must appear in the behaviour rule whereas the goal is absent. Therefore a *weakly deliberate behaviour rule* may have one of the following two forms:

$$current \; mental \; state \uparrow \implies action \downarrow$$

or

$$current\ mental\ state \uparrow \implies action \downarrow next\ mental\ state$$

The presence of the *next mental state* in the second form denotes a higher consciousness.

The weakly deliberate behaviour in patting the dog is modelled by one of the following two forms:

$$friendly(dog) \uparrow \implies pat(dog) \downarrow$$

or

$$friendly(dog) \uparrow \implies pat(dog) \downarrow happy(dog)$$

when there is a higher consciousness about the effect of our action on the dog.

3.2   Problem Solving

Problem solving makes use of reasoning and planning but also may possibly make assumptions on the external environment and mentally simulate behaviour. Therefore, during processing, STM needs not only to contain goals that drive the application of LTM rules and information that makes up the mental state, but also include

- special goals 'mgoal(*achievement*)', which we call *mental goals*, that drive the mental simulation of the rule application rather than its actual application;
- assumptions, defined by the keyword 'assume', about the external environment to be stored in STM;
- an *action plan* 'plan($act_1 \rightarrow act_2 \rightarrow \ldots \rightarrow act_n$)' that represents the result of mentally simulating the sequential execution of actions act_1, act_2, $\ldots act_n$.

We assume that the length of the action plan is reasonable in order to hold it in STM as a single chunk. If the action plan is too long or not chunkable, the problem solving task cannot be executed just mentally. In that case, we can assume that each of the planned actions is instead communicated to the external environment, for instance by writing it on paper, as soon as it is identified.

We consider one of the most important theories to explain problem solving, the *problem space theory*, which was developed by Newell and Simon [26] in 1972. The idea underlying this theory is to start from an initial state and generate the state space that allows us to solve the problem. To this purpose we have some operators that we can use to move from the initial state towards a goal state, which characterises a possible solution of the problem. We need some *heuristics* to select the operators and apply them in the right order. One successful heuristic is the *means-ends analysis*, which allows us to reduce the distance between the initial state and the goal state.

As an example, let's consider the problem of moving a box full of items from an initial position to a final position. We know that we can only move the box when it is empty and we know how to empty and fill the box. This behavioural knowledge may be expressed by the following three behaviour rules

$$\text{goal}(\text{at}(\text{final})) : \text{empty at}(\text{initial}) \uparrow \implies \text{moveBox} \downarrow \text{empty at}(\text{final}) \qquad (18)$$

$$\text{goal}(\text{empty}) : \text{full} \uparrow \implies \text{emptyBox} \downarrow \text{empty} \qquad (19)$$

$$\text{goal}(\text{full}) : \text{empty} \uparrow \implies \text{fillBox} \downarrow \text{full} \qquad (20)$$

where

- 'at(initial)' means that we know that the box is at the initial position;
- 'at(final)' means that we know that the box is at the final position;
- 'empty' means that we know that the box is empty;
- 'full' means that we know that the box is full;
- 'moveBox' is the action for the operator to move the box from the initial position to the final position;
- 'emptyBox' is the action for the operator to empty the box;
- 'fillBox' is the action for the operator to fill the box.

Each operator has a precondition and a result as defined in the behaviour rules: the precondition is the current mental state in the enabling part of the rule and the result is the next mental state in the performing part of the rule. For example 'moveBox' has 'empty' and 'at(initial)' as precondition and 'empty' and 'at(final)' as result.

Table 1 shows the steps for solving the problem:

1. At the initial state, STM contains two mental goals, 'mgoal(at(final))' and 'mgoal(full)', since we want to find out how to move the full box to the final position, and two assumption, 'assume(full)' and 'assume(at(initial))', since the box is assumed to be full in the initial position. This STM content does not enable any of the rules. We need to apply means-ends analysis and try to

Table 1. Moving a heavy box—Problem Solving

Step	STM Contents	Rule	Goal Produced
1	mgoal(at(final)) mgoal(full) assume(full) assume(at(initial))		mgoal(empty)
2	mgoal(at(final)) mgoal(full) mgoal(empty) assume(full) assume(at(initial)).	19	
3	mgoal(at(final)) mgoal(full) assume(at(initial) assume(empty) plan(emptyBox)	18	
4	mgoal(full) assume(at(final)) assume(empty) plan(emptyBox → moveBox)	20	
5	assume(at(final)) assume(full) plan(emptyBox → moveBox → fillBox)		

find an operator that can get us closer to the goal. Rules 18 and 20 would get us close to the goal, if enabled, since they produce respectively 'at(final)' and 'full' in STM. But in order to be enabled they require the STM to contain 'empty', which may be produced by rule 19. Therefore, we need to produce 'mgoal(empty)' in STM to enable the mental simulation of the application of rule 19.

2. The mental simulation of the application of rule 19 is now enabled and produces the initial version of the plan, containing action 'emptyBox', and replaces assumption 'assume(full)' with 'assume(empty)' in STM. Since the mental goal 'mgoal(empty)' is achieved, it is removed from STM.

3. the mental simulation of the application of rule 18 is now enabled and add action 'moveBox' to the plan and replace assumption 'assume(at(initial))' with 'assume(at(final))' in STM. Since the mental goal 'mgoal(at(final))' is achieved, it is removed from STM.

4. the mental simulation of the application of rule 20 is now enabled and add action 'fillBox' to the plan and replace assumption 'assume(empty)' with 'assume(full)' in STM. Since the mental goal 'mgoal(full)' is achieved, it is removed from STM.

5. The final assumptions in STM, 'assume(at(final))' and 'assume(full)', show that the problem is solved and its solution 'plan(emptyBox $\rightarrow$ moveBox $\rightarrow$ fillBox)' is also in STM.

4   Memory Processes: Modelling and Analysis

We can distinguish three kinds of memory processes:

information transfer processes which allow information to flow between memory components in a specific direction;

memory component processes which occur within a specific memory component;

complex processes which involve the combination of the previous two kinds of processes.

The following memory processes have been informally introduced in Sect. 1 and illustrated in Fig. 1:

perception the very short-term storage of information from the environment in sensory memory;

selective attention the selection of the information that is relevant from the content of sensory memory and its transfer to STM while ignoring all other information, which is described in details in Sect. 4.1;

rehearsal which is described in details in Sect. 4.2 and 4.3;

retrieval of which some aspects have been considered in Sect. 2.2;

We also discuss two further processes:

skill acquisition is described in Sect. 4.4;

closure is described in Sect. 4.5.

Figure 3 illustrates all these memory processes in relation to the human memory components.

We are not going to further discuss perception since it is a memory component process associated with sensory memory and we do not model sensory memory explicitly. In fact, we assume that all information present in the environment is directly available to the attention process, without any form of buffering.

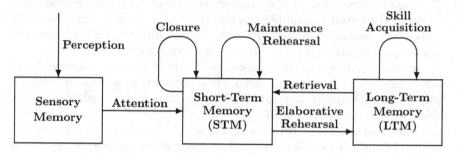

Fig. 3. Memory Processes

4.1   Selective Attention

Attention is an information transfer process that allows some of the information stored in sensory memory to be copied to STM before it decays. Since STM has a very limited capacity, only information that is relevant to the currently performed task is copied, possibly after some form of processing. Thus *attention* is a selective processing activity that aims to focus on one aspect of the environment while ignoring others. The effectiveness of selective attention depends on whether the

Table 2. Moving a heavy box—Physical Task

Step	STM Contents	Rule	Goal Produced	Action
1	goal(at(final)) goal(full) at(initial)	22		
2	goal(at(final)) goal(full) at(initial) full		goal(empty)	
3	goal(at(final)) goal(full) goal(empty) at(initial)) full	19		emptyBox.
4	goal(at(final)) goal(full) at(initial) empty	18		moveBox.
5	goal(full) at(final) empty	20		fillBox.
6	at(final) full			

information we need is salient in the environment. As we mentioned in Sect. 1, we distinguish two kinds of attention: *explicit attention* and *implicit attention*.

Explicit Attention focuses on goal-relevant stimuli in the environment that are associated with the current mental state. Moreover, the extent to which explicit attention works effectively depends on whether we have clear goals. The association between goal and stimuli should be stored somewhere in our LTM as the result of a learning process that has occurred over a long period. Therefore an *explicit attention rule* may have one of the following two forms:

$$goal : \ mental \ state \uparrow perception \implies \downarrow internalised/processed \ perception$$

or

$$goal : \uparrow perception \implies \downarrow internalised/processed \ perception$$

The presence of *mental state* in the first form denotes a higher consciousness. If we consider the example of problem solving in Sect. 3.2, rather than having just a mental task or deciding the sequence of actions to carry out afterwards, we can imagine to physically carry out each action as soon as it is identified. The first thing to do is then to perceive the weight of the box. With the goal of moving the box 'goal(at(final))', instead of the mental goal 'mgoal(at(final))', it is natural to focus on the perception of the weight of the box. This can be modelled by the following explicit attention rules:

$$goal(at(final)): \uparrow empty \implies \downarrow empty \tag{21}$$

$$goal(at(final)): \uparrow full \implies \downarrow full \tag{22}$$

The evolution of the STM and the action carried out for the physical task is given in Table 2.

Let's consider now the dog example. If our goal is to pat the dog, then our explicit attention will internalise the perception that the dog is wagging:

$$goal(pat(dog)): \uparrow wags(dog) \implies \downarrow wag(dog) \tag{23}$$

If we have some more familiarity with dog behaviour, then we can process the perception as part of the attention process and immediately realise that the dog is friendly:

$$goal(pat(dog)): \uparrow wags(dog) \implies \downarrow friendly(dog) \tag{24}$$

Implicit Attention is grabbed by sudden stimuli in the environment that are associated with the current mental state and/or carry emotional significance. The association between mental state or the emotional state and the stimuli should be stored somewhere in our LTM as the result of a learning process that has occurred over a long period. Therefore, an *implicit attention rule* has the following form:

$$mental \ state \uparrow perception \implies \downarrow internalised/processed \ perception$$

Let's consider the dog example again. If we are a dog lover, even without the explicit goal of patting the dog, our implicit attention will process the perception that the dog is wagging as part of the attention process:

$$\uparrow \text{wags(dog)} \implies \downarrow \text{friendly(dog)} \tag{25}$$

Finally, we observe that the focus determined by attention can cause *inattentional blindness*, that is, the fact that we miss some obvious details, which we cannot see though they are actually there. This is shown by Daniel J. Simons in two interesting videos titled "Selective Attention Test"[1] and "The Monkey Business Illusion"[2].

4.2   Maintenance Rehearsal

We have mentioned in Sect. 1.2 that among the information stored in STM we are interested in the one that may be verbalised (phonological loop). *Maintenance rehearsal* can be seen as phonological looping of the items to renew their representations within STM, thereby delaying signal decay. For example, by mentally repeating words that we have perceived and transferred to STM, their persistence in STM may be extended well beyond the normal STM decay time.

In 1962 Murdock [25] performed an experiment in which participants were presented with a list of words and then asked to recall them in any order immediately after the presentation. The result of the experiment were described by

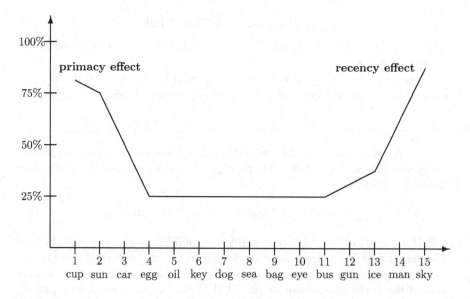

Fig. 4. Serial position curve

---

[1] https://www.youtube.com/watch?v=vJG698U2Mvo.
[2] https://www.youtube.com/watch?v=IGQmdoK_ZfY&t=16s.

a *serial position curve*, as the one in Fig. 4. This curve, which was described by Nipher as early as 1878 [27], shows that participant tend to remember the first few words (*primacy effect*) as well as the last few words (*recency effect*), whereas the middle words are mostly forgotten. An easy explanation for the recency effect is that the representation of the last words in STM did not decay at the time of the recall since they were still recent [1]. This explanation took into account later experiments in which recall is delayed by involving the participants in *distractor* activities, such as counting backwards or repeating nonsense words [20,34]. As shown in Fig. 5, a delay of 10 s considerably reduces the recency effect and a delay of 30 or more seconds makes it disappear completely. In fact, the representations of unrehearsed words decayed from STM due to the delay in recall. However, in both cases the primacy effect was basically unchanged.

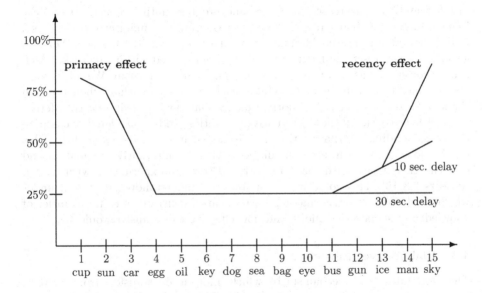

Fig. 5. Serial position curve

A more complex explanation can justify the primacy effect. Since participants were asked to remember the words, they actually rehearsed them, possibly unconsciously. As a result, the first few words were repeatedly rehearsed and persisted in STM determining the primacy effect. However, when approaching the middle of the sequence, there are too many words to rehearse and rehearsal cannot be carried out effectively. Therefore the memory of the middle words has mostly decayed at the time of recall. This explanation is based on Rundus experiments [35], which showed that primacy is reduced when the words are presented at a faster rate, thus preventing participants from properly rehearsing even the first words.

Clearly maintenance rehearsal extends the persistence of information in human memory. On the one hand such a persistence is rarely sustainable on the long-term but, on the other hand, it is essential to keep information in STM for the time needed to complete an ongoing task. We can also associate maintenance rehearsal with learning by heart, or *rote learning*, a form of learning that is unfortunately still used in school, but is boring, very time consuming and ineffective for consolidating knowledge on a long term and for comprehension. In fact, it is believed that maintenance rehearsal is normally not an information transfer process but mostly an STM-specific process.

In order to use BRDL to analyse maintenance rehearsal, we need to define a semantics that supports time progress. To this purpose, in previous work [15], items in STM are associated with two pieces of time information: a *lifetime*, which is the time that the item can persist in STM from production to natural decay, and a *lefttime*, which is the time left, at the current time, before the item decays. The lefttime equals the lifetime at the time of the item production in STM and then decreases with the time progress until it reaches 0 and the items decays, thus being removed from STM. However, maintenance rehearsal resets the lefttime to the lifetime every time the item is rehearsed. More in general, we can reset the lefttime when the item is used within the task, which can be considered as an implicit form of maintenance rehearsal. We might even assume that the lifetime increases a bit at each rehearsal and that, when a certain threshold is reached, then the information associated with the item is transferred from STM to LTM. All these alternative semantics can be considered to compare the corresponding alternative theories developed in cognitive psychology. This can be done by using in silico simulations with the alternative simulation and compare their result with the data gathered through experiments with human subjects [13,15]. This could also contribute to understanding how, and under which conditions, effective maintenance rehearsal contributes to the transfer of knowledge to semantic memory, and how effective this transfer would be.

4.3   Elaborative Rehearsal

The most important mechanism by which information transfers from STM to semantic memory is *elaborative rehearsal* [2]. This involves using the information representation within STM to access existing entries within semantic memory. This semantic association between items in STM and items in semantic memory is the deep processing that increases the chance that items in STM will become stored in LTM.

We can say that a large part of the content of semantic memory is knowledge that has been generated through elaborative rehearsal. From a BRDL perspective, we can say that fact representations, inference rules, planning rules, behaviour rules and, to some extent, explict attention rules model knowledge that is produced in semantic memory through elaborative rehearsal.

It is also possible to give BRDL a semantics that models the dynamics associations and links that are established during mental processing between information in STM and knowledge in semantic memory and can exploit such associations and links to synthesise new knowledge in semantic memory by modifying existing fact representations and rules and producing new ones. This would allow us to carry out in silico simulation of complex learning processes, which are normally difficult to study in reality because they occur over periods of many years. This is an important area of our current research using BRDL.

4.4   STM Skill Acquisition and Automatic Behaviour

In Sect. 3 we have considered the modelling and processing of behavioural knowledge. The processing of behavioural knowledge is the basis for all our deliberate activities. However, deliberate behaviour causes a high cognitive load and is very time consuming. In most of our daily activities we need a much more efficient form of information processing.

Imagine if in order to tie a shoe lace you had to rationally think about the process and consciously apply all rules needed for each single step. Although we might think that tying a shoe lace is a very trivial task, it is indeed a very complex one and, in fact, small children cannot do it and there are some people in their adulthood who still have difficulties or even cannot do it. Another activities that we take for granted is 'walking', but it is actually a very complex one. Then how can we perform such activities very efficiently while being totally unaware of the mental and motor processes underlying them?

To provide an answer to this question, Norman and Shallice [28] consider two levels of cognitive control:

Automatic Control
   fast processing activity that requires only *implicit attention* and is carried out outside awareness with no conscious effort implicitly, using rules and procedures stored in the procedural memory;

Deliberate Control
   processing activity triggered and focussed by *explicit attention* and carried out under the intentional control of the individual, who makes explicit use of factual knowledge and experiences stored in the declarative memory (semantic memory and episodic memory) and is aware and conscious of the effort required in doing so.

In addition to the apparently trivial task we considered above, automatic control is essential in more complex activities, such as riding a bike, playing a sport and driving a car. In order to effectively carry out such activities, we need to acquire a skill. Skill acquisition occurs through practice, often extensive and distributed over a long period of time, whereby, starting from a deliberate behaviour, the control of our behaviour evolves from deliberate to automatic. Once the skill is acquired, the task is carried out under automatic control, thus resulting in automatic behaviour.

For example, the skill of properly driving a car develops throughout a learning process based on deliberate control. During the learning process the driver has to make a conscious effort that requires explicit attention to use gear, indicators, etc. in the right way and to think about all road code rules before carrying out any action (deliberate control). In fact, the driver would not be able to carry out such an effort while talking or listening to the radio, since the deliberate control is entirely devoted to the driving task. Once automaticity in driving is acquired, the driver is no longer aware of low-level details and resorts to implicit attention to perform them (automatic control), while deliberate control and explicit attention may be devoted to other tasks such as talking or listening to the radio.

Therefore the process of skill acquisition is a complex process that modifies information from two forms of explicit memory, semantic memory and episodic memory, and moves it to procedural memory, which is the most known form of implicit memory. As for deliberate behaviour, automatic behaviour, which results from the process of skill acquisition, can be of three types: fully automatic, strongly automatic and weakly automatic.

Fully Automatic Behaviour. We say that the behaviour is *fully automatic* when it is totally driven by the perception, with no influence from the current mental state or a goal. For example, this is a kind of behaviour we have when we click 'ok' on a confirmation box associated with some routine interaction. In this case goal and mental state are totally ignored, thus they do not appear in the behaviour rule. Therefore, a *fully automatic behaviour rule* may have one of the following two forms:

$$\uparrow perception \implies action \downarrow$$

or

$$\uparrow perception \implies action \downarrow next \; mental \; state$$

The presence of the *next mental state* in the second form denotes a some form of consciousness about the potential effect of our behaviour.

The fully automatic behaviour of clicking 'ok' on a confirmation box is modelled by:

$$\uparrow button(ok) \implies click(ok) \downarrow$$

or

$$\uparrow button(ok) \implies click(ok) \downarrow confirmed$$

when there is some consciousness about the potential effect of our action. For example, while clicking on the confirmation box, we might get scared to make a mistake.

Strongly Automatic Behaviour. We say that the behaviour is *strongly automatic* when it is driven by a perception but also influenced by the current mental state. For example, this is a kind of behaviour we have when we click 'ok' on a confirmation box associated with a non-critical interaction. In this case the current mental state must appear in the behaviour rule whereas the goal is absent. This means that there is some consciousness about what we are doing. Therefore a *strongly automatic behaviour rule* may have one of the following two forms:

$$current \; mental \; state \uparrow perception \implies action \downarrow$$

or

$$current\ mental\ state \uparrow perception \implies action \downarrow next\ mental\ state$$

The presence of the *next mental state* in the second form denotes some form of consciousness about the potential effect of our behaviour.

The strongly automatic behaviour of clicking 'ok' on a confirmation box associated with a non-critical interaction is modelled by:

$$\text{non-critical(interaction)} \uparrow \text{button(ok)} \implies \text{click(ok)} \downarrow$$

or

$$\text{non-critical(interaction)} \uparrow \text{button(ok)} \implies \text{click(ok)} \downarrow \text{confirmed}$$

when there is some consciousness that we have confirmed.

Weakly Automatic Behaviour. We say that the behaviour is *weakly automatic* when it is influenced by the goal and possibly the current mental state. For example, this is a kind of behaviour we have when we click 'ok' on a confirmation box while deliberatly trying to save a file. In this case the goal must appear in the behaviour rule. This means that there is a higher consciousness about what we are doing. Therefore a *weakly automatic behaviour rule* may have one of the following four forms:

$$goal : \ current\ mental\ state \uparrow perception \implies action \downarrow$$

or

$$goal : \ current\ mental\ state \uparrow perception \implies action \downarrow next\ mental\ state$$

or

$$goal : \uparrow perception \implies action \downarrow$$

or

$$goal : \uparrow perception \implies action \downarrow next\ mental\ state$$

The presence of the *current mental state* in the first and second forms denotes some form of awareness about the context of our activity. The presence of the *next mental state* in the second and fourth forms denotes some form of consciousness about the potential effect of our behaviour.

If the automatic behaviour only occurs within non-critical interactions, the weakly automatic behaviour of clicking 'ok' on a confirmation box when trying to save a file is modelled by:

$$\text{goal(save)} : \text{non-critical(interaction)} \uparrow \text{button(ok)} \implies \text{click(ok)} \downarrow$$

or

$$\text{goal(save)} : \text{non-critical(interaction)} \uparrow \text{button(ok)} \implies \text{click(ok)} \downarrow \text{confirmed}$$

when there is some consciousness that we have confirmed.

If the automatic behaviour occurs independently of any awareness about the criticality of the interaction, the weakly automatic behaviour of clicking 'ok' on a confirmation box when trying to save a file is modelled by:

$$\text{goal(save)} : \uparrow \text{button(ok)} \Longrightarrow \text{click(ok)} \downarrow$$

or

$$\text{goal(save)} : \uparrow \text{button(ok)} \Longrightarrow \text{click(ok)} \downarrow \text{confirmed}$$

when there is some consciousness that we have confirmed.

Example of Skill Acquisition. Let's now model the car driving task of turning left at a crossing equipped with a traffic light, which requires to give way when turning left, assuming that we drive on the right side of the road. A novice who is still learning to drive will carry out the task using the following rules:

$$\uparrow \text{red(light)} \Longrightarrow \text{stop} \downarrow \text{waiting(green(light)))} \tag{26}$$

$$\text{waiting(green(light))} \uparrow \text{green(light)} \Longrightarrow \downarrow \text{green(light)} \tag{27}$$

$$\text{goal(turn(left))} : \text{green(light)} \uparrow \text{crossing(free)} \Longrightarrow \downarrow \text{crossing(free)} \tag{28}$$

$$\text{goal(turn(left))} : \text{crossing(free)} \uparrow \Longrightarrow \text{turn(left)} \downarrow \tag{29}$$

Rule 26 requires the driver to stop at a red traffic light and start waiting for a green light. The information 'waiting(green(light))' focuses the attention of the driver on the traffic light. Rule 27 models the implicit attention of the driver and leads to the internalisation that the light is green. This internalisation is modelled by the production of information 'green(light)' in STM. Such information drives the explicit attention of driver on the crossing to check whether it is free. This is a form of explicit attention because it is explicitly driven by the goal 'goal(turn(left))'. In fact, in absence of this goal, the driver would have probably just gone straight. Finally, the internalisation that the crossing is free drives the deliberate action of turning left. This novice behaviour consists of 3 automatic behaviour rules (26, 27 and 28) and one deliberate behaviour rule (29).

After the skill of driving is fully acquired, rules 28 and 29 are merged in the following automatic rule:

$$\text{goal(turn(left))} : \text{green(light)} \uparrow \text{crossing(free)} \Longrightarrow \text{turn(left)} \downarrow \tag{30}$$

Therefore, the deliberate rule is no longer used and the task is modelled by just automatic rules.

4.5   STM Closure

We have already said that once a goal is achieved, it is removed from STM. However, the achievement of the goal has been normally attained by exploiting a large amount of information that has been stored in STM and used for mental processing. Although most of this information has finally decayed once reached the lifetime, at the time of the goal achievement there is normally still some information in STM that was essential in achieving the goal but is now no longer needed. The presence of this information from the completed task keeps the *cognitive load* (that is, the amount of information stored in STM) high. This decreased available space in STM prevents information needed for new tasks to be stored. Moreover, if the usage of information in mental processing really increases its lifetime in STM, as we hypothized in Sect. 4.2, we cannot expect a fast decay for the leftover information.

Due to this reason, a memory process called *STM closure* aims at removing information that is no longer needed from STM. This subconscious removal is essential for the use of STM, but may cause human errors as we see in Sect 5.3. Moreover, the fact that such errors normally occur only when the cognitive load is high suggests that also closure may occur only when the cognitive load is high. However, how exactly this is carried out is not fully understood and a number of alternative hypotheses have been proposed. There are several questions on how STM closure is carried out: how much information is removed? under which circumstances? which information is removed first? Different answers to these questions lead to different hypotheses, whose implementations can provide distinct formal semantics for BRDL. Quantitative aspects may also be introduced at the semantic level, such as STM capacity and storage and retrieval times, as well as the persistence time information (lifetime and left time) that we discussed in Sect. 4.2. These semantics variants have been used to compare alternative cognitive psychology theories [13,15].

As an example of closure, let's consider the task of using an ATM (automatic teller machine). Let's assume that the user will normally use the ATM either to withdraw cash ('cash') or to get a statement ('stat'). Let's also assume that the user would like to select the note values when withdrawing cash. We can model this ATM task with the following rules:

$$\uparrow \text{requested}(\text{card}) \implies \text{insert}(\text{card}) \downarrow \text{thought}(\text{collect}(\text{card})) \qquad (31)$$

$$\uparrow \text{request}(\text{pin}) \implies \text{enter}(\text{pin}) \downarrow \qquad (32)$$

$$\text{goal}(\text{collect}(\text{cash})) : \uparrow \text{requested}(\text{selection}) \implies \text{select}(\text{cash}) \downarrow \text{decided}(\text{notes})$$
$$(33)$$

$$\text{goal}(\text{collect}(\text{stat})) : \uparrow \text{requested}(\text{selection}) \implies \text{select}(\text{stat}) \downarrow \qquad (34)$$

$$\text{decided}(\text{notes}) \uparrow \text{requested}(\text{values}) \implies \text{select}(\text{values}) \downarrow \qquad (35)$$

$$\uparrow \text{delivered}(\text{cash}) \implies \text{collect}(\text{cash}) \downarrow \qquad (36)$$

$$\uparrow \text{delivered}(\text{stat}) \implies \text{collect}(\text{stat}) \downarrow \qquad (37)$$

$$\text{thought}(\text{collect}(\text{card})) \uparrow \text{returned}(\text{card}) \implies \text{collect}(\text{card}) \downarrow \qquad (38)$$

In rule 31 the user reacts to the request of the ATM to insert the card not only by inserting the card but also thinking that the card will have to be retrieved. In rule 32 the user reacts to the request of the ATM to enter the pin by entering the pin. Rules 33 and 34 are the only deliberate rules, driven by the respective goals for withdrawing cash and getting a statement. When selecting cash withdrawal, the user will also decide which note values they would like to have and rule 35 implements such a selection. In rules 36 and 37 the user reacts to the perception of delivered cash and delivered statement, respectively. Finally, in rule 38 the user is triggered by the thought of collecting the card and performs such an action. We can notice that when withdrawing cash in the interaction with an ATM that does not offer the possibility to select the note values, rule 35 cannot be applied.

When the goal is achieved by performing rule 36, in which the user collects the cash, the user's thought 'thought(collect(card))' is still in STM. At this point, the STM closure process causes the removal of that thought from STM.

5   Informal and Formal Analysis

We can say that BRDL is a semi-formal notation. It has a precise syntax in terms of the structure of the rules, but it is very flexible in terms of the quality and structure of the rule components. Thanks to this syntactic flexibility, BRDL may be used at various levels of formality. It can be informally used to discuss human thinking and behaviour, as we illustrate in Sect. 5.1, and to analyse interaction, as we illustrate in Sect. 5.3.

Moreover, the same syntax may be associated with alternative formal semantics, thus supporting the comparison of alternative memory theories and other cognitive theories. Such full formalisations of BRDL may be formally used to analyse memory theories and cognitive theories, as we illustrate in Sect. 5.2, and to formally verify interactive systems, as we illustrate in Sect. 5.4. More information and examples on the use of BRDL in formal analysis can be found on the BRDL website[3].

5.1   Informally Analysing Cognition

Using formal methods is not only important for producing a formal model that can be used in a formal analysis process, possibly supported by semi-automatic or automatic tools. In fact, in software engineering, a key role of the formalisation process is to get rid of ambiguities and clarify aspects of the process or system we are investigating. When we use a precise, semi-formal notation to model human thinking and behaviour, we can exploit the formalisation process to understand and clarify a lot of aspects of human cognition. Building a formal model means describing structure and behaviour in a precise way and this can be successfully done only if we deeply understand the object of our modelling process.

Let's consider the driving task of a learner we introduced in Sect. 4.4. In order to build the LTM rules, we need to identify all cognitive elements of the task: the traffic light and its lights and the crossing, which needs to be free for us to turn left. In order to select the appropriate rule formats, we have to consider our focus changes while carrying out the task:

---

[3] https://antoniocerone.github.io/BRDL/.

- the initial focus on the traffic light waiting for the green light independently of the goal of turning to the left;
- once the traffic light is green, switching the focus to the crossing, driven by the goal of turning left.

These considerations lead to the formal description of the task using rules 26–29, but also to a deep understanding of the task itself.

Then we can consider the four rules and see that the two rules with a goal, 28 and 29, may be merged in one, rule 30, thus illustrating the skill acquisition process that allows a learner to become an expert driver, with respect to this specific task. We can then start asking ourself questions on the effect of this skill acquisition process.

A first question is whether the skilled behaviour is more efficient than the learner's behaviour. The fact that the number of rules is reduced from four to three already tells us that there is a reduction in the task complexity. Moreover, as it is always the case, the skill behaviour does not include deliberate behaviour rules, whereas the learner's behaviour includes deliberate behaviour rule 28.

A second question is whether the skilled behaviour is safer than the learner's behaviour. An intuitive answer would probably be that the learner's behaviour is better thought and less hurried and it is thus expected to be safer. However, the skilled driver has some consciousness that the traffic light is green while turning left, since 'green(light)' is in the mental state, whereas the learner's behaviour is only aware that the crossing is free while turning left. In fact, the skilled driver turns left as soon as the crossing is free without spending time in thinking about the give-way rule. Instead, during the time spent by the learner in reflecting on the road-code give-way rule in behaviour rule 28, the light might have become red again, thus causing a hazard. Therefore, as a conclusion, we can say that the skilled behaviour is safer than the learner's behaviour.

5.2   Formally Analysing Cognition

In psychology, theories of memory, cognition and human behaviour are developed and verified through the analysis of data collected using observations, questionnaires, interviews and experiments. Such theories are usually conceptual models, very informal and difficult to transform into computational models. BRDL helps provide a more precise description of such conceptual models, with the definition of alternative semantics that can be used to perform in silico experiments and compare their results with real-world data to understand which theory best reflects the reality.

In Sect. 4.2, we have discussed how to provide BRDL with a semantics that supports time progress. We adopted this approach in previous work [15] and we used it to perform in silico experiments to compare alternative quantitative implementations of conceptual hypotheses on the functioning of maintenance rehearsal. For example, we considered Burgess and Hitch's two parallel learning mechanisms [3,4], a 'fast' short-term learning process that is the basis of STM and is associated with trace decay, and a 'slow' learning process that gradually leads to LTM. These two processes proceed in parallel and, in our approach, are controlled by the two time information associated with items in STM. The 'fast' short-term learning process is controlled by the lefttime of the item, which determine its decay, while the parallel slow learning mechanism is represented by an increase in the lifetime.

In Sect. 4.3 we mentioned that it is possible to give BRDL a semantics that models the dynamic associations and links that are established during mental processing between information in STM and knowledge in semantic memory. We can then exploit such associations and links to build fact representations and rules that model the new knowledge created in semantic memory, thus enabling the in silico simulation of complex learning processes that in reality occur over periods of many years.

In Sect. 4.4 we mentioned that skill acquisition is a complex process that modifies information from semantic memory and episodic memory and moves it to procedural memory. The driving task example shows us that the merging of rules (rules 28 and 29 in the example) is a mechanical process that can be described algorithmically. We can then define a semantics that equip BRDL with this rule transformation process, thus implementing skill acquisition. As for knowledge learning, also skill acquisition occurs in reality over a long time period and, in such a context, in silico simulation can contribute to a better understanding of the phenomenon.

In Sect. 4.5, we mentioned several research questions about the STM closure process. Let's discuss possible semantics associated to these questions:

How much information is removed? The simplest answer to this question is that we completely flash out STM. But then, what about goals? If we have achieved a subgoal, we should not remove the main goal, which is not yet achieved. Think about the physical task of moving a heavy box shown in Table 2: we cannot remove the goal of moving the box once the goal of emptying the box is achieved. The most obvious solution is that closure does not remove any goal other that the one achieved. But are we sure that it is not the case that in some situations some other goals could be actually removed, possibly determining a human error as an outcome? Well, we need to make sure that we do not use too strict a semantics thus ruling out some potential human errors. After all, one important aim of analysing cognition is the identification of human errors. Finally, should we remove all non-goal information or just the information associated with the achieved goal? If we aim at the latter, then we must in some way link information in STM to one or more goals in order to select the information to remove.

Under which circumstances is information removed? We might possibly think that STM closure occurs every time the goal is achieved. Or we might think that it only occurs when there is need to make space in STM, that is, when the cognitive load is high. We discuss this issue in relation to human error in Sect. 5.3.

Which information is removed first? If we do not remove all information, how do we select the information to remove first? We already said that we could just remove the information associated with the achieved goal. But if we want to remove only part of such information, how do we select it? One possible choice would be to remove the oldest information. But since the oldest information might decay soon anyway, maybe it would be more effective to remove the most recent information. And how does rehearsal effect closure? Is rehearsed information more difficult to remove, especially when we define a semantics in which maintenance rehearsal increases the lifetime?

Different answers to these questions lead to different hypotheses, whose implementations can provide distinct formal semantics for BRDL. Quantitative aspects may also be introduced at the semantic level, such as STM capacity and storage and retrieval times, as well as the persistence time information (lifetime and left time) that we discussed in Sect. 4.2. These semantics variants have been used to compare alternative cognitive psychology theories [13,15].

We conclude this section by observing that cognitive aspects may sometimes be formalised as property of a behaviour, rather than characterised through BRDL semantics. For example, we may expect that a given task might fail for a number of different reasons. Psychologists may then try to identify all human behavioural patterns that lead to the failure. In this context, formal analysis may help by formally verifying if the taxonomy of the behavioural patterns that lead to the failure is a correct and complete decomposition of the task failure. This approach has been successfully applied to an air traffic control task [8,9].

5.3   Informally Analysing Interaction

There are many techniques for informally analysing interactive systems [18]. Such techniques come from the areas of software engineering and human-computer interaction and from synergetic aspects of these two areas. Due to the central role of the user in interaction, many techniques are based on the user's participation in the system evaluation process in general, and in testing the system in particular. However, selecting and involving the right users is a difficult and expensive process, both in terms of resources and time.

For this reason techniques based on expert analysis have also been developed. There is no user participation in these techniques, but evaluators have to consider user's cognition. In fact the evaluators are often experts in cognition or, at least, have some background in cognitive psychology. BRDL can offer a great contribution to these techniques and introduce rigour in modelling cognition.

One important technique based on expert analysis is *cognitive walkthrough*. This technique was introduced by Polson *et al.* in 1992 [33]. It originates from code walkthrough and consists in going through the sequence of actions that the interface requires the user to perform in order to accomplish some specific task, with a strong focus on learnability. BRDL could be used by the evaluator to describe the cognitive aspects of the actions consistently with the kind of knowledge and experience that the evaluator assumes about the user and provide a precise description of a representative task. For example, an expert user would be modelled mosty using automatic rules whereas a novice users would be modelled using a large number of deliberate rules.

When we focus on a specific task, BRDL can help identify problems associated with that task, which is also an important purpose of cognitive walkthrough. Let's consider the ATM example introduced in Sect. 4.5. Although closure is useful to get rid of the cognitive load caused by a task, once the goal is achieved, it may also cause some human errors, which can have serious consequences. If the task defined by rules 31–38 in Sect. 4.5 is performed with the goal of withdrawing cash using an ATM that delivers the cash after returning the card, then 'thought(collect(card))' is still in STM when rule 38 is performed at the end of the task. However, if the ATM delivers the cash before returning the card, the achievement of the goal may determine the STM closure and remove 'thought(collect(card))' from STM, so that rule 38 is not enabled and cannot be performed. This causes a *post-completion error*, so called because it occurs after the completion of the task, because a subsidiary subtask cannot be carried out. Post-completion error can be avoided if the action that determines the goal achievement is the last to be performed, as it is the case for the ATM that delivers the cash after returning the card.

In some application domains, such as air transportation, post-completion errors may potentially have catastrophic consequences. On 24 May 2013, during take off from London Heathrow, the fan cowl doors from both engines of an Airbus A319-131 detached from the aircraft, causing much damage, including a fuel leak, which resulted in development of an external fire. Although the aircraft managed to return to Heathrow and land safely with nobody injured, the consequences of the accident could have been catastrophic.

The investigation[4] determined that the fan cowl doors on both engines were left unlatched after a scheduled overnight maintenance. This is a post-completion error, since latching the fan cowl doors is a subsidiary task to be carried out after the goal of performing maintenance is achieved. This was the first time that post-completion error was identified in an aircraft accident, but it was also discovered that a number of previous accidents were caused by the same kind of error.

5.4   Formally Analysing Interaction

As shown by the aircraft accident described in Sect. 5.3, human error may have catastrophic consequences in interactive system used in safety-critical areas such as medicine, transportation, air traffic control, nuclear power and chemical plants. For this reason the attempt to use formal methods in the analysis of interactive system is not new [19].

Initial works on the application of formal methods to interactive systems and human-computer interaction considered either the formal description of expected effective operator behaviour [31] or the formal analysis of errors performed by the operator as reported by accident analysis [21]. However, human behaviour

---

[4] https://www.gov.uk/aaib-reports/aircraft-accident-report-1-2015-airbus-a319-131-g-euoe-24-may-2013.

essentially emerges from cognitive processes and, on the one hand, limiting the model of the human component to the modelling of expected or already observed behaviour does not provide a sufficient coverage of potential human errors while, on the other hand, enabling the emergence of all potential behaviours would result in an infinite or intractable state space.

The introduction of the notion of *cognitively plausible user behaviour*, based on formal assumptions to bind the way users act driven by cognitive processes [5], resulted in the appropriate compromise to select the aspects of user's cognition to be modelled. The cognitive model is then composed in parallel with the system model, thus generating a predicted behaviour whose state space is finite and sufficiently small to be effectively analysed but still allows human errors to emerge. This approach well-suits the use of BRDL. In fact, the cognitive model defined using BRDL may be composed in parallel with models of a physical/computer system and the properties of the interaction can be analysed at various levels of abstraction, for example abstracting from time versus modelling time explicitly.

The analysis is carried out using *model checking* [16], either directly searching the predicted behaviour for specific states or sets of states or by using some logical notations, normally *temporal logic* [32], to define system properties and exhaustively checking their validity on the predicted behaviour. In previous work [14], we adopted this approach and implemented BRDL constructs by using Real-Time Maude, a formal modelling language based on rewrite systems and equipped with a model checker [22,29,30].

Acknowledgment. We would like to thank Graham Pluck, Ben Tyler and Olzhas Zhalgendinov for helpful discussions and the research assistants who contributed to the implementation of the tools based on BRDL: Anel Mengdigali, Diana Murzagaliyeva, Nuray Nabiyeva and Temirlan Nurbay.

A   BRDL Syntax

In this appendix we summarise the BRDL syntax by using squared brackets '[' and ']' to enclose optional parts:

Fact Representations
   knowledge domain : category $|\longrightarrow|$ *label(category/attribute)*
Inference Rules
   premise $\uparrow \implies \downarrow consequence$
Planning Rules
   goal : current stage $\uparrow \implies \downarrow next\ stage$
Explicit Attention Rules
   goal : [*mental state*] $\uparrow perception \implies \downarrow internalised/processed\ perception$
Implicit Attention Rules
   [*mental state*] $\uparrow perception \implies \downarrow internalised/processed\ perception$
Fully Deliberate Behaviour Rules
   goal : $\uparrow \implies action \downarrow$ [*next mental state*]

Strongly Deliberate Behaviour Rules

$goal:$ $current\ mental\ state \uparrow \implies action \downarrow [next\ mental\ state]$

Weakly Deliberate Behaviour Rules

$current\ mental\ state \uparrow \implies action \downarrow [next\ mental\ state]$

Fully Automatic Behaviour Rules

$\uparrow perception \implies action \downarrow [next\ mental\ state]$

Strongly Automatic Behaviour Rules

$current\ mental\ state \uparrow perception \implies action \downarrow [next\ mental\ state]$

Weakly Automatic Behaviour Rules

$goal:$ $[current\ mental\ state] \uparrow perception \implies action \downarrow [next\ mental\ state]$

References

1. Atkinson, R.C., Shiffrin, R.M.: Human memory: a proposed system and its control processes. In: Spense, K.W. (ed.) The Psychology of Learning and Motivation: Advances in Research and Theory II, pp. 89–195. Academic Press (1968)
2. Atkinson, R.C., Shiffrin, R.M.: The control of short-term memory. Sci. Am. **225**(2), 82–90 (1971)
3. Burgess, N., Hitch, G.J.: Memory for serial order: a network model of the phonological loop and its timing. Psychol. Rev. **106**(3), 551–581 (1999)
4. Burgess, N., Hitch, G.J.: A revised model of short-term memory and long-term learning of verbal sequences. J. Mem. Lang. **55**(4), 627–652 (2006)
5. Butterworth, R., Blandford, A.E., Duke, D.: Demonstrating the cognitive plausability of interactive systems. Form. Asp. Comput. **12**, 237–259 (2000)
6. Campoy, G.: Evidence for decay in verbal short-term memory: a commentary on Berman, Jonides, and Lewis (2009). J. Exp. Psychol. Learn. Mem. Cogn. **38**(4), 1129–1136 (2012)
7. Castro, N., Siew, C.S.Q.: Contributions of modern network science to the cognitive sciences: revisiting research spirals of representation and process. In: Proceedings of the Royal Society A, vol. 476. The Royal Society (2020). https://doi.org/10.1098/rspa.2019.0825
8. Cerone, A., Connelly, S., Lindsay, P.: Formal analysis of human operator behavioural patterns in interactive surveillance systems. Softw. Syst. Model. **7**(3), 273–286 (2008)
9. Cerone, A.: A cognitive framework based on rewriting logic for the analysis of interactive systems. In: De Nicola, R., Kühn, E. (eds.) SEFM 2016. LNCS, vol. 9763, pp. 287–303. Springer, Cham (2016). https://doi.org/10.1007/978-3-319-41591-8_20
10. Cerone, A.: Behaviour and Reasoning Description Language (BRDL). In: Camara, J., Steffen, M. (eds.) SEFM 2019. LNCS, vol. 12226, pp. 137–153. Springer, Cham (2020). https://doi.org/10.1007/978-3-030-57506-9_11
11. Cerone, A.: A BRDL-based framework for motivators and emotions. In: SEFM 2022 Collocated Workshops, Lecture Notes in Computer Science, vol. 13765, pp. 351–365. Springer, Cham (2023). https://doi.org/10.1007/978-3-031-26236-4_28
12. Cerone, A., Mengdigali, A., Nabiyeva, N., Nurbay, T.: A web-based tool for collaborative modelling and analysis in human-computer interaction and cognitive science. In: Proceeding of DataMod 2021, Lecture Notes in Computer Science, vol. 13268, pp. 175–192. Springer, Cham (2022). https://doi.org/10.1007/978-3-031-16011-0_12

13. Cerone, A., Murzagaliyeva, D., Nabiyeva, N., Tyler, B., Pluck, G.: In silico simulations and analysis of human phonological working memory maintenance and learning mechanisms with Behavior and Reasoning Description Language (BRDL). In: SEFM 2021 Collocated Workshops, Lecture Notes in Computer Science, vol. 13230. Springer, Cham (2022). https://doi.org/10.1007/978-3-031-12429-7_3

14. Cerone, A., Ölveczky, P.C.: Modelling human reasoning in practical behavioural contexts using Real-Time Maude. In: Sekerinski, E., et al. (eds.) FM 2019. LNCS, vol. 12232, pp. 424–442. Springer, Cham (2020). https://doi.org/10.1007/978-3-030-54994-7_32

15. Cerone, A., Pluck, G.: A formal model for emulating the generation of human knowledge in semantic memory. In: Bowles, J., Broccia, G., Nanni, M. (eds.) DataMod 2020. LNCS, vol. 12611, pp. 104–122. Springer, Cham (2021). https://doi.org/10.1007/978-3-030-70650-0_7

16. Clarke, E.M., Henzinger, T.A., Veith, H., Bloem, R. (eds.): Handbook of Model Checking. Springer, Cham (2018). https://doi.org/10.1007/978-3-319-10575-8

17. Collins, A.M., Quillian, M.R.: Retrieval time from semantic memory. J. Verbal Learn. Verbal Behav. 8, 240–247 (1969)

18. Dix, A., Finlay, J., Abowd, G., Beale, R.: Human-Computer Interaction. Pearson Education, 3rd edn. (2004)

19. Dix, A.J.: Formal Methods for Interactive Systems. Academic Press, Cambridge (1991)

20. Glanzer, M., Cunitz, A.R.: Two storage mechanisms in free recall. J. Verbal Learn. Verbal Behav. 5(4), 351–360 (1966). https://doi.org/10.1016/S0022-5371(66)80044-0

21. Johnson, C.: Reasoning about human error and system failure for accident analysis. In: Proceedings of INTERACT 1997, pp. 331–338. Chapman and Hall (1997)

22. Martí-Oliet, N., Meseguer, J.: Rewriting logic: roadmap and bibliography. Theoret. Comput. Sci. 285(2), 121–154 (2002)

23. Miller, G.A.: The magical number seven, plus or minus two: some limits on our capacity to process information. Psychol. Rev. 63(2), 81–97 (1956)

24. Mueller, S.T., Krawitz, A.: Reconsidering the two-second decay hypothesis in verbal working memory. J. Math. Psychol. 53(1), 14–25 (2009)

25. Murdock, B.B.J.: The serial position effect of free recall. J. Exp. Psychol. 64(5), 482–488 (1962)

26. Newell, A., Simon, H.: Human Problem Solving. Prentice Hall, Hoboken (1972)

27. Nipher, F.E.: Lecture experiment. Nature 18(447), 94–95 (1878)

28. Norman, D.A., Shallice, T.: Attention to action – willed and automatic control of behavior. In: Davidson, R.J., Schwartz, G.E., Shapiro, D. (eds.) Consciousness and Self-Regulation. Springer (1986). https://doi.org/10.1007/978-1-4757-0629-1_1

29. Ölveczky, P.C.: Designing Reliable Distributed Systems. UTCS, Springer, London (2017). https://doi.org/10.1007/978-1-4471-6687-0

30. Ölveczky, P.C., Meseguer, J.: Semantics and pragmatics of Real-Time Maude. Higher-Order Symb. Comput. 20(1–2), 161–196 (2007)

31. Palanque, P., Bastide, R., Paterno, F.: Formal specification as a tool for objective assessment of safety-critical interactive systems. In: Proceedings of INTERACT 1997, pp. 323–330. Chapman and Hall (1997)

32. Pnueli, A.: The temporal logic of programs. In: Proceedings of FOCS 1977, pp. 46–57. IEEE (1977)

33. Polson, P., Lewis, C., Rieman, J., Wharton, C.: Cognitive walkthroughs: a method for theory-based evaluation of user interfaces. Int. J. Man-Mach. Stud. 36, 742–773 (1992)

34. Postman, L., Phillips, L.W.: Short-term temporal changes in free recall. Q. J. Exp. Psychol. **17**(2), 132–138 (1965). https://doi.org/10.1080/17470216508416422
35. Rundus, D.: Analysis of rehearsal processes in free recall. J. Exp. Psychol. **89**(1), 63–77 (1971). https://doi.org/10.1037/h0031185
36. Wason, P.C.: Reasoning. In: Foss, B.M. (ed.) New Horizons in Psychology. Penguin (1966)

Object-Centric Process Mining: An Introduction

Wil M. P. van der Aalst(✉)

Process and Data Science (PADS), RWTH Aachen University, Aachen, Germany
wvdaalst@pads.rwth-aachen.de
https://www.vdaalst.com/

Abstract. Initially, the focus of process mining was on processes evolving around a single type of objects, e.g., orders, order lines, payments, deliveries, or customers. In this simplified setting, each event refers to precisely one object and the automatically discovered process models describe the lifecycles of the selected objects. Dozens of process-discovery and conformance-checking techniques have been developed using this simplifying assumption. However, real-life processes are more complex and involve objects of multiple types interacting through shared activities. Object-centric process mining techniques start from event logs consisting of events and objects without imposing the classical constraints, i.e., an event may involve multiple objects of possibly different types. This paper introduces object-centric event logs and shows that many of the existing process-discovery and conformance-checking techniques can be adapted to this more holistic setting. This provides many opportunities, as demonstrated by examples and the tool support we developed.

Keywords: Object-Centric Process Mining · Process Discovery · Conformance Checking · Event Data · Process Mining

1   Introduction

More than half of the Fortune 500 companies are already using process mining to analyze and improve their business processes. Process mining starts from event logs extracted from data stored in information systems [1]. Some information systems record explicit audit trails ready to be used for process mining. However, this is the exception. Taking a closer look at contemporary information systems shows that most center around a database composed of dozens, hundreds, or even thousands of database tables. Looking at these tables, one will witness that most of these tables contain timestamps or dates, e.g., when the order was created, when the patient was admitted, when the data were entered into the system, etc. Hence, *event data are everywhere* [5].

According to Gartner, there are now over 40 process mining vendors, e.g., Celonis, Signavio (now part of SAP), ProcessGold (now part of UiPath), Fluxicon, Minit, LanaLabs (now part of Appian), MyInvenio (now part of IBM), QPR, Apromore, Everflow, etc. [30].[1] Most of these systems assume that *each event refers to a single case*

---

[1] See the website www.processmining.org for an up-to-date overview of existing tools.

© The Author(s), under exclusive licence to Springer Nature Switzerland AG 2023
A. Cerone (Ed.): ICTAC 2021, LNCS 13490, pp. 73–105, 2023.
https://doi.org/10.1007/978-3-031-43678-9_3

and has a *timestamp* and *activity*. This is also the standard assumption made in literature [1]. Also the official IEEE standard for storing event data, called XES (eXtensible
Event Stream) [28], makes this assumption.

It is very natural to assume that an event has indeed a timestamp and refers to an
activity: What happened and when did it happen? However, the assumption that each
event refers to precisely one case may cause problems [3]. *Object-Centric Event Logs*
(OCEL) aim to overcome this limitation [26]. In OCEL, an event may refer to any
number of objects (of different types) rather than a single case. Object-centric process
mining techniques may produce Petri nets with different types of objects [8] or artifact-
centric process models [21,22,35].

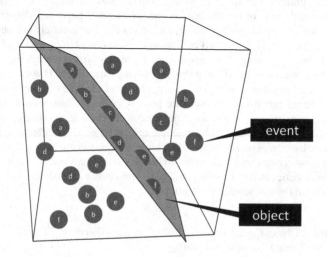

Fig. 1. An event may refer to any number of objects and the same object may be involved in
multiple events. The classical case notion assumes that each event refers to a single case. Object-
centric process mining drops this assumption to analyze and improve a much larger class of
processes.

Large-scale process mining users, vendors, and researchers acknowledge that the
case-notation is limiting the application of process mining. Also, the preprocessing of
raw data to create event data satisfying the requirements may take up to 80% of the time.
One can use the following metaphor to explain the problem. Existing techniques use
two-dimensional (2D) event logs and models. In object-centric process mining, we use
three-dimensional (3D) event logs and models (see Fig. 1). The first two dimensions are
activities and time while considering only one type of objects. Object-centric process
mining adds a third dimension because multiple object types are considered and one
event may refer to any number of objects.

For people familiar with *Colored Petri Nets* (CPNs) [9,29], it is fairly easy to imagine a process model with multiple types of interacting objects. In a CPN tokens resid-
ing in places may represent different types of objects (products, people, machines, storage
locations, etc.). Transitions in a CPN may connect places of different types and can thus

represent activities involving multiple types of objects. However, it is far from trivial to discover such models. Traditional process mining approaches assume that each event refers to a single case. As a result, cases can be considered *independent* of each other. This leads to process models that describe the lifecycle of a case *in isolation*.

A range of process discovery approaches using the "single-case assumption" have been proposed [4]. These can be grouped in "bottom-up" approaches like the Alpha algorithm [1, 10, 13, 14, 16, 38, 41] and "top-down" approaches like the inductive mining approaches [31–33]. See [12] for a recent survey of process discovery techniques.

There are many techniques for conformance checking, but most of these also make the "single-case assumption". The two most frequently used approaches are *token-based replay* [37] and *alignments* [6, 17]. The approach in [24] is a notable exception using so-called *proclets* [7]. Proclets and most of the artifact-centric approaches [22] assume that process instances (case, artifact, proclet, etc.) are interacting. Object-centric process mining assumes that events share objects, i.e., objects are not interacting as autonomous entities, but may be involved in common events. This simplifies the problem as is illustrated by the recently developed object-centric process mining techniques and tools, the OCEL standard, and the simplicity of the definitions presented in this tutorial paper.

The advantages of using object-centric process mining are threefold:

- *Data extraction is only done once.* There is no longer a need to pick a case notion when extracting data. The extraction of objects and events does not depend on the viewpoint.
- *Relations between objects of possibly multiple types are captured and analyzed.* In traditional process mining (with a focus on individual cases), interactions between objects are abstracted away.
- *Object-centric process models provide a three-dimensional view of processes and organizations.* In one process model multiple object types and their relations are visualized. Moreover, by selecting subsets of object types and activities, it is possible to change viewpoint and get new insights.

The goal of this paper is not to explain a specific process-discovery or conformance-checking technique. Instead, we provide a *tutorial-style introduction* to the topic and will show that there are a few general principles that allow lifting process mining techniques from the "single-case" to the "multi-object" level. This paper is based on a tutorial and keynote given in the context of *18th International Colloquium on Theoretical Aspects of Computing* (ICTAC 2021) in September 2021.

The remainder is organized as follows. Section 2 introduces the input needed for object-centric process mining, followed by a brief introduction to process discovery and conformance checking for event logs assuming a single case notion (Sect. 3). Section 4 presents a baseline approach for object-centric process discovery building upon existing techniques. The topic of object-centric conformance checking is covered in Sect. 5. Process mining is not limited to process discovery and conformance checking. Hence, Sect. 6 briefly discusses the impact of object-centricity on other types of analysis. Section 7 discusses concerns related to the complexity caused by looking at many object types and activities. Section 8 concludes the paper.

2 Object-Centric Event Data

Traditional process mining approaches assume that each event is related to precisely one object (called case). This tutorial paper shows that *relaxing* this requirement allows for a major step forward in data-driven process analytics. For example, we can now look at processes and organizations *from any angle* using a *single source of truth*, i.e., there is no need to extract new data when changing the viewpoint of analysis. Looking at different types of objects at the same time allows us to discover novel and valuable insights that live at the intersection points of processes and departments. The transition from traditional process mining to object-centric process mining is similar to moving from 2D to 3D. Before we discuss novel 3D process mining techniques, this section first introduces *object-centric event logs*, i.e., collections of *related events and objects*.

An event e can have any number of attributes. $\#_x(e)$ is the value of attribute x for event e. We require the following two attributes to be present for any event: activity $\#_{act}(e)$, and timestamp $\#_{time}(e)$. An object o can also have any number of attributes, but these may change over time. For example, object o represents a specific patient that has a birth date that does not change, but also has an address, phone number, weight, and blood pressure that may change. $\#_x^t(o)$ is the value of attribute x for object o at time t. There is a mandatory object attribute *type* with value $\#_{type}^t(o)$ representing the type of object. $\#_{type}^t(o)$ does not change over time, so we can also write $\#_{type}(o)$. There is a many-to-many relation R between events and objects. $(e, o) \in R$ if and only if object o is involved in event e. To formalize object-centric event logs, we first introduce several universes.

Definition 1 (Universes). $\mathcal{U}_{ev}$ *is the universe of events,* $\mathcal{U}_{obj}$ *is the universe of objects* $(\mathcal{U}_{ev} \cap \mathcal{U}_{obj} = \emptyset)$, $\mathcal{U}_{act}$ *is the universe of activities,* $\mathcal{U}_{time}$ *is the universe of timestamps,* $\mathcal{U}_{type}$ *is the universe of object types,* $\mathcal{U}_{att} = \{act, time, type, \ldots\}$ *is the universe of attributes,* $\mathcal{U}_{val}$ *is the universe of values, and* $\mathcal{U}_{map} = \mathcal{U}_{att} \nrightarrow \mathcal{U}_{val}$ *is the universe of attribute-value mappings. We assume that* $\mathcal{U}_{act} \cup \mathcal{U}_{time} \cup \mathcal{U}_{type} \subseteq \mathcal{U}_{val}$ *and* $\perp \notin \mathcal{U}_{val}$. *For any* $f \in \mathcal{U}_{map}$, *if* $x \notin dom(f)$, *we write* $f(x) = \perp$ *to denote that there is no attribute value.*

Using these universes, we define an event log as follows.

Definition 2 (Event Log). *An event log is a tuple* $L = (E, O, \#, R)$ *consisting of a set of events* $E \subseteq \mathcal{U}_{ev}$, *a set of objects* $O \subseteq \mathcal{U}_{obj}$, *a mapping* $\# \in (E \rightarrow \mathcal{U}_{map}) \cup (O \rightarrow (\mathcal{U}_{time} \rightarrow \mathcal{U}_{map}))$, *and a relation* $R \subseteq E \times O$, *such that for all* $e \in E$, $\#(e)(act) \in \mathcal{U}_{act}$ *and* $\#(e)(time) \in \mathcal{U}_{time}$, *and for all* $o \in O$ *and* $t, t' \in \mathcal{U}_{time}$, $\#(o)(t)(type) = \#(o)(t')(type) \in \mathcal{U}_{type}$.

An event log consists of a set of events E and a set of objects O connected through R. Events have an activity and a timestamp, and objects have a type. To make the notation more intuitive, we use $\#_x$ or $\#_x^t$ to refer to attribute values. Formally: $\#_x(e) = \#(e)(x)$ and $\#_x^t(o) = \#(o)(t)(x)$, e.g., $\#_{act}(e)$ is the activity of event e, $\#_{time}(e)$ is the timestamp of event e, $\#_{type}^t(o)$ is the type of object o at time t. Since the type of an object cannot change, we can drop t and write $\#_{type}(o)$.

Events are ordered by their timestamps. Without loss of generality, we can assume that there is a total order on events, i.e., we assume an arbitrary (but fixed) order for events that have the same timestamp.

Definition 3 (Event Order). *Let $L = (E, O, \#, R)$ be an event log. $\prec_L \subset E \times E$ is a total order such that for any pair of events $e_1, e_2 \in E$: $e_1 \prec_L e_2$ implies $e_1 \neq e_2$ and $\#_{time}(e_1) \leq \#_{time}(e_2)$.*

Figure 2 shows a visualization of an event log. The black circles represent events labeled with the corresponding activity. Objects flow through the graph from start ▶ to end ■ grouped and colored per object type. Exploiting the total order $\prec_L$ we can think of objects as a "line" visiting different events, i.e., pick an object o and the corresponding events visited by o form a sequence. Note that all objects entering an event are also exiting an event and vice versa.

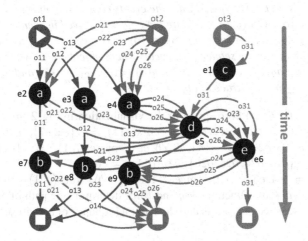

Fig. 2. visualization of an event log $L = (E, O, \#, R)$ with nine events $E = \{e1, e2, \ldots, e9\}$, ten objects $O = \{o11, o12, \ldots, o31\}$, three object types (e.g., $\#_{type}(o11) = ot1$, $\#_{type}(o21) = ot2$, and $\#_{type}(o31) = ot3$), and five activities a, b, c, d, and e. The connections show the flow of objects. $R = \{(e1, o31), (e2, o11), (e2, o21), (e2, o22), (e3, o12), (e3, o23), (e4, o13), (e4, o24), (e4, o25), (e4, o26), \ldots, (e9, o26)\}$ relates events and objects.

The formalization $L = (E, O, \#, R)$ abstracts from the way the information is stored. A possible realization to store event data would be to have three database tables:

- An *event table* with one row per event and a column for each event attribute (e.g., activity and timestamp and optional attributes like costs), next to the event identifier as the primary key.
- An *object update table* with one row per object update and a column for each object attribute (including object type), next to the object identifier and timestamp (the combination of the latter two is the primary key).
- A *relation table* connecting event identifiers and object identifiers.

The *Object-Centric Event Log (OCEL)* standard [26] provides two storage formats for such data: *JSON-OCEL* and *XML-OCEL* (cf. `ocel-standard.org`). The only difference between our formalization and OCEL is that OCEL assumes that objects have fixed attributes. The idea is that a new object is created if its attributes change. Moreover, OCEL types attributes, e.g., string, integer, float, and timestamp. In this paper, we introduce object-centric process mining at a conceptual level, not assuming a particular syntax. However, our tools use OCEL as a concrete storage format.

In the remainder, we will use the following functions to query event logs and to extract the "path" of a particular object.

Definition 4 (Notations). *For an event log $L = (E, O, \#, R)$, we introduce the following notations.*

- $act(L) = \{\#_{act}(e) \mid e \in E\}$ *is the set of activities,*
- $types(L) = \{\#_{type}(o) \mid o \in O\}$ *is the set of object types,*
- $events(o) = \{e \in E \mid (e, o) \in R\}$ *are the events containing object $o \in O$,*
- $objects(e) = \{o \in O \mid (e, o) \in R\}$ *are the objects involved in event $e \in E$,*
- $seq(o) = \langle e_1, e_2, \ldots, e_n \rangle$ *such that $events(o) = \{e_1, e_2, \ldots, e_n\}$ and $e_i \prec_L e_j$ for any $1 \leq i < j \leq n$ is the sequence of events where object $o \in O$ was involved in,*
- $trace(o) = \langle a_1, a_2, \ldots, a_n \rangle$ *such that $seq(o) = \langle e_1, e_2, \ldots, e_n \rangle$ and $a_i = \#_{act}(e_i)$ for any $1 \leq i \leq n$ is the trace of object $o \in O$.*

Let $L = (E, O, \#, R)$ correspond to the visualization in Fig. 2. $act(L) = \{a, b, c, d, e\}$, $types(L) = \{ot1, ot2, ot3\}$, $events(o11) = \{e2, e7\}$, $events(o21) = \{e2, e5, e7\}$, $events(o26) = \{e4, e5, e6, e9\}$, $objects(e1) = \{o11, o21, o22\}$, $objects(e4) = \{o13, o24, o25, o26\}$, $seq(o11) = \langle e2, e7 \rangle$, $seq(o21) = \langle e2, e5, e7 \rangle$, $seq(o26) = \langle e4, e5, e6, e9 \rangle$, $trace(o11) = \langle a, b \rangle$, $trace(o21) = \langle a, d, b \rangle$, and $trace(o26) = \langle a, d, e, b \rangle$. Functions seq and $trace$ determine the path of an object: the former returns a sequence of events and the latter a sequence of activities.

3   Traditional Process Mining

As mentioned in the introduction, most process mining techniques assume that each event corresponds to precisely one case. This implies that there is just one object type *case* and relation R is a function. In terms of the visualization in Fig. 2 this means that every event has precisely one ingoing and one outgoing arc. This implies that an event log can be seen as a *multiset of traces* where each *trace is a sequence of activities* corresponding to a specific case.

Figure 3 visualizes the lifecycle of each object. There are ten objects $O = \{o11, o12, \ldots, o31\}$ distributed over three object types. When we are forced to pick a single case notion, we pick an object type and use the corresponding subset of sequences depicted in Fig. 3. Note that the same event may appear in different lifecycles leading to the so-called convergence problem.

In this section, we show how to extract a classical event log from an object-centric event log and discuss filtering, basic process discovery, and conformance checking starting from a multiset of traces.

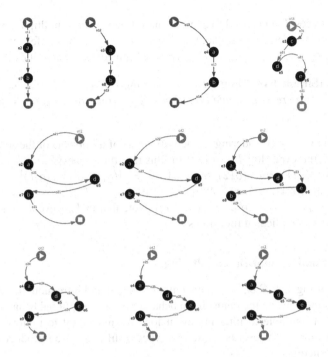

Fig. 3. A visualization of the lifecycle of each object based on Fig. 2. Note that some events are replicated, e.g. $e4$ appears four times, because $objects(e4) = \{o13, o24, o25, o26\}$. Due to the total ordering of events, each object corresponds to a sequence of activities, e.g., $trace(o11) = \langle a, b\rangle$, $trace(o21) = \langle a, d, b\rangle$, and $trace(o26) = \langle a, d, e, b\rangle$.

3.1 Preliminaries

In the remainder, we use basic mathematical notations, including sequences, sets, multisets, and functions. $\sigma = \langle x_1, x_2, \ldots, x_n\rangle \in X^*$ is a sequence of length n over a set X. $\mathcal{P}(X) = \{Y \mid Y \subseteq X\}$ is the powerset of X, i.e., all subsets of X. $f \in X \nrightarrow Y$ is a partial function with domain $dom(f)$ and range $rng(f) = \{f(x) \mid x \in dom(f)\}$. $f \in X \to Y$ is a total function with domain $dom(f) = X$. $\mathcal{B}(X) = X \to \mathbf{N}$ is the set of all multisets over X. We use square brackets to denote concrete multisets, e.g., $X = [a^2, b^7, c] \in \mathcal{B}(\{a, b, c\})$ is a multiset with 10 elements such that $X(a) = 2$, $X(b) = 7$, and $X(c) = 1$. As usual, multisets can be mapped to ordinary sets if needed. Some examples assuming $X = [a^2, b^7, c]$: $\{x \in X\} = \{a, b, c\}$, $X \cup [c^2, d^5] = [a^2, b^7, c^3, d^5]$, $X \cap [b^2, c^5, d^3] = [b^2, c]$, $[f(x) \mid x \in X] = [(f(a))^2, (f(b))^7, f(c)]$, $\sum_{x \in X} f(x) = 2f(a) + 7f(b) + f(c)$.

3.2 Creating a Classical Event Log for a Specific Object Type

To relate object-centric event logs to classical case-centric event logs, we can simply pick a single object type and then create a trace for each object using the function *trace* introduced before. Note that multiple objects may have the same trace, therefore we get a multiset of traces. Events need to be replicated if they refer to multiple objects of the selected type. Consider, for example, Fig. 3. The bottom six object lifecycles define the simple event log $[\langle a, d, b \rangle^2, \langle a, d, e, b \rangle^4]$ when we consider only activities.

Definition 5 (Simple Event Log). *For an event log $L = (E, O, \#, R)$ and object type $ot \in types(L)$, we create a simple event log $L_{ot} = [trace(o) \mid o \in O \wedge \#_{type}(o) = ot] \in \mathcal{B}(\mathcal{U}_{act}^*)$.*

L_{ot} is obtained by considering the activity paths of all objects of the selected type. Again we use the event log L in Fig. 2 to illustrate this. $types(L) = \{ot1, ot2, ot3\}$ $L_{ot1} = [trace(o11), trace(o12), trace(o13)] = [\langle a, b \rangle, \langle a, b \rangle, \langle a, b \rangle] = [\langle a, b \rangle^3]$. $L_{ot2} = [trace(o21), \ldots trace(o26)] = [\langle a, d, b \rangle, \ldots \langle a, d, e, b \rangle] = [\langle a, d, b \rangle^2, \langle a, d, e, b \rangle^4]$. $L_{ot3} = [trace(o31)] = [\langle c, d, e \rangle]$. Note that in L_{ot2} event $e5$ is replicated six times and $e6$ is replicated four times.

3.3 Activity and Variant-Based Filtering

A simple event log $L \in \mathcal{B}(\mathcal{U}_{act}^*)$ may contain frequent and infrequent behaviors. Process mining may focus on the mainstream behavior or on exceptional behaviors. Therefore, we need to be able to filter the event log. We may want to remove infrequent activities or variants. To describe these two types of filtering, we introduce projection and ranking functions.

Definition 6 (Projection Functions). *Let $L \in \mathcal{B}(\mathcal{U}_{act}^*)$ be an event log, $A \subseteq \mathcal{U}_{act}$ a set of activities, and $V \subseteq \mathcal{U}_{act}^*$ a set of variants (i.e. traces).*

- $L \Uparrow V = [\sigma \in L \mid \sigma \in V]$ *is the projection of L on V, and $L \Uparrow \overline{V} = [\sigma \in L \mid \sigma \notin V]$ removes all variants in V.*
- $\sigma \uparrow A$ *projects a trace $\sigma \in \mathcal{U}_{act}^*$ on A, i.e., $(\sigma \cdot \langle a \rangle) \uparrow A = \sigma \uparrow A \cdot \langle a \rangle$ if $a \in A$, and $(\sigma \cdot \langle a \rangle) \uparrow A = \sigma \uparrow A$ if $a \notin A$. $\sigma \uparrow \overline{A}$ removes all activities in A from trace $\sigma \in \mathcal{U}_{act}^*$, i.e., $\sigma \uparrow \overline{A} = \sigma \uparrow (\mathcal{U}_{act} \setminus A)$.*
- $L \uparrow A = [\sigma \uparrow A \mid \sigma \in L]$ *is the projection of L on A and $L \uparrow \overline{A} = [\sigma \uparrow \overline{A} \mid \sigma \in L]$ removes all A events.*

Consider the example log $L = [\langle a, b, c, d \rangle^{10}, \langle a, c, b, d \rangle^5, \langle a, e, d \rangle^3]$. $L \Uparrow \{\langle a, e, d \rangle\} = [\langle a, e, d \rangle^3]$. $L \Uparrow \overline{\{\langle a, e, d \rangle\}} = [\langle a, b, c, d \rangle^{10}, \langle a, c, b, d \rangle^5]$. $L \uparrow \{a, d\} = [\langle a, d \rangle^{18}]$. $L \uparrow \overline{\{a, d\}} = [\langle b, c \rangle^{10}, \langle c, b \rangle^5, \langle e \rangle^3]$. Next, we rank the activities and variants based on their frequency.

Definition 7 (Ranking Functions). *Let $L \in \mathcal{B}(\mathcal{U}_{act}^*)$ be an event log.*

- $afreq_L(A) = \sum_{\sigma \in L \uparrow A} |\sigma|$ *counts the number of $A \subseteq \mathcal{U}_{act}$ events in event log L.*
- $vfreq_L(V) = |L \Uparrow V|$ *counts the number of $V \subseteq \mathcal{U}_{act}^*$ traces in event log L.*
- $act(L) = \cup_{\sigma \in L} \{a \in \sigma\}$ *are the activities in L.*
- $var(L) = \{\sigma \in L\}$ *are the variants in L.*
- $arank(L) = \langle a_1, a_2, \ldots, a_n \rangle \in \mathcal{U}_{act}^*$ *such that $afreq_L(\{a_i\}) \geq afreq_L(\{a_j\})$ and $a_i \neq a_j$, for any $1 \leq i < j \leq n$ and $\{a_1, a_2, \ldots, a_n\} = act(L)$.*

- $vrank(L) = \langle \sigma_1, \sigma_2, \ldots, \sigma_m \rangle \in (\mathcal{U}_{act}{}^*)^*$ *such that* $vfreq_L(\{\sigma_i\}) \geq vfreq_L(\{\sigma_j\})$ *and* $\sigma_i \neq \sigma_j$, *for any* $1 \leq i < j \leq m$ *and* $\{\sigma_1, \sigma_2, \ldots, \sigma_m\} = var(L)$.

There may be activities and variants that have the same frequency. In this case, we rank these in some fixed order, e.g., alphabetically. For event log $L = [\langle a, b, c, d \rangle^{10},$ $\langle a, c, b, d \rangle^5, \langle a, e, d \rangle^3]$, we have $arank(L) = \langle a, d, b, c, e \rangle$ and $vrank(L) = \langle \langle a, b, c, d \rangle,$ $\langle a, c, b, d \rangle, \langle a, e, d \rangle \rangle$. The ranking of activities and variants can be used to select the most frequent activities and variants covering a given percentage $cov \in [0, 1]$ of the events or traces in the event log.

Definition 8 (Filtering Functions). *Let* $L \in \mathcal{B}(\mathcal{U}_{act}{}^*)$ *be an event log with arank* $(L) = \langle a_1, a_2, \ldots, a_n \rangle$ *and* $vrank(L) = \langle \sigma_1, \sigma_2, \ldots, \sigma_m \rangle$. *Given a threshold* $cov \in$ $[0, 1]$, *we can filter the log as follows.*

- $afilter_L(cov) = L \uparrow \{a_1, a_2, \ldots, a_k\}$ *where* $1 \leq k \leq n$ *is the smallest number such that* $afreq_L(\{a_1, a_2, \ldots, a_k\}) \geq cov \times afreq_L(act(L))$.
- $vfilter_L(cov) = L \Uparrow \{\sigma_1, \sigma_2, \ldots, \sigma_k\}$ *where* $1 \leq k \leq m$ *is the smallest number such that* $vfreq_L(\{\sigma_1, \sigma_2, \ldots, \sigma_k\}) \geq cov \times vfreq_L(var(L))$.

Again we use event log $L = [\langle a, b, c, d \rangle^{10}, \langle a, c, b, d \rangle^5, \langle a, e, d \rangle^3]$ to illustrate the two filtering functions. $afilter_L(0.5) = [\langle a, d \rangle^{18}]$ (covering 36 of 69 events, i.e., 52%), $afilter_L(0.8) = [\langle a, b, c, d \rangle^{10}, \langle a, c, b, d \rangle^5, \langle a, d \rangle^3]$ (covering 66 of 69 events, i.e., 95%), $vfilter_L(0.5) = [\langle a, b, c, d \rangle^{10}]$ (covering 10 of 18 traces, i.e., 55%), and $vfilter_L(0.8) = [\langle a, b, c, d \rangle^{10}]$ (covering 15 of 18 traces, i.e., 83%).

Most process mining tools provide sliders to seamlessly simply models by leaving out infrequent activities and/or variants.

3.4 Discovering a Directly-Follows Graph (DFG)

Dozens of process discovery techniques are able to learn process models from event data based on the "multiset of traces" abstraction, i.e., event logs of the form $L \in$ $\mathcal{B}(\mathcal{U}_{act}{}^*)$. These process models provide a representation describing a set of traces, i.e., they describe behavior of the form $B \subseteq \mathcal{U}_{act}{}^*$. Examples include "bottom-up" approaches like the Alpha algorithm [1, 10] producing Petri nets and 'top-down' approaches like the inductive mining approaches [31–33] producing process trees. Both Petri nets and process trees are able to describe concurrency and can be translated into *Business Process Model and Notation* (BPMN) models [20, 36]. There are also approaches not able to uncover concurrency. These approaches typically produce *Directly-Follows Graphs* (DFGs).

DFGs simply visualize the "directly-follows" relation between activities. This typically leads to underfitting process models [2]. When activities appear out of sequence, loops are created, thus leading to Spaghetti-like diagrams suggesting repetitions that are not supported by the data. However, DFGs are easy to compute, also in a distributed manner, using a single pass through the event data [1]. This explains why they are widely used.

Definition 9 (Directly Follows Graph). *A Directly Follows Graph (DFG) $G = (A, F)$ is composed of a multiset of activities $A \in \mathcal{B}(\mathcal{U}_{act})$ and a set of weighted edges $F \in \mathcal{B}((A \cup \{\blacktriangleright\}) \times (A \cup \{\blacksquare\}))$ such that $\{\blacktriangleright, \blacksquare\} \cap A = \emptyset$ and for any $a \in A$: $|[b \mid (b, a) \in F]| = |[b \mid (a, b) \in F]| = A(a)$ and there exists a path $\sigma = \langle \blacktriangleright, a_1, \ldots a_n, \blacksquare \rangle$ such that $(a_i, a_{i+1}) \in F$ for $1 \leq i < n$ and $a \in \{a_1, \ldots a_n\}$.*

In a DFG $G = (A, F)$, A represents the multiset of activities, i.e., $A(a)$ denotes the frequency of activity $a \in A$. Recall that $\mathcal{B}(\mathcal{U}_{act}) = \mathcal{U}_{act} \to \mathbb{N}$. F is also a multiset. $F(a, b)$ is the frequency of the connection between activities a and b. The process starts with a symbolic activity $\blacktriangleright$ and ends with a symbolic activity $\blacksquare$. Therefore, each regular activity $a \in A$ needs to be on a path from $\blacktriangleright$ to $\blacksquare$. Finally, the frequency of activity a should match the sum of the frequencies on the input arcs and should also match the sum of the frequencies on the output arcs. This is expressed by the requirement $|[b \mid (b, a) \in F]| = |[b \mid (a, b) \in F]| = A(a)$ for any regular activity a. Note that this implies that $|[a \mid (\blacktriangleright, a) \in F]| = |[a \mid (a, \blacksquare) \in F]| > 0$, i.e., the frequencies of the symbolic start and end match, because the rest of the graph is balanced.

Given an event log L, we can create the corresponding DFG $G(L) = (A, F)$ as follows.

Definition 10 (Directly Follows Graph for an Event Log). *For a simple event log $L \in \mathcal{B}(\mathcal{U}_{act}^*)$, the Directly Follows Graph (DFG) $G(L) = (A, F)$ is composed of a multiset of activities $A = \bigcup_{\sigma \in L} [a \in \sigma]$, a start activity $\blacktriangleright \notin A$, an end activity $\blacksquare \notin A$, a flow relation $F = [(a_i, a_{i+1}) \mid \sigma = \langle a_1, a_2, \ldots, a_n \rangle \in L \land a_0 = \blacktriangleright \land a_{n+1} = \blacksquare \land 0 \leq i \leq n]$.*

It is easy to see that the construction in Definition 10 leads to a DFG satisfying the requirements in Definition 9.

Figure 4 shows three DFGs based on the object-centric event log in Fig. 2. There is one DFG for each of the object types. Using Definition 5 the following three simple event logs are created: $L_{ot1} = [\langle a, b \rangle^3]$, $L_{ot2} = [\langle a, d, b \rangle^2, \langle a, d, e, b \rangle^4]$, and $L_{ot3} = [\langle c, d, e \rangle]$. Using Definition 10, a DFG is created for each of these logs. $G_{ot1} = (A_{ot1}, F_{ot1})$ with $A_{ot1} = [a^3, b^3]$ and $F_{ot1} = [(\blacktriangleright, a)^3, (a, b)^3, (b, \blacksquare)^3]$ is the DFG computed for object type $ot1$. $G_{ot2} = (A_{ot2}, F_{ot2})$ with $A_{ot2} = [a^6, b^6, d^6, e^4]$ and $F_{ot2} = [(\blacktriangleright, a)^6, (a, d)^6, (d, b)^2, (d, e)^4, (e, b)^4, (b, \blacksquare)^6]$ is the DFG computed for object type $ot2$. $G_{ot3} = (A_{ot3}, F_{ot3})$ with $A_{ot3} = [c, d, e]$ and $F_{ot3} = [(\blacktriangleright, c), (c, d), (d, e), (e, \blacksquare)]$ is the DFG computed for object type $ot3$.

Definition 11 (Accepting Traces of a DFG). *Let $G = (A, F)$ be a DFG. $\sigma = \langle a_1, a_2, \ldots, a_n \rangle$ is an accepting trace of G if $(\blacktriangleright, a_1) \in F$, $(a_n, \blacksquare) \in F$, and $(a_i, a_{i+1}) \in F$ for $1 \leq i < n$. $lang(G)$ is the set of all accepting traces.*

The three DFGs in Fig. 4 are acyclic and therefore have a finite number of accepting traces: $lang(G_{ot1}) = \{\langle a, b \rangle\}$, $lang(G_{ot2}) = \{\langle a, d, b \rangle, \langle a, d, e, b \rangle\}$, and $lang(G_{ot3}) = \{\langle c, d, e \rangle\}$. DFGs cannot capture concurrency. To illustrate this, we first introduce *accepting Petri nets*.

Note that activity-based filtering using $afilter_L(cov)$ and variant-based filtering using $vfilter_L(cov)$ can be applied to the event log before computing the DFG. In our

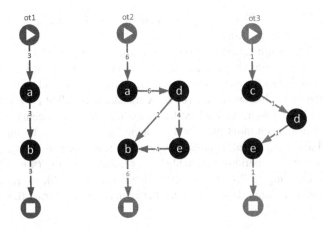

Fig. 4. Three Directly Follows Graphs (DFG) based on the simple event logs $L_{ot1} = [\langle a, b \rangle^3]$, $L_{ot2} = [\langle a, d, b \rangle^2, \langle a, d, e, b \rangle^4]$, and $L_{ot3} = [\langle c, d, e \rangle]$.

formalization $G = (A, F)$, the edges in a DFG have frequencies (F is a multiset). This can also be used for filtering. However, frequencies do not affect the set of accepting traces $lang(G)$. Hence, they are also ignored for conformance checking. It is assumed that the DFG only contains the relevant directly-follows relations.

3.5   Accepting Petri Net

There exist many different process modeling notations able to capture concurrency, e.g., UML activity diagram, UML statecharts, Petri nets, process algebras, BPMN (Business Process Model and Notation) models, etc. The Petri net formalism provides a graphical but also formal language and was the first formalism to adequately capture concurrency. See [18, 19] for a more extensive introduction. Other notations, like BPMN and UML activity diagrams, often have semantics involving "playing the token game" and build on Petri net concepts.

Because traces in an event log have a clear start and end, we use *accepting* Petri nets.

Definition 12 (Accepting Petri Net). *An accepting Petri net is a triplet $AN = (N, M_{init}, M_{final})$ where $N = (P, T, F, l)$ is a labeled Petri net, $M_{init} \in \mathcal{B}(P)$ is the initial marking, and $M_{final} \in \mathcal{B}(P)$ is the final marking. A labeled Petri net is a tuple $N = (P, T, F, l)$ with P the set of places, T the set of transitions, $P \cap T = \emptyset$, $F \subseteq (P \times T) \cup (T \times P)$ the flow relation, and $l \in T \nrightarrow \mathcal{U}_{act}$ a labeling function.*

The left-hand side of Fig. 5 shows an accepting Petri net AN_1. There are eight places $P = \{p1, p2, p3, p4, p5, p6, p7, p8\}$ (represented by circles) and six transitions $T = \{t1, t2, t3, t4, t5, t6\}$ (represented by squares). The flow relation $F = \{(p1, t1), (t1, p2), (t1, p3), \ldots, (t6, p8)\}$ list the connections between places and transitions. The labeling function is a partial function, i.e., there may be transitions without a label. However, in AN_1 all transitions have a label: $l(t1) = a, l(t2) = b, l(t3) = c, l(t4) = d,$

$l(t5) = e$, and $l(t6) = f$. The accepting Petri net in Fig. 5 has an initial marking $M_{init} = [p1]$ and a final marking $M_{final} = [p8]$.

States in Petri nets are called *markings* and mark certain places with *tokens* (represented by black dots). Formally, a marking M is a multiset of places, i.e., $M \in \mathcal{B}(P)$. Tokens in the initial marking are denoted using small triangles ▶ and tokens in the final marking are denoted using small squares ■. A transition is called *enabled* if each of the input places has a token. An enabled transition may *fire* (i.e., occur), thereby consuming a token from each input place and producing a token for each output place. In the initial marking $M_{init} = [p1]$, transition $t1$ can fire resulting in marking $[p2, p3, p4]$. In this marking, three transitions are enabled: $t2$, $t3$, and $t4$. Firing $t4$ results in marking $[p2, p3, p7]$ enabling $t2$, $t3$, and $t5$. After also firing $t2$ and $t3$, we reach marking $[p5, p6, p7]$. In this marking, there is a choice between $t5$ and $t6$. Firing $t6$ results in the final marking $M_{final} = [p8]$.

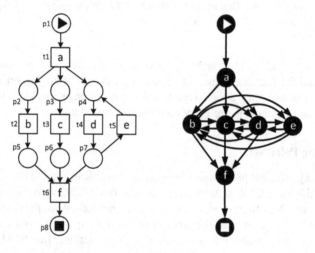

Fig. 5. Accepting Petri net AN_1 (left) and DFG G_1 (right).

A *firing sequence* is a sequence of transition occurrences obtained by firing enabled transitions and moving from one marking to the next. A *complete* firing sequence starts in the initial marking and ends in the final marking. AN_1 in Fig. 5 has infinitely many complete firing sequences because of the loop involving $t5$ and $t4$. Examples of such complete firing sequences are $\langle t1, t2, t3, t4, t6 \rangle$, $\langle t1, t4, t3, t2, t5, t4, t6 \rangle$, and $\langle t1, t3, t2, t4, t5, t4, t5, t4, t6 \rangle$. Note that when starting in the initial marking M_{init} it is possible to fire the transitions in the order indicated (i.e., the transition are enabled in the intermediate markings) ending in the final marking M_{final}.

Definition 13 (Accepting Traces of an Accepting Petri Net). *Let $AN = (N, M_{init}, M_{final})$ be an accepting Petri net with $N = (P, T, F, l)$ and $FS \subseteq T^*$ the set of all* *complete firing sequences.* $lang(AN) = \{l(\sigma) \mid \sigma \in FS\}$ *is the set of all accepting traces.*[2]

For AN_1 in Fig. 5 there are infinitely many accepting traces $lang(AN_1) = \{\langle a, b, c, d, f\rangle, \langle a, d, c, b, e, d, f\rangle, \langle a, c, b, d, e, d, e, d, f\rangle, \ldots\}$.

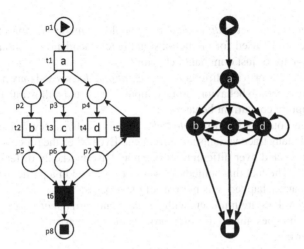

Fig. 6. Accepting Petri net AN_2 (left) and DFG G_2 (right). Note that the accepting Petri net has two silent transitions $t5$ and $t6$.

Accepting Petri net AN_2 in Fig. 6 has the same network structure as AN_1 but a different labeling function l_2. $dom(l_2) = \{t1, t2, t3, t4\}$, i.e., $t5$ and $t6$ do not have a label and are called silent. This means that these transitions cannot be observed in the corresponding accepting traces. $lang(AN_2) = \{\langle a, b, c, d\rangle, \langle a, d, c, b, d\rangle, \langle a, c, b, d, d, d\rangle, \ldots\}$.

Figures 5 and 6 also show the corresponding DFGs: G_1 and G_2. Since DFGs cannot express concurrency, it is impossible to create DFGs that have the same set of accepting traces as the accepting Petri nets AN_1 and AN_2. Note that $lang(AN_1) \subset lang(G_1)$ and $lang(AN_2) \subset lang(G_2)$ and the differences are significant. In AN_1 and AN_2 there is always one b and one c in each accepting trace. However, in G_1 and G_2 there can be any number of b's and c's.

This explains why DFGs tend to be severely underfitting. Whenever activities do not happen in a fixed sequence, loops are introduced. However, DFGs, in combination with filtering, can be used to get a valuable first impression of the underlying process.

3.6 Conformance Checking

The goal of process discovery is to find a process model whose behavior is "close" to the behavior seen in the event log. Conformance-checking techniques aim to measure

---

[2] Note that labeling function l is applied to a sequence of transitions, i.e., $l(\langle\rangle) = \langle\rangle$, $l(\langle t\rangle) = \langle l(t)\rangle$ if $t \in dom(l)$, $l(\langle t\rangle) = \langle\rangle$ if $t \notin dom(l)$, and $l(\sigma \cdot \langle t\rangle) = l(\sigma) \cdot l(\langle t\rangle)$ for any $\sigma \in T^*$.

the distance between an event log and a process model. These techniques can be used to evaluate the quality of a discovered or hand-made process model. Here, we focus on the simplified setting where we have an event log $L \in \mathcal{B}(\mathcal{U}_{act}^*)$ and a process model PM having $lang(PM) \in \mathcal{P}(\mathcal{U}_{act}^*)$ as accepting traces. We have seen DFGs and accepting Petri nets as examples. Despite the simplified setting, there are many challenges. Some examples:

- A process model may serve *different goals*. Should the model summarize past behavior, or is the model used for predictions and recommendations? Should the model show all behavior or just dominant behavior?
- Different notations provide different *representational biases* and may make it impossible to express certain behaviors. For example, Figs. 5 and 6 illustrate that DFGs are unable to capture concurrent behavior.
- An event log contains just *example behavior*. Typically, a few trace variants are frequent and many trace variants are infrequent. Even when the process is stable, two event logs collected over different periods may have markedly different infrequent trace variants. The fact that something was not observed in a particular period does not mean it cannot happen or is not part of the process.
- Although event logs are multisets with *frequent* and *infrequent* traces, most process discovery techniques aim to discover process models that are "binary", i.e., a trace is possible or not.

These challenges show that it is impossible to restrict conformance to a single measure. In [1], the following four *quality dimensions* to evaluate a process model PM in the context of an event log L were identified.

- *Recall*, also called (replay) fitness, aims to quantify the fraction of observed behavior that is allowed by the model.
- *Precision* aims to quantify the fraction of behavior allowed by the model that was actually observed (i.e., avoid "underfitting" the event data).
- *Generalization* aims to quantify the probability that new unseen cases will fit the model (i.e., avoid "overfitting" the event data).
- *Simplicity* refers to Occam's Razor and can be made operational by quantifying the complexity of the model (number of nodes, number of arcs, understandability, etc.).

In this paper, we do not focus on a single measure and use the following generic definition.

Definition 14 (Conformance Measure). *A conformance measure is a function conf $\in \mathcal{B}(\mathcal{U}_{act}^*) \times \mathcal{P}(\mathcal{U}_{act}^*) \rightarrow [0, 1]$. conf$(L, lang(PM))$ quantifies conformance for an event log $L \in \mathcal{B}(\mathcal{U}_{act}^*)$ and a process model PM having $lang(PM) \in \mathcal{P}(\mathcal{U}_{act}^*)$ as accepting traces (higher is better).*

Let $L \in \mathcal{B}(\mathcal{U}_{act}^*)$ and $lang(PM) \in \mathcal{P}(\mathcal{U}_{act}^*)$. Some example measures are:

- Trace-based recall: $conf_1(L, lang(PM)) = \frac{|[\sigma \in L | \sigma \in lang(PM)]|}{|L|}$, i.e., the fraction of observed traces that fit into the model.

- Trace-based precision: $conf_2(L, lang(PM)) = \frac{|\{\sigma \in lang(PM) \mid \sigma \in L\}|}{|lang(PM)|}$, i.e., the fraction of modeled traces that were observed.
- DF-based recall: $conf_3(L, lang(PM)) = \frac{|\{(a,b) \in DF_L \mid (a,b) \in DF_{PM}\}|}{|DF_L|}$ with $DF_L = [(a_i, a_{i+1}) \in \mathcal{U}_{act} \times \mathcal{U}_{act} \mid \sigma = \langle a_1, a_2, \ldots, a_n \rangle \in L \wedge a_0 = \blacktriangleright \wedge a_{n+1} = \blacksquare \wedge 0 \le i \le n]$ and $DF_{PM} = \{(a_i, a_{i+1}) \in \mathcal{U}_{act} \times \mathcal{U}_{act} \mid \sigma = \langle a_1, a_2, \ldots, a_n \rangle \in lang(PM) \wedge a_0 = \blacktriangleright \wedge a_{n+1} = \blacksquare \wedge 0 \le i \le n\}$, i.e., the fraction of observed directly-follows relationships that also exist in the model.
- DF-based precision: $conf_4(L, lang(PM)) = \frac{|\{(a,b) \in DF_{PM} \mid (a,b) \in DF_L\}|}{|DF_{PM}|}$, i.e., the fraction of observed directly-follows relationships that also exist in the model.

The four conformance functions are just examples: $conf_1$ and $conf_3$ aim to measure recall (i.e., the fraction of observed behavior that is allowed by the model) and $conf_2$ and $conf_4$ aim to measure precision (i.e., the fraction of behavior allowed by the model that was actually observed). $conf_1$ and $conf_2$ consider complete traces and $conf_3$ and $conf_4$ compare direct successions in model and log. Note that $conf_2$ is problematic because $conf_2(L, lang(PM)) = 0$ if the model has a loop, no matter how large the event log is.

There are dozens (if not hundreds) of process-discovery and conformance-checking techniques, all assuming a simple event log based on a fixed case notion. A complete overview is out of scope. The goal of this tutorial is to show that these techniques can be lifted to object-centric process mining techniques. See [1] for a comprehensive introduction into process discovery and conformance checking.

3.7 Convergence and Divergence

In Sect. 3.2, we showed that any object-centric event log $L = (E, O, \#, R)$ can be converted to a simple event log L_{ot} by projecting events onto a single object type $ot \in types(L)$. We often call this the *flattening of an event log* into an event log where we again have *precisely one* case object per event. Figure 3 visualizes this process.

To better understand what happens with events during the flattening of an event log, consider an arbitrary event $e \in E$ with objects $O_e = \{o \in objects(e) \mid \#_{type}(o) = ot\}$ of type ot.

- If $|O_e| = 0$, then event e will not appear in L_{ot}. This is referred to as the *deficiency problem*. Potentially relevant events may disappear from the event log in this way.
- If $|O_e| = 1$, then event e appears precisely one in L_{ot}. This case is easy to interpret.
- If $|O_e| = k > 1$, then event e appears k times in L_{ot}, i.e., the same event is replicated. This may lead to confusing diagnostics and is known as the *convergence problem*. For example, based on Fig. 4 one may think that a happened 6 times. However, in reality it happened only 3 times. This shows that many Key Performance Indicators (KPIs) computed based on the flatted event log will be misleading (e.g., costs, rework, mean duration, etc.)

The *divergence problem* is caused by the fact that after flattening the event log, we are unable to distinguish events referring to the same case and activity. Consider an object o of the selected object type ot and o_1 o_2, and o_3 three objects of another type (not selected). Let $events(o) = \langle e_1, e_2, e_3, e_4, e_5, e_6, e_7, e_8 \rangle$, $events(o_1) = \langle e_2, e_3 \rangle$, $events(o_2) = \langle e_4, e_7 \rangle$, and $events(o_3) = \langle e_5, e_6 \rangle$, with $\#_{act}(e_1) = a$, $\#_{act}(e_2) = b$, $\#_{act}(e_3) = c$, $\#_{act}(e_4) = b$, $\#_{act}(e_5) = b$, $\#_{act}(e_6) = c$, $\#_{act}(e_7) = c$, and $\#_{act}(e_8) = d$. Hence, $trace(o) = \langle a, b, c, b, b, c, c, d \rangle$, $trace(o_1) = \langle b, c \rangle$, $trace(o_2) = \langle b, c \rangle$, and $trace(o_3) = \langle b, c \rangle$. When considering only o of the selected object type ot, it seems that activities b and c occur in random order (note that in $trace(o)$, b is followed by c and b and c is followed by b, c, and d). However, when considering o_1 o_2, and o_3 it becomes clear that b is always followed by c. This information gets lost on the flattened event log. The divergence problem leads to misleading process models that do *not* show the actual causalities. The resulting models often have loops because unrelated events are connected.

These problems are omnipresent when dealing with real-world processes and information systems. They illustrate the need for object-centric process mining.

4   Object-Centric Process Discovery

In Sect. 3, we showed that an object-centric event log $L = (E, O, \#, R)$ can be converted into a collection of simple event logs. For each object type $ot \in types(L)$, one can create a traditional simple event log $L_{ot} = [trace(o) \mid o \in O \wedge \#_{type}(o) = ot] \in \mathcal{B}(\mathcal{U}_{act}^*)$. For each L_{ot} we can create a process model, e.g., a DFG $G = (A, F)$ or an accepting Petri net $AN = (N, M_{init}, M_{final})$. In this section, we show that these models can be folded into object-centric process models.

Note that in prior work, an abundance of event-logging formats and models have been proposed. Consider, for example, proclets [7], object-centric behavioral constraint models [11,34], composite state machines [21], and various flavors of artifact-centric process models [23,24,35]. It is impossible to be complete here. Most of these models and approaches turned out to be too complex to be practically feasible. Therefore, we decided to resort to the simple representation proposed in [3] and standardized in the form of OCEL (ocel-standard.org). Unlike many of the artifact- and proclet-based approaches, we do not consider interacting entities (i.e., objects or artifact), but shared events only, i.e., one event may refer to multiple objects. It turns out that this approach helps to leverage existing techniques for process discovery and conformance checking. This is illustrated in the remainder.

Before introducing the folding operation, we first introduce some functions that help us to characterize the relationship between events, activities, objects, and object types. A central element is the "mix" of object types involved in the occurrence of an activity. Consider an activity *meeting* and three related object types *person*, *room* and *project*. If a *meeting* activity *occurs* in *mode* $[person^5, room, project^2]$, then this refers to an event referring to activity *meeting* and 8 objects: 5 objects of type *person*, 1 object of type *room*, and two objects of type *project*. We refer to such an event as *activity occurrence* $(meeting, [person^5, room, project^2])$. Other examples of activity occurrences are $(meeting, [person^{20}, room, project])$, $(clean\ room, [person^2, room])$, and $(approve\_project, [person^3, project])$. Note that there may be many events with the same activity occurrence. An event log can be transformed into a multiset of activity occurrences, e.g., $occ(L) = [(meeting, [person^5, room, project^2])^3, (clean\ room, [person^2, room])^2, \ldots]$.

Definition 15 (Activity Characteristics). *For an event log $L = (E, O, \#, R)$ with activities $A = act(L)$ and object types $OT = types(L)$ we define the following concepts and functions:*

- *An execution mode $m \in \mathcal{B}(OT)$ is a multiset of object types and characterizes the types of objects and their count involved in an event.*
- *An activity occurrence $(a, m) \in A \times \mathcal{B}(OT)$ refers to an activity a executed in mode m.*
- *$aot(L) = \{(\#_{act}(e), \#_{type}(o)) \mid e \in E \land o \in objects(e)\} \subseteq A \times OT$ is the set of all activity-object-type combinations in event log L.*
- *$occ(L) = [(\#_{act}(e), [\#_{type}(o) \mid o \in objects(e)]) \mid e \in E] \in \mathcal{B}(A \times \mathcal{B}(OT))$ is the multiset of activity occurrences present in event log L.*
- *$mode_L(a) = [m \mid (a', m) \in occ(L) \land a' = a] \in \mathcal{B}(OT)$ is the multiset of execution modes of $a \in A$.*
- *$min_L(a, ot) = \min_{m \in mode_L(a)} m(ot) \in \mathbf{N}$ is the minimum number of $ot \in OT$ objects of involved when executing activity $a \in A$.*
- *$max_L(a, ot) = \max_{m \in mode_L(a)} m(ot) \in \mathbf{N}$ is the maximum number of $ot \in OT$ objects of involved when executing activity $a \in A$.*
- *$mean_L(a, ot) = \frac{\sum_{m \in mode_L(a)} m(ot)}{|mode_L(a)|}$ is the mean number of $ot \in OT$ objects involved when executing activity $a \in A$.*

To illustrate these measures, we use an example event log $L = (E, O, \#, R)$ with 22080 events and 11300 objects. A small fragment of the event log in tabular format is shown in Fig. 7. $E = \{e_1, e_2, \ldots, e_{22080}\}$ are the 22080 events. Figure 7 shows the properties and related objects of events e_{13226} until e_{13244}, e.g., $\#_{act}(e_{13233}) = place\ order$ and $objects(e_{13233}) = \{991222, 884950, 884951, 884952\}$. There are three object types *order*, *item*, and *package*: order numbers start with "99", item numbers start with "88", and package numbers start with "66". Figure 7 also shows the timestamp of each event and two additional attributes: *price* and *weight*.

	activity	time	orders	items	packages	price	weight
13226	pick item	2022-09-27 17:08:09	{}	{884875}	{}	€ 129,99	0,98
13227	item out of stock	2022-09-27 17:18:12	{}	{884873}	{}	€ 2.200,00	1,25
13228	pick item	2022-09-27 17:26:02	{}	{884872}	{}	€ 129,99	0,98
13229	pick item	2022-09-27 17:29:36	{}	{884939}	{}	€ 495,00	0,48
13230	create package	2022-09-27 17:29:36	{}	{884826,884790,884827,884824,884914,884913,884915,884916,884822}	{660768}	€ 10.231,99	5,81
13231	package delivered	2022-09-27 17:34:30	{}	{884828,884834,884830,884832,884829,884833}	{660763}	€ 1.924,96	3,15
13232	pick item	2022-09-27 17:40:24	{}	{884858}	{}	€ 129,99	0,98
13233	place order	2022-09-27 17:53:09	{991222}	{884950,884951,884952}	{}	€ 5.534,00	2,95
13234	pay order	2022-09-27 17:55:19	{991094}	{}	{}	€ 3.463,98	2,90
13235	send package	2022-09-27 19:05:09	{}	{884788,884904,884889,884902,884903,884886,884887,884885,884787}	{660767}	€ 2.674,98	2,55
13236	place order	2022-09-27 20:15:42	{991223}	{884953,884954,884955}	{}	€ 9.117,97	7,17
13237	pick item	2022-09-27 20:24:50	{}	{884923}	{}	€ 99,99	0,78
13238	send package	2022-09-27 21:47:44	{}	{884826,884790,884827,884824,884914,884913,884915,884916,884822}	{660768}	€ 10.231,99	5,81
13239	place order	2022-09-27 23:07:38	{991224}	{884956}	{}	€ 134,00	0,50
13240	confirm order	2022-09-28 08:54:07	{991223}	{}	{}	€ 2.674,98	2,55
13241	place order	2022-09-28 08:57:24	{991225}	{884957,884958,884959,884960,884961}	{}	€ 2.431,98	2,37
13242	pick item	2022-09-28 09:13:17	{}	{884905}	{}	€ 29,99	0,38
13243	pick item	2022-09-28 09:17:41	{}	{884817}	{}	€ 699,00	0,17
13244	pick item	2022-09-28 09:25:34	{}	{884851}	{}	€ 495,00	0,48

Fig. 7. Small fragment of a larger object-centric event log with 22080 events and 11300 objects (200 orders, 8003 items, and 1297 packages).

Event e_{13233} represents an activity occurrence $(place\ order, [order, item^3])$, i.e., one order and three items are involved in the execution of activity *place order*. Some more examples: event e_{13226} represents an activity occurrence $(pick\ item, [item])$, event e_{13231} represents an activity occurrence $(package\ delivered, [item^6, package])$, and event e_{13239} represents an activity occurrence $(place\ order, [order, item^5])$. We can also compute $|mode_L(a)|$ (number of a events), $min_L(a, ot)$ (the minimum number of ot objects involved in a events), $mean_L(a, ot)$ (the average number of ot objects involved in a events), and $max_L(a, ot)$ (the maximum number of ot objects involved in a events). Table 1 shows the corresponding values for all activity/object-type combinations. For example, $min_L(place\ order, item) = 1$, $mean_L(place\ order, item) = 4.0$, $max_L(place\ order, item) = 13$, $min_L(create\ package, item) = 1$, $mean_L(create\ package, item) = 6.17$, and $max_L(create\ package, item) = 19$.

Table 1. The characteristics of activities for the event log partially shown in Fig. 7.

| activity | frequency | object type | | | | | | | | |
| | | $ot = order$ | | | $ot = item$ | | | $ot = package$ | | |
a	$|mode_L(a)|$	$min_L(a, ot)$	$mean_L(a, ot)$	$max_L(a, ot)$	$min_L(a, ot)$	$mean_L(a, ot)$	$max_L(a, ot)$	$min_L(a, ot)$	$mean_L(a, ot)$	$max_L(a, ot)$
confirm order (co)	2000	1	1	1	0	0	0	0	0	0
create package (cp)	1297	0	0	0	1	6.17	19	1	1	1
failed delivery (fd)	345	0	0	0	1	5.98	19	1	1	1
item out of stock (is)	1645	0	0	0	1	1	1	0	0	0
package delivered (pd)	1297	0	0	0	1	6.17	19	1	1	1
pay order (py)	2000	1	1	1	0	0	0	0	0	0
payment reminder (pr)	551	1	1	1	0	0	0	0	0	0
pick item (pi)	8003	0	0	0	1	1	1	0	0	0
place order (po)	2000	1	1	1	1	4.00	13	0	0	0
reorder item (ri)	1645	0	0	0	1	1	1	0	0	0
send package (sp)	1297	0	0	0	1	6.17	19	1	1	1

After showing some descriptive statistics, we create three events logs using Definition 5: L_{order}, L_{item}, and $L_{package}$. Recall that $L_{ot} = [trace(o) \mid o \in O \land \#_{type}(o) = ot] \in \mathcal{B}(\mathcal{U}_{act}^*)$.

$L_{order} = [\langle po, co, py\rangle^{1565}, \langle po, co, pr, py\rangle^{338}, \langle po, co, pr, pr, py\rangle^{80}, \langle po, co, pr, pr, pr, py\rangle^{15}, \langle po, co, pr, pr, pr, pr, py\rangle^2]$ when we use the short names introduced in Table 1, e.g., pr refers to $payment\ reminder$ and py refers to $pay\ order$. Figure 8(left) shows the DFG created for L_{order} by applying Definition 10.

$L_{item} = [\langle po, pi, cp, sp, pd\rangle^{5231}, \langle po, is, ri, pi, cp, sp, pd\rangle^{1330}, \langle po, pi, cp, sp, fd, pd\rangle^{766}, \langle po, pi, cp, sp, fd, fd, pd\rangle^{271}, \langle po, is, ri, pi, cp, sp, fd, pd\rangle^{218}, \langle po, pi, cp, sp, fd, fd, fd, pd\rangle^{68}, \langle po, is, ri, pi, cp, sp, fd, fd, pd\rangle^{65}, \langle po, is, ri, pi, cp, sp, fd, fd, fd, pd\rangle^{24}, \langle po, pi, cp, sp, fd, fd, fd, fd, fd, pd\rangle^{12}, \langle po, pi, cp, sp, fd, fd, fd, fd, pd\rangle^{10}, \langle po, is, ri, pi, cp, sp, fd, fd, fd, fd, pd\rangle^7, \langle po, is, ri, pi, cp, sp, fd, fd, fd, fd, fd, pd\rangle^1]$. The 8003 items are distributed over 12 variants. Figure 8(middle) shows the DFG created for L_{item} by applying Definition 10. $L_{package} = [\langle cp, sp, pd\rangle^{1060}, \langle cp, sp, fd, pd\rangle^{161}, \langle cp, sp, fd, fd, pd\rangle^{53}, \langle cp, sp, fd, fd, fd, pd\rangle^{16}, \langle cp, sp, fd, fd, fd, fd, pd\rangle^5, \langle cp, sp, fd, fd, fd, fd, fd, pd\rangle^2]$. The 1279 packages are distributed over 12 variants. Figure 8(left) shows the DFG created for $L_{package}$.

Next, we combine the information in Table 1 and the three DFGs in Fig. 8 into the *Object-Centric Directly Follows Graph* (OC-DFG) shown in Fig. 9. The basic idea is as follows: An OC-DFG can be seen as a set of "stacked" or "folded" DFGs. The arcs and start and end activities always refer to a specific object type. The connections are realized through shared activities. The activity frequencies correspond to the *actual* frequencies. This helps to avoid the convergence and divergence problems mentioned

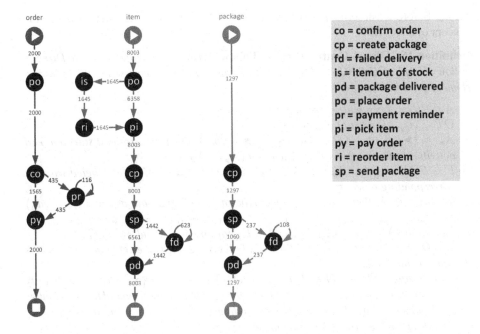

Fig. 8. Three DFGs created for the flattened event logs L_{order} (left), L_{item} (middle), and $L_{package}$ (right).

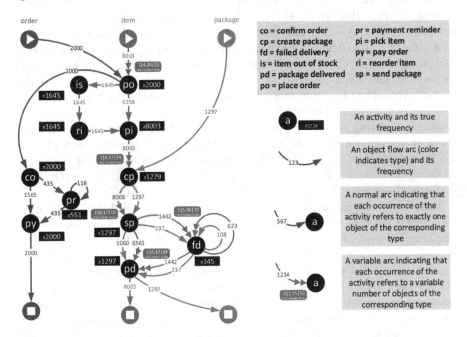

Fig. 9. An object-centric DFG based on the information in Table 1 and three DFGs in Fig. 8. The three colors refer to the three object types.

before. Before we describe how to create the OC-DFG in Fig. 9, we first formalize the concept of a OC-DFG.

Definition 16 (Object-Centric Directly Follows Graph). *An Object-Centric Directly Follows Graph (OC-DFG) $OG = (A, OT, F, min, max)$ is composed of the following elements:*

- *$A \in \mathcal{B}(\mathcal{U}_{act})$ is a multiset of activities,*
- *$OT \subseteq \mathcal{U}_{type}$ is a set of object types,*
- *$A_{\blacktriangleright} = \{\blacktriangleright_{ot} \mid ot \in OT\}$ and $A_{\blacksquare} = \{\blacksquare_{ot} \mid ot \in OT\}$ are artificial start and end activities (one per object type) such that $(A_{\blacktriangleright} \cup A_{\blacksquare}) \cap A = \emptyset$,*
- *$F \in \mathcal{B}(OT \times (A \cup A_{\blacktriangleright}) \times (A \cup A_{\blacksquare}))$ is a weighted set of edges labeled with the corresponding object type,*
- *for any $a \in A$: there exists an object type $ot \in OT$ and path $\sigma_{ot} = \langle a_1, \ldots, a_n \rangle$ such that $(ot, a_i, a_{i+1}) \in F$ for $1 \leq i < n$, $a_1 = \blacktriangleright_{ot}$, $a_n = \blacksquare_{ot}$, and $a \in \sigma_{ot}$.*
- *$|[b \mid (ot, b, a) \in F]| = |[b \mid (ot, a, b) \in F]|$ for any $a \in A$ and $ot \in OT$,*
- *$aot(OG) = \{(a, ot) \in A \times OT \mid \exists_{b \in A} \, (ot, b, a) \in F\}$ is the set of activity-object-type combinations,*
- *$min \in aot(OG) \to \mathbf{N}$ and $max \in aot(OG) \to \mathbf{N} \cup \{\infty\}$ define cardinality constraints, i.e., for $(a, ot) \in aot(OG)$: $min(a, ot)$ is a lower bound for the number of ot objects involved in events corresponding to activity a, $max(a, ot)$ is an upper bound (of course $min(a, ot) \leq max(a, ot)$).*

Comparing Definition 16 (OC-DFG) with Definition 9 (DFG), shows the following. Both are composed of nodes corresponding to activities and weighted edges connecting these activities. However, in an OC-DFG there are separate edges and start and end activities *per object type*. For each object type ot, $\blacktriangleright_{ot}$ denotes the start of ot objects and $\blacksquare_{ot}$ the end. $A(a)$ denote the real frequency of activity a. $F(ot, a, b)$ denotes how often an object of type ot "moved" from a to b. Since each edge refers to an object type, we can talk about ot-paths $\sigma_{ot} = \langle a_1, \ldots, a_n \rangle$ with $(ot, a_i, a_{i+1}) \in F$ for $1 \leq i < n$ connecting $\blacktriangleright_{ot} = a_1$ to $\blacksquare_{ot} = a_n$ using only ot-edges. Each activity should be on one of such paths. The requirement $|[b \mid (ot, b, a) \in F]| = |[b \mid (ot, a, b) \in F]|$ for any $a \in A$ and $ot \in OT$ states that the sum of the frequencies of the input arcs of an activity a matches the sum of the frequencies of the output arcs of a for each individual object type ot. Note that these numbers may be different from $A(a)$ and that $|[b \mid (ot, b, a) \in F]| = |[b \mid (ot, a, b) \in F]| = 0$ if $(a, ot) \notin aot(OG)$ and $|[b \mid (ot, b, a) \in F]| = |[b \mid (ot, a, b) \in F]| > 0$ if $(a, ot) \in aot(OG)$.

There is the special case that $min(a, ot) = max(a, ot) = 1$, i.e., the number of ot objects involved in events corresponding to activity a is precisely one. We call these *simple activity-object-type combinations*, denoted by $saot(OG) = \{(a, ot) \in aot(OG) \mid min((a, ot) = max((a, ot) = 1\}$. Note that for $(a, ot) \in saot(OG)$: $|[b \mid (ot, b, a) \in F]| = |[b \mid (ot, a, b) \in F]| = A(a)$. This is similar to the requirement in Definition 9 (DFG). In a normal DFG, the number of ot objects involved in events corresponding to activity a is precisely one. Figure 9 uses *single-headed* arcs for simple activity-object-type combinations. For other activity-object-type combinations, *double-headed* arcs are used. The property is always attached to the incoming arc. To simplify language, we refer to these as *normal arcs* (single-headed) and *variable arcs* (double-headed). However, it is a property of the activity-object-type combination.

Definition 17 (Object-Centric Directly Follows Graph Discovery). *Let $L = (E, O,$ $\#, R)$ be an object-centric event log. $OG(L) = (A, OT, F, min, max)$ is the corresponding Object-Centric Directly Follows Graph (OC-DFG) and is defined as follows:*

- *$A = [\#_{act}(e) \mid e \in E]$ is the multiset of activities,*
- *$OT = types(L)$ is the set of object types,*
- *$F = [(ot, a_i, a_{i+1}) \mid o \in O \wedge ot = \#_{type}(o) \wedge trace(o) = \langle a_1, a_2, \ldots, a_n \rangle \wedge a_0 =$ $\blacktriangleright_{ot} \wedge a_{n+1} = \blacksquare_{ot} \wedge 0 \leq i \leq n]$ is the weighted set of edges labeled with the corresponding object type,*
- *$min \in aot(L) \rightarrow \mathbf{N}$ and $max \in aot(L) \rightarrow \mathbf{N}$ such that for $(a, ot) \in aot(L)$: $min(a, ot) = min_L(a, ot)$ and $max(a, ot) = max_L(a, ot)$ (see Definition 15).*

Applying Definition 17 to the event log L partially shown in Fig. 7 (i.e., the event log with 22080 events and 11300 objects) results in the OC-DFG shown in Fig. 9. Using the short names, we obtain $OG(L) = (A, OT, F, min, max)$ with

- $A = \{(co, 2000), (cp, 1297), (fd, 345), (is, 1645), (pd, 1297), (po, 2000), (pr,$ $551), (pi, 8003), (py, 2000), (ri, 1645), (sp, 1297)\}$,
- $OT = \{order, item, package\}$,
- $F = [(order, \blacktriangleright_{order}, po)^{2000}, (item, \blacktriangleright_{item}, po)^{8003}, (package, \blacktriangleright_{package}, cp)^{1297},$ $(order, po, co)^{2000}, (item, po, is)^{1645}, (item, po, pi)^{6358}, (package, cp, sp)^{1297},$ $(item, cp, sp)^{8003}, \ldots, (item, pd, \blacksquare_{item})^{8003}, (package, pd, \blacksquare_{package})^{1297}]$
- $min = \{((po, order), 1), ((co, order), 1), ((pr, order), 1), ((py, order), 1),$ $((po, item), 1), ((is, item), 1), ((ri, item), 1), ((pi, item), 1), ((cp, item), 1),$ $((sp, item), 1), ((fd, item), 1), ((pd, item), 1), ((cp, package), 1),$ $((sp, package), 1), ((fd, package), 1), ((pd, package), 1)\}$
- $max = \{((po, order), 1), ((co, order), 1), ((pr, order), 1), ((py, order), 1),$ $((po, item), 16), ((is, item), 1), ((ri, item), 1), ((pi, item), 1), ((cp, item), 19),$ $((sp, item), 19), ((fd, item), 19), ((pd, item), 19), ((cp, package), 1),$ $((sp, package), 1), ((fd, package), 1), ((pd, package), 1)\}$

Note that Definition 17 only computes cardinality constraints for activity-object-type combinations. There are many ways to extend the model with more fine-grained information. For example, Fig. 9 also shows the mean number of $ot \in OT$ objects of involved when executing activity $a \in A$, i.e., the $mean_L(a, ot) = \frac{\sum_{m \in mode_L(a)} m(ot)}{|mode_L(a)|}$ value already introduced in Definition 15.

Instead of cardinality constraints, it is also possible to define an *allowed set of execution modes*. This allows us to relate the frequencies of different object types. For example, the number of objects of one type matches the number of objects of another type. In Definition 15, we already showed how such information can be extracted from event logs.

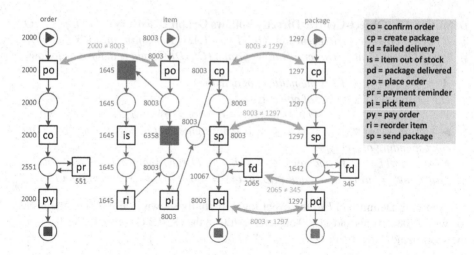

Fig. 10. Three accepting Petri nets created for the flattened event logs L_{order} (left), L_{item} (middle), and $L_{package}$ (right). Note that the accepting Petri net in the middle has two silent activities. The gray bidirectional arcs show disagreements between the different models and logs. For example, activity *po* (place order) occurs 2000 times in L_{order} (left) and 8003 times in L_{item} (middle), and activity *cp* (create package) occurs 8003 times in L_{item} (middle) and 1287 times in $L_{package}$ (right). When folding the accepting Petri nets, these differences need to be addressed.

The same principles can be applied to other representations and discovery algorithms. The only limitation is that activities have to be unique, i.e., it is not possible to have models where two nodes (e.g., transitions in a Petri net) refer to the same activity.

We use the same event log to illustrate the folding of accepting Petri nets. Figure 10 shows three accepting Petri nets discovered for the three flattened event logs created before: L_{order} (left), L_{item} (middle), and $L_{package}$ (right). Each transition is annotated with the frequency in the corresponding flattened event log. The places indicate how often a token was produced and later consumed in that place (i.e., the token-flow frequency). Using exactly the same principles as before, we can fold the three accepting Petri nets resulting in the *Object-Centric Accepting Petri Net* (OC-APN) shown in Fig. 11.

The object-centric accepting Petri net is obtained as follows. The three accepting Petri nets are joined, assuming that all places and arcs are disjoint. The only thing shared are visible transitions with the same label. Silent transitions are never merged. Then the actual frequencies are added. These are obtained from the original event log. Next all activity-object-type combinations (a, ot) are inspected (as before). If the number of ot objects is always precisely one for activity a, then we use normal arcs (single-headed). If the number of ot objects is not always precisely one for activity a, then we use variable arcs (double-headed) and also add additional information. Figure 11 shows the minimum, mean, and maximum number of objects involved.

In Sect. 3.3, we introduced *activity* and *variant-based filtering*. These can be easily combined with the approach in this section. Moreover, it is also possible to *filter for particular activity-object-type combinations*. For example, one could selectively remove

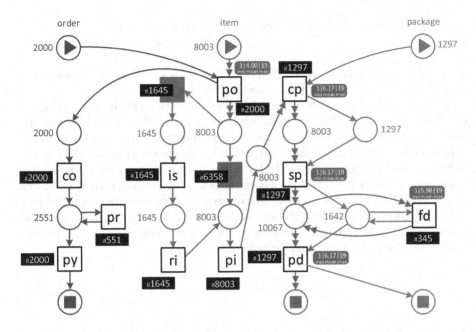

Fig. 11. An object-centric accepting Petri net based on the three accepting Petri nets in Fig. 10. The transitions are labeled with the correct frequencies, e.g., activity *po* (place order) occurs 2000 times and activity *cp* (create package) occurs 1297 times. The silent transitions do not need to be merged and can therefore reuse the frequencies shown in Fig. 10. All other transitions have the frequency found in the original object-centric event log. The double-headed arcs indicate that, when firing the transition, possibly a variable number of objects is consumed and produced (i.e., not always precisely one). For transitions having double-headed arcs, additional statistics are added, e.g., occurrences of *po* (place order) involve between 1 and 13 items with a mean of 4.00 and occurrences of *cp* (create package) involve between 1 and 19 items with a mean of 6.17.

item objects from the activities *sp* (send package) and *fd* (failed delivery), but keep the *item* objects for activity *pd* (package delivered) to measure flow times.

Note that object-centric DFGs and object-centric accepting Petri net are just examples illustrating the basic principles of object-centric process discovery. This shows that techniques for classical process discovery (using a single case notion) can be lifted to multiple object types and a variable number of objects involved in the execution of activities. This leads to a more holistic view avoiding convergence and divergence problems discussed before.

5 Object-Centric Conformance Checking

Now we consider the situation where we have both an object-centric event log and an object-centric process model. Without going onto details, we argue that we can use a similar approach as for process discovery. We can project both the event log and the process model on each of the object types and apply classical conformance-checking techniques. On top of that, we need to check the cardinality constraints.

In Definition 14, we defined a conformance measure to be a function $conf \in \mathcal{B}(\mathcal{U}_{act}^*) \times \mathcal{P}(\mathcal{U}_{act}^*) \rightarrow [0,1]$. $conf(L, lang(PM))$ quantifies conformance for an event log $L \in \mathcal{B}(\mathcal{U}_{act}^*)$ and a process model PM having $lang(PM) \in \mathcal{P}(\mathcal{U}_{act}^*)$ as accepting traces (higher is better). We provided examples such as trace-based recall, trace-based precision, DF-based recall, and DF-based precision.

Given an object-centric process model PM, we assume it is possible to extract a process model PM_{ot} for each object type. This requires an unfolding of the object-centric process model. For example, the object-centric accepting Petri net shown in Fig. 11 is unfolded into the three accepting Petri nets in Fig. 10. The object-centric DFG shown in Fig. 9 is unfolded into the three DFGs in Fig. 8. Of course, we should ignore the frequencies added to the process models during discovery. Frequencies only come into play when a concrete event log is considered and are not part of the normative process model. However, cardinality constraints are part of the model. Figure 12 illustrates this. Note that the object-centric process model does not show frequencies. The only annotations that are kept are the upper and lower bounds.

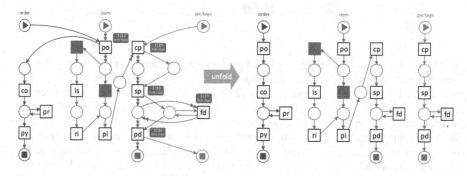

Fig. 12. Unfolding an object-centric accepting Petri net into one accepting Petri net per object type. Note the cardinality constraints, e.g., activity *po* always involves precisely one *order* object and between 1 and 13 *item* objects, activity *cp* always involves precisely one *package* object and between 1 and 19 *item* objects. These cannot be checked in the unfolded models, but can be checked on the original event log.

Using the flattened event logs (L_{ot}) and unfolded models (PM_{ot}), we can apply different conformance measures of the form $conf(L_{ot}, lang(PM_{ot}))$. These can be considered separately or aggregated in an overall measure.

By checking conformance using a collection of flattened event logs and unfolded models, we do not check the interactions between object types and also do not check cardinalities. However, these can be checked directly on the object-centric event log. Consider an event log $L = (E, O, \#, R)$ with activities $A = act(L)$ and object types $OT = types(L)$. In Definition 15, we introduced $occ(L) = [(\#_{act}(e), [\#_{type}(o) \mid o \in objects(e)]) \mid e \in E]$ as the multiset of activity occurrences present in event log L and $mode_L(a) = [m \mid (a', m) \in occ(L) \land a' = a]$ as the multiset of execution modes of $a \in A$.

Now assume that the process model PM defines a *set of allowed activity occurrences* $aocc(PM) \subseteq A \times \mathcal{B}(OT)$. If $(a, m) \in aocc(PM)$, then activity a can be executed in mode m. To illustrate this consider the cardinality constraints in Fig. 12(left). In this example: $aocc(PM) = \{(po, [order, item^k]) \mid 1 \leq k \leq 13\} \cup \{(cp, [item^k, package]) \mid 1 \leq k \leq 19\} \cup \{(sp, [item^k, package]) \mid 1 \leq k \leq 19\} \cup \{(fd, [item^k, package]) \mid 1 \leq k \leq 19\} \cup \{(pd, [item^k, package]) \mid 1 \leq k \leq 19\} \cup \{(co, [order]), (pr, [order]), (py, [order]), (is, [item]), (ri, [item]), (pi, [item])\}$. This shows that it is quite easy to add graphical annotations to object-centric process models describing the set of allowed activity occurrences. Activity-occurrence-based recall computes the fraction of observed activity occurrences allowed according to the process model.

Definition 18 (Checking Allowed Activity Occurrences). *Let $L = (E, O, \#, R)$ be an object-centric event log with an observed multiset of activity occurrences $occ(L)$ and PM an object-centric process model with $aocc(PM) \subseteq A \times \mathcal{B}(OT)$ as the set of allowed activity occurrences. $conf_{occ}(L, PM) = \frac{|[(a,m) \in occ(L) \mid (a,m) \in aocc(PM)]|}{|occ(L)|}$ is activity-occurrence-based recall.*

Note that $conf_{occ}(L, PM) \in [0, 1]$. For the running example, $conf_{occ}(L, PM) = 1$. However, if we make the cardinality constraints more strict (e.g., an order or package contains at most 5 items), then $conf_{occ}(L, PM) < 1$.

To summarize the above. Object-centric conformance checking takes as input an object-centric event log and an object-centric process model. Then two complementary checks are conducted: (1) for each object type, a flattened event log and unfolded model are created that are checked using traditional conformance-checking techniques (see Sect. 3.6) and (2) the observed multiset of activity occurrences $occ(L)$ is compared with the allowed set of activity occurrences $aocc(PM)$. These checks can be used to provide detailed diagnostics and can also be combined in an overall measure (e.g., a weighted average).

6   Other Forms of Object-Centric Process Mining

Process mining is not limited to process discovery and conformance checking and includes a wide variety of topics ranging from data quality problems specific for event data to action-oriented process mining where machine learning techniques are used to predict problems and automatically take action. The broadness of the spectrum (including connections to neighboring fields like simulation, data management, artificial intelligence, and machine learning) also applies to object-centric process mining, as is shown in Fig. 13.

The process mining tasks described in Fig. 13 have been researched during the past two decades. However, the focus was always on simple event logs, i.e., event logs assuming a single case notion. Like for process discovery and conformance checking, these tasks may become very challenging when dealing with multiple object types and a variable number of objects involved in events. Although it is often possible to lift existing approaches to the multi-object level (as was illustrated in the previous sections), many new challenges emerge when we drop the assumption of having a single case notion.

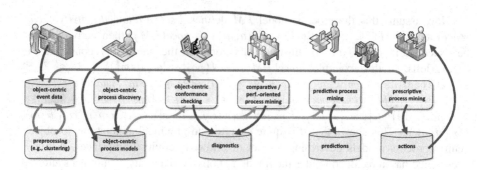

Fig. 13. Object-centric process mining is not limited to process discovery and conformance checking.

Consider, for example, the topic of *trace clustering* [27,39,40], which has been investigated in-depth for simple event logs. The goal of trace clustering is to find groups of cases that have similar characteristics. This can be used to partition the event log into multiple smaller, more homogeneous, event logs. These can be used to discover a collection of process models that are easier to analyze and interpret. These ideas cannot be easily transferred to object-centric event logs. Of course, one can try to cluster objects. However, objects share events and the log cannot be nicely partitioned based on clustered objects.

The same challenges can be seen when considering predictive process mining and prescriptive process mining. Often cases are assumed to be independent and this is no longer possible. This also shows that traditional process mining approaches fail to capture the interactions between different objects.

7   Handling Complexity

As mentioned in the introduction of this paper, the advantages of using object-centric process mining are threefold: (1) data extraction is only done once, (2) relations between objects of possibly multiple types are captured and analyzed, and (3) a three-dimensional view of processes and organizations comes into reach. However, because data exaction is only done once, the complexity of input data is typically far more complex than in traditional process mining. Traditionally, scoping is done before turning the data from source systems (e.g., SAP's 800.000 database tables) into an event log with a single case notion. Moreover, sliders and filters need to be reinvented for the new setting with multiple object types and events that refer to multiple objects.

An important tool to tackle complexity is the so-called *Event-Type-Object-Type* (ETOT) matrix. Recall that $act(L) = \{\#_{act}(e) \mid e \in E\}$ is the set of event types (i.e., activities) and $types(L) = \{\#_{type}(o) \mid o \in O\}$ is the set of object types. An ETOT matrix determines which *event-type* and *object-type combinations* are in focus. Given an event log and an ETOT matrix, we create an event log that retains only the event types, object types, and relations selected.

Definition 19 (Event-Type-Object-Type Matrix). *Let $L = (E, O, \#, R)$ be an event log. An Event-Type-Object-Type (ETOT) matrix is a relation $M \subseteq \{(act(e), \#_{type}(o)) \mid (e, o) \in R\}$. $L{\uparrow}M = (E', O', \#', R')$ is the projected event log based on M with $E' = \{e \in E \mid act(e) \in \{et \mid (et, ot) \in M\}\}$, $O' = \{o \in O \mid \#_{type}(o) \in \{ot \mid (et, ot) \in M\}\}$, $dom(\#') = E' \cup O'$, $\#'(e) = \#(e)$ for $e \in E'$, $\#'(o) = \#(o)$ for $o \in O'$, and $R' = \{(e, o) \in R \mid (act(e), \#_{type}(o)) \in M\}$.*

Table 2. The maximal Event-Type-Object-Type (ETOT) matrix based on the event log partially shown in Fig. 7.

event type (activity)	object type		
	$ot = order$	$ot = item$	$ot = package$
confirm order (**co**)	✓		
create package (**cp**)		✓	✓
failed delivery (**fd**)		✓	✓
item out of stock (**is**)		✓	
package delivered (**pd**)		✓	✓
pay order (**py**)	✓		
payment reminder (**pr**)	✓		
pick item (**pi**)		✓	
place order (**po**)	✓	✓	
reorder item (**ri**)		✓	
send package (**sp**)		✓	✓

Note that an Event-Type-Object-Type (ETOT) matrix M can be visualized as a matrix. This is illustrated in Table 2. The example ETOT matrix is maximal, i.e., $M = \{(act(e), \#_{type}(o)) \mid (e, o) \in R\}$. Table 3 shows another ETOT matrix where many event-type and object-type combinations have been removed. The corresponding discovered object-centric accepting Petri net is shown in Fig. 14. Note that the object type *package* was completely removed. Also, activities such as *payment reminder* were removed. The resulting process model is, therefore, much simpler.

Table 3 and Fig. 14 show that it is easy to scope analysis; just select the event-type and object-type combinations that need to be included. An ETOT matrix M can be considered as an "analysis profile" or "view" on the processes and organization. These may be predefined and reusable. Depending on the questions one has, one pick such a predefined profile/view.

Selecting the ETOT matrix can be seen as a first step in the analysis process. However, one can consider further filter or projection steps based on picking subsets of objects. It is recommended to include an object completely or not at all, otherwise, results are difficult to interpret. This leads to another subsequent log projection based on a set of selected objects O_{sel}.

Table 3. An Event-Type-Object-Type (ETOT) matrix M used to create an event log focusing on a subset of event types and object types.

event type (activity)	object type		
	$ot = order$	$ot = item$	$ot = package$
confirm order (**co**)	✓		
create package (**cp**)			
failed delivery (**fd**)			
item out of stock (**is**)		✓	
package delivered (**pd**)		✓	
pay order (**py**)	✓		
payment reminder (**pr**)			
pick item (**pi**)		✓	
place order (**po**)	✓	✓	
reorder item (**ri**)		✓	
send package (**sp**)			

Definition 20 (Object Selection). *Let $L = L'{\uparrow}M = (E, O, \#, R)$ be an event log obtained by selecting event-type and object-type combinations as defined by ETOT matrix M starting from event log L'. Let $O_{sel} \subseteq O$ be a set of selected objects. Projecting L on these selected objects O_{sel} yields $L{\uparrow}O_{sel} = (E', O', \#', R')$ with $O' = O_{sel}$, $R' = \{(e, o) \in R \mid o \in O'\}$, $E' = \{e \mid (e, o) \in R'\}$, $dom(\#') = E' \cup O'$, $\#'(e) = \#(e)$ for $e \in E'$, and $\#'(o) = \#(o)$ for $o \in O'$.*

Note that events without selected objects are removed in Definition 20. Object selection can be used to implement *sliders that seamlessly simplify process models*. For example, objects are sorted per object type based on the frequency of the corresponding trace variant (note that each object defines a sequence of activities). If the slider is set to, for example, 80%, then one can pick 80% of the objects per object type (starting with the objects following the most frequent variant). Using $L{\uparrow}O_{sel}$ as defined in Definition 20, one obtains a new event log covering, by definition, 80% of all objects. Such a slider has a clear interpretation and predictable effects. However, relationships between objects are ignored. This can be problematic, as can be explained using our running example.

Assume we have orders, items, and packages as objects. We select orders, items, and packages based on the frequencies of the corresponding variants. This may result in "orphan objects", e.g., orders without items, items without a corresponding order, packages without items, or items without a corresponding package. This is caused by the fact that dependencies between objects are ignored. One way to solve this is to use the notion of *leading objects*. One starts with a set of leading objects, e.g., all orders following the five most frequent variants, and all transitively related objects are included.

Definition 21 (Object Selection Based on Leading Objects). *Let $L = L'{\uparrow}M = (E, O, \#, R)$ be an event log obtained by selecting event-type and object-type combi-*

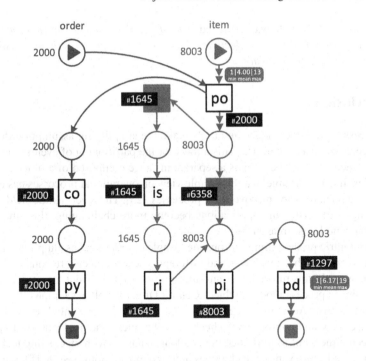

Fig. 14. An object-centric accepting Petri net based on event log $L{\uparrow}M$ created using the ETOT matrix M in Table 3.

nations as defined by ETOT matrix M starting from event log L'. $O2O = \{(o_1, o_2) \in O \times O \mid \exists_{e \in E} \{(e, o_1), (e, o_2)\} \subseteq R\}$. $O2O^*$ is the transitive closure of relation $O2O$. Let $O_{lead} \subseteq O$ be the selected set of leading objects. $O_{sel} = \{o \in O \mid \exists_{o' \in O_{lead}} (o', o) \in O2O^*\}$ is the set of objects transitively connected to at least one leading object. Projecting L based on these objects connected to leading objects yields again $L{\uparrow}O_{sel} = (E', O', \#', R')$ with $O' = O_{sel}$, $R' = \{(e, o) \in R \mid o \in O'\}$, $E' = \{e \mid (e, o) \in R'\}$, $dom(\#') = E' \cup O'$, $\#'(e) = \#(e)$ for $e \in E'$, and $\#'(o) = \#(o)$ for $o \in O'$.

Definition 21 allows us to pick a set of orders as leading objects and include all items included in these orders. It is also possible to select a set of packages and include all corresponding items and orders. Note that due to the transitive closure, too many objects may be included. Hence, further refinements or a well-chosen ETOT matrix are needed to obtain the desired projected event log. However, Definition 20 and Definition 21, in combination with the ETOT matrix, provide the basic tools that can be used to implement sliders and filters. For example, we may want to create the process model based on all orders with a value of more than €8000, having items that are hazardous, shipped in packages with more than five items. Such questions require careful definitions to avoid misleading interpretations. However, the data set used as input is always the same. In traditional non-object-centric approaches, such selections are often done before loading the event data in a process mining tool. As a result, transparency is missing and analysts need to guess how the data was extracted. *Therefore, using object-centric process mining, we can handle complexity effectively. Moreover, we can also create transparency based on a single source of truth.*

8   Conclusion

Most process mining techniques and tools make the simplifying assumption that each event refers to precisely one case. This allows for the partitioning of events over different cases. Each case can be seen as a separate instance composed of a timed sequence of activities. It is remarkable that this simple view on operational processes has enabled so many organizations to improve their processes [25]. However, as the field of process mining is maturing and applications become more challenging, this simplifying assumption is no longer reasonable.

Object-centric process mining drops the "single case notion" assumption. An event may refer to any number of objects and different types of objects are considered in an integral manner. In this tutorial, we introduced object-centric event logs and two types of object-centric process models: Object-Centric Directly-Follows Graphs (OC-DFGs) and Object-Centric Accepting Petri Nets (OC-APNs). We presented a few baseline process-discovery and conformance-checking techniques. The goal was not to present specific techniques, but to introduce the challenges and show how existing techniques can be leveraged. For example, techniques and implementations, see [8,15], the OCEL standard (`ocel-standard.org`), and the OCPM toolset. The insights provided are also valuable when using existing process mining software not supporting object-centric event logs. Also, practitioners should know about convergence and divergence problems, because these phenomena occur in almost any real-world process mining project.

Object-centric process mining is a new rapidly-growing subdiscipline with many exciting research challenges. Things like filtering, clustering, prediction, etc. become more challenging when considering object-centric event logs. However, the general principles used for object-centric process discovery and conformance checking presented in this tutorial can also be applied to most other process mining tasks.

Acknowledgments. The author thanks the Alexander von Humboldt (AvH) Stiftung for supporting his research. Funded by the Deutsche Forschungsgemeinschaft (DFG) under Germany's Excellence Strategy, Internet of Production (390621612).

References

1. van der Aalst, W.M.P.: Process Mining. Data Science in Action. Springer, Heidelberg (2016). https://doi.org/10.1007/978-3-662-49851-4
2. van der Aalst, W.M.P.: A practitioner's guide to process mining: limitations of the directly-follows graph. Procedia Comput. Sci. **164**, 321–328 (2019). Part of specital issue: International Conference on Enterprise Information Systems, CENTERIS 2019
3. Aalst, W.M.P.: Object-centric process mining: dealing with divergence and convergence in event data. In: Ölveczky, P.C., Salaün, G. (eds.) SEFM 2019. LNCS, vol. 11724, pp. 3–25. Springer, Cham (2019). https://doi.org/10.1007/978-3-030-30446-1_1

4. van der Aalst, W.M.P.: Foundations of process discovery. In: van der Aalst, W.M.P., Carmona, J. (eds.) Process Mining Handbook. Lecture Notes in Business Information Processing, vol. 448, pp. 37–75. Springer, Cham (2022). https://doi.org/10.1007/978-3-031-08848-3_2

5. van der Aalst, W.M.P.: Process mining: a 360 degrees overview. In: van der Aalst, W.M.P., Carmona, J. (eds.) Process Mining Handbook. Lecture Notes in Business Information Processing, vol. 448, pp. 3–34. Springer, Cham (2022). https://doi.org/10.1007/978-3-031-08848-3_1

6. van der Aalst, W.M.P., Adriansyah, A., van Dongen, B.: Replaying history on process models for conformance checking and performance analysis. WIREs Data Min. Knowl. Discov. 2(2), 182–192 (2012)

7. van der Aalst, W.M.P., Barthelmess, P., Ellis, C.A., Wainer, J.: Proclets: a framework for lightweight interacting workflow processes. Int. J. Coop. Inf. Syst. 10(4), 443–482 (2001)

8. van der Aalst, W.M.P., Berti, A.: Discovering object-centric Petri nets. Fund. Inform. 175(1–4), 1–40 (2020)

9. van der Aalst, W.M.P., Stahl, C.: Modeling Business Processes: A Petri Net Oriented Approach. MIT Press, Cambridge (2011)

10. van der Aalst, W.M.P., Weijters, A.J.M.M., Maruster, L.: Workflow mining: discovering process models from event logs. IEEE Trans. Knowl. Data Eng. 16(9), 1128–1142 (2004)

11. Artale, A., Kovtunova, A., Montali, M., van der Aalst, W.M.P.: Modeling and reasoning over declarative data-aware processes with object-centric behavioral constraints. In: Hildebrandt, T., van Dongen, B.F., Röglinger, M., Mendling, J. (eds.) BPM 2019. LNCS, vol. 11675, pp. 139–156. Springer, Cham (2019). https://doi.org/10.1007/978-3-030-26619-6_11

12. Augusto, A., et al.: Automated discovery of process models from event logs: review and benchmark. IEEE Trans. Knowl. Data Eng. 31(4), 686–705 (2019)

13. Augusto, A., Conforti, R., Marlon, M., La Rosa, M., Polyvyanyy, A.: Split miner: automated discovery of accurate and simple business process models from event logs. Knowl. Inf. Syst. 59(2), 251–284 (2019)

14. Bergenthum, R., Desel, J., Lorenz, R., Mauser, S.: Process mining based on regions of languages. In: Alonso, G., Dadam, P., Rosemann, M. (eds.) BPM 2007. LNCS, vol. 4714, pp. 375–383. Springer, Heidelberg (2007). https://doi.org/10.1007/978-3-540-75183-0_27

15. Berti, A., van der Aalst, W.: Extracting multiple viewpoint models from relational databases. In: Ceravolo, P., van Keulen, M., Gómez-López, M.T. (eds.) SIMPDA 2018-2019. LNBIP, vol. 379, pp. 24–51. Springer, Cham (2020). https://doi.org/10.1007/978-3-030-46633-6_2

16. Carmona, J., Cortadella, J., Kishinevsky, M.: A region-based algorithm for discovering Petri nets from event logs. In: Dumas, M., Reichert, M., Shan, M.-C. (eds.) BPM 2008. LNCS, vol. 5240, pp. 358–373. Springer, Heidelberg (2008). https://doi.org/10.1007/978-3-540-85758-7_26

17. Carmona, J., van Dongen, B., Solti, A., Weidlich, M.: Conformance Checking. Relating Processes and Models. Springer, Cham (2018). https://doi.org/10.1007/978-3-319-99414-7

18. Desel, J., Esparza, J.: Free choice Petri nets. In: Cambridge Tracts in Theoretical Computer Science, vol. 40. Cambridge University Press, Cambridge (1995)

19. Desel, J., Reisig, W.: Place/transition Petri nets. In: Reisig, W., Rozenberg, G. (eds.) ACPN 1996. LNCS, vol. 1491, pp. 122–173. Springer, Heidelberg (1998). https://doi.org/10.1007/3-540-65306-6_15

20. Dumas, M., La Rosa, M., Mendling, J., Reijers, H.: Fundamentals of Business Process Management. Springer, Heidelberg (2018). https://doi.org/10.1007/978-3-662-56509-4

21. van Eck, M.L., Sidorova, N., van der Aalst, W.M.P.: Guided interaction exploration and performance analysis in artifact-centric process models. Bus. Inf. Syst. Eng. 61(6), 649–663 (2019)

22. Fahland, D.: Describing behavior of processes with many-to-many interactions. In: Donatelli, S., Haar, S. (eds.) PETRI NETS 2019. LNCS, vol. 11522, pp. 3–24. Springer, Cham (2019). https://doi.org/10.1007/978-3-030-21571-2_1
23. Fahland, D., de Leoni, M., van Dongen, B.F., van der Aalst, W.M.P.: Behavioral conformance of artifact-centric process models. In: Abramowicz, W. (ed.) BIS 2011. LNBIP, vol. 87, pp. 37–49. Springer, Heidelberg (2011). https://doi.org/10.1007/978-3-642-21863-7_4
24. Fahland, D., de Leoni, M., van Dongen, B.F., van der Aalst, W.M.P.: Conformance checking of interacting processes with overlapping instances. In: Rinderle-Ma, S., Toumani, F., Wolf, K. (eds.) BPM 2011. LNCS, vol. 6896, pp. 345–361. Springer, Heidelberg (2011). https://doi.org/10.1007/978-3-642-23059-2_26
25. Galic, G., Wolf, M.: Global Process Mining Survey 2021: Delivering Value with Process Analytics - Adoption and Success Factors of Process Mining. Deloitte (2021)
26. Ghahfarokhi, A.F., Park, G., Berti, A., van der Aalst, W.M.P.: OCEL Standard (2021). www.ocel-standard.org
27. Greco, G., Guzzo, A., Pontieri, L., Saccà, D.: Discovering expressive process models by clustering log traces. IEEE Trans. Knowl. Data Eng. **18**(8), 1010–1027 (2006)
28. IEEE Task Force on Process Mining. XES Standard Definition (2016). www.xes-standard.org
29. Jensen, K., Kristensen, L.M.: Coloured Petri Nets. Springer, Heidelberg (2009). https://doi.org/10.1007/b95112
30. Kerremans, M., Srivastava, T., Choudhary, F.: Market Guide for Process Mining. Research Note G00737056. Gartner (2021). www.gartner.com
31. Leemans, S.J.J., Fahland, D., van der Aalst, W.M.P.: Discovering block-structured process models from event logs - a constructive approach. In: Colom, J.-M., Desel, J. (eds.) PETRI NETS 2013. LNCS, vol. 7927, pp. 311–329. Springer, Heidelberg (2013). https://doi.org/10.1007/978-3-642-38697-8_17
32. Leemans, S.J.J., Fahland, D., van der Aalst, W.M.P.: Discovering block-structured process models from event logs containing infrequent behaviour. In: Lohmann, N., Song, M., Wohed, P. (eds.) BPM 2013. LNBIP, vol. 171, pp. 66–78. Springer, Cham (2014). https://doi.org/10.1007/978-3-319-06257-0_6
33. Leemans, S.J.J., Fahland, D., van der Aalst, W.M.P.: Scalable process discovery and conformance checking. Softw. Syst. Model. **17**(2), 599–631 (2018)
34. Li, G., de Carvalho, R.M., van der Aalst, W.M.P.: Automatic discovery of object-centric behavioral constraint models. In: Abramowicz, W. (ed.) BIS 2017. LNBIP, vol. 288, pp. 43–58. Springer, Cham (2017). https://doi.org/10.1007/978-3-319-59336-4_4
35. Lu, X., Nagelkerke, M., van de Wiel, D., Fahland, D.: Discovering interacting artifacts from ERP systems. IEEE Trans. Serv. Comput. **8**(6), 861–873 (2015)
36. OMG: Business Process Model and Notation (BPMN), Version 2.0.2. Object Management Group (2014). www.omg.org/spec/BPMN/
37. Rozinat, A., van der Aalst, W.M.P.: Conformance checking of processes based on monitoring real behavior. Inf. Syst. **33**(1), 64–95 (2008)
38. Solé, M., Carmona, J.: Process mining from a basis of state regions. In: Lilius, J., Penczek, W. (eds.) PETRI NETS 2010. LNCS, vol. 6128, pp. 226–245. Springer, Heidelberg (2010). https://doi.org/10.1007/978-3-642-13675-7_14
39. Song, M., Günther, C.W., van der Aalst, W.M.P.: Trace clustering in process mining. In: Ardagna, D., Mecella, M., Yang, J. (eds.) BPM 2008. LNBIP, vol. 17, pp. 109–120. Springer, Heidelberg (2009). https://doi.org/10.1007/978-3-642-00328-8_11

40. De Weerdt, J., De Backer, M., Vanthienen, J., Baesens, B.: Leveraging process discovery with trace clustering and text mining for intelligent analysis of incident management processes. In: IEEE Congress on Evolutionary Computation, CEC 2012, pp. 1–8. IEEE Computer Society (2012)
41. van der Werf, J.M.E.M., van Dongen, B.F., Hurkens, C.A.J., Serebrenik, A.: Process discovery using integer linear programming. Fund. Inform. **94**, 387–412 (2010)

Model-Based Engineering for Robotics with RoboChart and RoboTool

Ana Cavalcanti$^{(\boxtimes)}$, Ziggy Attala, James Baxter, Alvaro Miyazawa,
and Pedro Ribeiro

Department of Computer Science, University of York, York, UK
`Ana.Cavalcanti@york.ac.uk`

Abstract. Use of simulation to support the design of software for robotic systems is pervasive. Typically, roboticists draw a state machine using an informal notation (not precise or machine checkable) to convey a design and guide the development of a simulation. This involves writing code for a specific simulator (using C, C++, or some proprietary language and API). Verification is carried out using simulation runs and testing the deployed system. The RoboStar technology supports a model-based, rather than this (simulation) code-centered, approach to development. Models are written using domain-specific notations in line with those accepted by roboticists. In this tutorial, we focus on modelling and verification using RoboChart, our design notation, and its tool, called RoboTool. In RoboChart, software controllers are described by timed state machines. The semantics is defined using a process algebra, namely, tock-CSP, which we can use for verification by model checking or theorem proving. Use of RoboChart complements simulation and testing.

1 Introduction

With a very large and expanding global market, robotics has attracted a lot of attention in both academia and industry. For numerous applications of interest, it is envisaged that robots work side-by-side, assisting or collaborating with humans. In this context, many concerns arise: applicability and scalability of control techniques, adaptability and evolution, costs of development, and so on. Our focus is on Software Engineering, and its modern and rigorous techniques for design and verification with solid mathematical foundations.

Several groups are working on tailoring Software Engineering techniques to the needs of robotics [10]. Just like many other application areas, robotics can benefit from model-driven software development. Model-based techniques foster reuse and cost-effective automated generation of several artefacts: simulations, code, and tests, among others. Verification is a central concern[1], but full verification is beyond the state of the art. Challenges are imposed by many aspects of the heterogeneous cyber-physical nature of a robotic system.

---

[1] verifiability.org.

A. Cerone (Ed.): ICTAC 2021, LNCS 13490, pp. 106–151, 2023.
https://doi.org/10.1007/978-3-031-43678-9_4

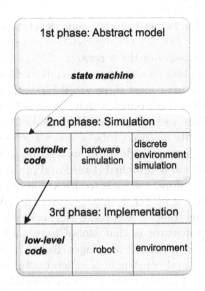

Fig. 1. Common approach to development

Current approaches to the development of software for robotic systems typically focus on simulation (see Fig. 1), if not directly on deployment and coding. A state-machine drawing is often used as a basis to develop (or explain) a simulation; many examples can be found in the literature [13,28,31,32,34]. In these drawings, informal annotations often record events and actions, as well as times and probabilities. The drawing gives an overview of the simulation code, but is not rigorously connected to it (by a code generation process, for example).

Simulations are written for reactive simulators using proprietary languages or general programming languages such as C or C++, and simulator-dependent customised programming interfaces for simulation of the robotic platform and of the environment. There is generally no portability between simulators.

The simulation code can be used as a basis to develop an implementation. During deployment, however, a common problem is the reality gap [6]. It happens when behaviour observed during deployment does not match the behaviour exhibited by the simulations. At this point, a developer can fix the problems only by modifying the low-level code. Cycles of trial and error follow. At the end, the only guarantee is that no more errors have been found, not that they are not present. There is no assurance of required properties.

In this tutorial, we present RoboChart [23,25], the notation of the RoboStar framework[2] for platform-independent modelling of controller software. With RoboChart and RoboStar, software development can start with the definition of verified RoboChart models, which can then be used to generate simulations and tests. Verification uses an automatically generated semantics for model checking or theorem proving. In this context, changes due the reality gap or to evolution

---

[2] robostar.cs.york.ac.uk.

can be made at the model, rather than the code, level. In addition, the development process gives rise to, besides the deployed code, several artefacts that can provide evidence of the quality of the software.

Compared to other notations and approaches, RoboChart and the RoboStar framework are distinctive in at least three ways. First, they complement, rather than replace, use of existing techniques widely adopted by roboticists, in particular use of state machines and simulation. With RoboChart, instead of simply drawing a (sketch of a) state machine, roboticists can define a precise machine or collection of machines. These provide an unambiguous account of requirements for the robotic platform, and of designed (timed and probabilistic) behaviours of the software. We can, therefore, use tools to check that the machines are syntactically correct, well typed, and well formed, for instance. We can also generate automatically simulations (models and code) that conform to the designs.

A second distinctive feature is that RoboChart, and the other RoboStar notations, are simple domain-specific languages. RoboChart, for example, avoids the use of many concepts and constructs of general notations like UML [30] and SysML [29], which make the semantics more challenging. With this, we lower the learning curve of the notations and improve understandability of models. Thirdly, from RoboChart we can automatically generate a mathematical model, which can be used for mechanical validation and verification by proof with the mathematical model used to justify soundness of the techniques.

Use of RoboChart is supported by a set of Eclipse plug-ins called RoboTool[3]. It provides support for modelling, validation, verification, simulation, and testing using RoboChart and other RoboStar notations. In this tutorial, we focus on the use of RoboTool for defining and verifying RoboChart models: we present the non-probabilistic version of RoboChart and use of its automatically generated process algebraic semantics for model checking. Use of RoboChart to model and verify probabilistic algorithms is covered in [39]. A detailed account of the whole RoboChart notation is provided in the reference manual [26].

We assume basic knowledge of state-machine notations, but describe in detail the novel features of RoboChart. An account of the notation for state machines used in UML, for example, is in [30]. The RoboChart core notation for state machines is based on that of UML. RoboChart, however, has, on one hand, eliminated features of complex semantics, and, on the other, adopts a component-model and includes constructs for modelling time properties: clocks and deadlines. In the next section, we give an overview of RoboChart and RoboTool. Section 3 provides the more substantial example of an autonomous segway. Verification supported by RoboTool is the topic of Sect. 4. We conclude in Sect. 5, where we also describe additional resources for use of RoboStar technology.

2   Overview of RoboChart and RoboTool

In this section, we present RoboChart and RoboTool via the segway example detailed in Sect. 3. To follow the explanations, it is useful to install RoboTool,

---

[3] robostar.cs.york.ac.uk/robotool/.

and create a project and a diagram as indicated in a complementary step-by-step tutorial[4]. In what follows, besides giving an overview of RoboChart, we briefly explain how RoboTool can be used to develop and validate a model.

RoboChart is concerned with the last level of the design of a control software for a robotic system. It has a simple component model, based on notions of modules, controllers, state machines, and operations that provide guidance on the development of models. In defining the components, it is possible to take a functional view, with different components capturing different aspects of the functionality identified by the requirements. It is also possible to reflect concurrency and distribution of computation in a (prospective) implementation.

Section 2.1 describes module blocks and the associated blocks that define robotic platforms. Controllers, state machines, and operations are presented in Sect. 2.2. Finally, in Sect. 2.3 we describe the RoboChart facilities to model time properties in the definition of state machines and operations.

2.1 Modules and Platforms

The main structuring component in a RoboChart model is the module. It describes the control software for a single robotic system, and is characterised by a robotic platform: a block describing services that can be used by the software. To specify the software behaviour, a module includes one or more controllers.

Figure 2 is a screenshot of RoboTool showing a module called Segway for our example. The screenshot in this and in other figures to follow give an idea of the kind of support offered by RoboTool, but we refer to a different tutorial for details[5]. Here, we do not rely on the specific textual content displayed in the screenshots. The diagram editor of RoboTool shows a palette on the right with diagram edition tools. To create a module, we need to select the Module tool in the Architectural Constructs section of that palette. The diagram itself is in the graphical area at the centre. As we construct the model, guidance is provided at the bottom panel. The problems view indicates any infelicities or missing elements that still need to be modelled. In Fig. 2, the messages indicate that every module must have a robotic platform and one or more controllers.

The services of a robotic platform are described by events, operations, and variables that can be shared with the software. These are abstractions for sensors and actuators, and possibly an embedded API, of an actual platform. Any physical platform that implements these services can use the software defined by the module. So, a robotic-platform block records assumptions about the robot hardware and its embedded software. A platform block may also declare (loose) constants, which are parameters of the model if their value is not defined.

For example, the platform for the Segway module provides two operations setLeftMotorSpeed and setRightMotorSpeed, both with a parameter speed of type real. As detailed in the next section, these operations are abstractions for actual motors that control the segway wheels, and software facilities to set their speed.

---

[4] robostar.cs.york.ac.uk/robotool/tutorial-16-08-2021/tutorial.pdf.

[5] robostar.cs.york.ac.uk/robotool/tutorial-16-08-2021/tutorial.pdf.

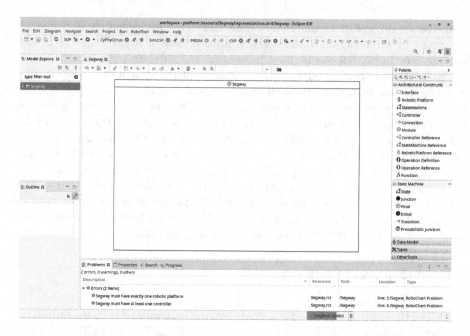

Fig. 2. Creating a module: **Segway**. We have the diagram in the graphical area at the centre, a palette of edition tools on the right, and a problems view at the bottom. The model explorer on the left shows just the Segway project. The outline view on the bottom left gives an overview of the contents of the whole graphical area. Here, it contains just the module block being shown.

Variables (including constants, which are special forms of variables that cannot be the target of an assignment), events, and operations can be added either directly to a robotic platform block, or indirectly by provided or defined interfaces. The notion of interface here is different from that in UML. RoboChart interfaces group variables, operations, and clocks, or events. Interfaces can be provided, required, or defined by robotic platforms, controllers, state machines or operations. In the case of a robotic platform, interfaces can be just provided or defined, because a platform is a service provider: it cannot require any services.

Figure 3 shows the creation of an interface MotorsI of the segway model. It declares the operations setLeftMotorSpeed and setRightMotorSpeed mentioned above. To create an interface using RoboTool, we select the Interface edition tool in the Architectural Constructs section of the palette, and click on the editor to position the interface. To add an operation to an interface, we use the Operation signature edition tool in the Data Model section, and click on the interface. Similarly, to add an event or clock, we use the Event or the Clock tool.

Provided and required interfaces represent dependencies between the platform, controllers, state machines and operations, and can contain variables and operations, which can be shared between components. Events are locally defined and are connected explicitly. Defined interfaces simply declare its variables and

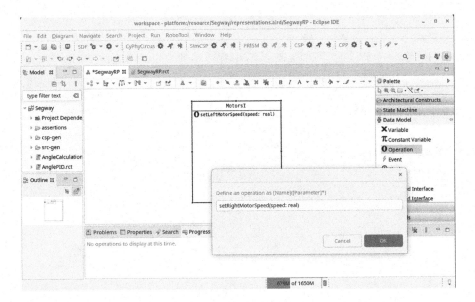

Fig. 3. Creating an interface: MotorsI declaring two operations, namely, the operation setLeftMotorSpeed(speed: real) already in the interface block labelled MotorsI, and setRightMotorSpeed(speed:real) in the dialogue box of the Operation tool in Data Model section of the palette of edition tools. The model explorer view on the left lists various folders and files in the Segway project.

events in the component (platform, controller, machine, or operation) as if the variables and events were declared individually. As detailed in the next section, in the case of operations defined in a controller, required interfaces can contain clocks, which must be declared by the machines calling those operations. A machine can declare a clock directly or via a defined interface.

In Fig. 4, we show an interface IMUI declaring four events angle, gyroX, gyroY, and gyroZ for inputting the orientation and angular velocities of the segway. These are abstractions for an accelerometer and a gyroscope. The platform declares IMUI as a defined interface. In this way, its events, providing inputs from the sensors, are made available for the controllers to use.

Defined interfaces cannot contain operations. This is because no component can or need to declare an operation locally. First, modules do not have local declarations. The data model of a module is given by its robotic platform. Second, in a robotic platform, operations are either provided, as opposed to defined, by the platform, and not further defined in the module. Thirdly, in a controller, operations are either required or defined, not just declared, locally. In more detail, operations in a controller are themselves independent components local to a controller that need to specified by state machines, and not just declared (in an interface). In this case, the declaration of the controller operation is by an operation block, not in an interface. (The next section provides examples of

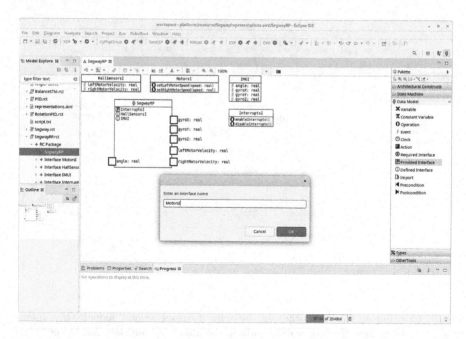

Fig. 4. Creating a robotic platform: SegwayRP. In the graphical area, we have four interfaces: blocks named HallSensorsI, MotorsI, IMUI, and InterruptsI. We also have the robotic-platform block SegwayRP. It declares InterruptsI as a provided interface (indicated by the symbol 🅿), and HallSensorsI and IMUI as defined interfaces (indicated by the symbol ①). A dialogue box of the Provided Interface edition tool indicates MotorsI is to be declared as provided in SegwayRP.

controller operations.) Finally, in a state machine or operation, we can require operations, but not declare or define them locally.

In defining the platform of a module, we can include it directly inside the module block. Alternatively, we can define the robotic platform block independently, and then add a reference to it inside the module block. In any case, in RoboTool, to create a platform, we select the Robotic Platform edition tool in the Architectural Constructs section of the palette, and click on the editor to position the platform. Figure 4 illustrates the creation of SegwayRP, the platform for our example, and the declaration of MotorsI as a provided interface in that platform.

As shown, the Provided Interface (or Defined Interface) tool in the Data Model section of the palette can be used to declare an interface in a platform. Additionally, events, variables and operations can be added to platforms in the same way as for interfaces. If the platform block is created outside a module, the Robotic Platform Reference edition tool in the Architectural Constructs section of the palette can be used to include a reference to the platform in the module.

The robotic platform determines the only means available to the control software for exchange of information with the environment of the robotic system. It is via the platform that the behaviour of the control software of a robotic

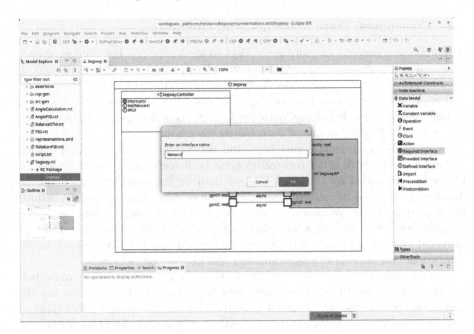

Fig. 5. Creating a controller: SegwayController. In the graphical area, we have the Segway module already including its controller called SegwayController. The robotic platform is eclipsed by a dialogue box for the Required Interface tool. It is being used to declare MotorsI as a required interface of SegwayController.

system can be observed. So, the changes of values of variables of the platform, the occurrence of events of the platform, and calls to operations of the platform characterise the visible behaviour of the module. We recall that these are abstractions for sensors, actuators, and embedded API of a physical platform, reflecting services realised using a range of devices.

While we expect the robotic platform used in the deployment of the system to be principally a robot (that is, specialised hardware with sensing and actuation capabilities), there may be more to it than that. First, as said, there may be a significant embedded API. Moreover, the robot may be connected to laptops and servers, for instance, used to provide additional services: database management or image processing, for example. For the purposes of a platform-independent model, like those described in RoboChart, however, all these components should be abstracted away as part of the robotic-platform block. The abstraction should not, and cannot, identify or differentiate computational units of a particular deployment platform in any way. As described next, however, the identification of the controllers of a module may reflect the availability of computational units.

2.2 Controllers, State Machines, and Operations

A module contains one or more controllers to model specific behaviours or code executed in a particular computational unit. To create a controller in RoboTool, we select the Controller tool in the Architectural Constructs section of the palette, and click on the editor to position the controller. Figure 5 shows the definition of the controller block SegwayController for our example, and in particular the declaration of MotorsI as one of its required interfaces.

A controller can declare variables (and constants), operations, and events. Variables shared with other controllers must be declared in required interfaces. Operations provided by the platform and used by the controller must also be declared in required interfaces. Events must be declared directly or in a defined interface. Constants, variables, operations, and events define a data model for a component. In a module, everything that is required by a controller, must be provided by the platform. Controllers cannot provide variables or operations. No component can provide events, which are just interaction points.

Events defined in the robotic-platform block of a module can be connected, via directed arrows, to events of controllers in the module. For that, we use the Connection tool in the Architectural Constructs section of the RoboTool palette. The direction of the connection arrows indicate the events the platform inputs, and the events the platform outputs to the software. These connections are all asynchronous, since the software does not block the platform. Figure 5 shows two of the connections between the SegwayController for our example and the events of the robotic platform SegwayRP previously discussed. Of course, not all controllers need to require or connect to all services of the platform.

Communication between controllers can be synchronous or asynchronous. Normally, communication between computational units are asynchronous, but we can use synchronous communications for abstraction. In this case, an implementation of the design represented by the model needs to define a protocol to implement the communication ensuring synchronicity.

Behaviour is defined by state machines. Multiple machines can characterise independent functions or define several threads of behaviour. In addition, state machines can be used to define operations that can be required and used by the state machines that define the threads of behaviour of the controller.

In line with practice in the robotics community, state machines are the main behavioural specification construct in RoboChart. They are self-contained components describing a data model (variables, events, operations, and clocks required or defined) and associated behaviour. In RoboChart, modules, controllers, state machines, and operations are all self-contained components that can be analysed in isolation. As mentioned above, in the case of a module, the visible behaviour is defined by its robotic platform. For controllers, machines, and operations, the visible behaviour is characterised by the values of their shared (required) variables, occurrence of events, and calls to the required operations.

As standard in state machines, the next step of behaviour is defined according to the current state. The notion of state is used to capture the consequences of

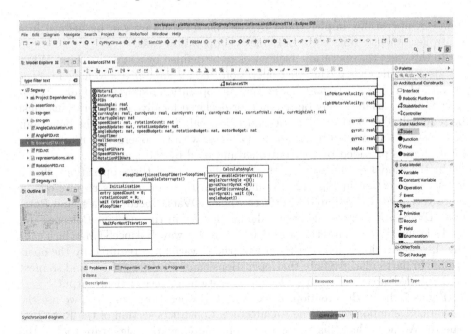

Fig. 6. Creating a state machine: BalanceSTM. In the graphical area, we have just the state-machine block. It has two parts: at the top, we define the data model of the machine via the declaration of required interfaces (indicated by the symbol ⑧), a few constants (𝝅) and variables (✖), a clock called loopTimer (indicated by the symbol ⓒ), and a few defined interfaces (indicated by an ①). In the bottom of the state-machine block, we have the machine itself. Here, it has an initial junction and three states with transitions between them.

the behaviour up to a certain point. Figure 6 shows the creation of the machine BalanceSTM for the segway model using RoboTool. For that, we use the State Machine tool in the Architectural Constructs section of the RoboTool palette.

To connect the events of the controller and of the machine, we use the Connection tool in the Architectural Constructs section. To add an initial junction to the state machine, we use the Initial junction tool in the State Machine section of the palette. In the same section, the State, Transition, and Action tools support the definition of a complete machine with (composite) states, with entry, during, and exit actions, and (labelled) transitions, with triggers, guards, and actions. These concepts are the same adopted in UML or SysML, for example. As mentioned, we assume here familiarity with these core state-machine concepts.

Operations provided by the robotic platform do not need to be defined in the RoboChart model. The services of a robotic-platform block are assumed as given and reliable, and so not subject to verification. There is, therefore, no need to provide a model for operations of the platform. If there is a service of the platform that is a concern, it should be modelled as part of the controllers specification, not as a service of the robotic platform. As already mentioned, however, operations implemented by the control software can be defined in a controller, for use in its state machines via operation calls.

In this case, the operation itself needs to be defined by a state machine. When a state machine calls a controller operation, the machine needs to have in scope all variables, operations, and clocks, that the operation requires, and all events it defines. The variables may be required or declared locally. The operations must be required. The clocks and events must be local. To summarise, the behaviour of a controller is defined by its state machines, with the operations representing local services provided by the controller and used by the machines.

In the model of the segway, the controller defines three operations shown in the next section in Figs. 12, 13, and 14. All these operations require one or more variables, via required interfaces AnglePIDVars, SpeedPIDVars, and RotationPIDVars. All these variables are defined locally in the machine BalanceSTM, by declaring the same interfaces as defined. In this way, BalanceSTM, which calls the three operations, defines the services (here, variables) required by the operations. In particular, we note that operations cannot return values, and so most of the shared variables are used by the operations to record their output.

Figure 7 shows the creation of the AnglePID operation. For that, we use the Operation Definition tool of the Architectural Constructs section of the RoboTool palette. We note that this is different from the Operation signature tool of the Data Model section, which creates just an operation declaration in an interface. Here, we are not declaring, but we are defining an operation. Creating the machine that defines the operation can be done in the way already explained.

Just like for robotic platforms, a module block can include a controller block directly, or a reference to a controller block defined outside the module. Similarly, controllers can include references to state machines and operations defined outside the module. RoboTool has a notion of package (similar to that of Java, for example) that can be used to organise diagrams.

The RoboChart type system is that of Z [1]. So, there is support for modelling using abstract given types, about which no further information is provided. There is also support for abstract data types, such as, sets, sequences, functions, and so on. This use of the Z notation ensures a simple encoding of the semantics for theorem proving. For pragmatic reasons, however, RoboTool provides some types such as booleans, arrays, and real numbers, which can be encoded in Z [2].

The Z mathematical toolkit provides a rich collection of functions. In addition, RoboChart, like Z, allows the definition of new functions via pre and post-conditions. The notation is similar to that adopted in OCL or JML [5]. These definitions are useful for documentation and proof. For model checking and simulation, constructive definitions of the functions need to be provided.

2.3   Time

Distinctively, RoboChart machines provide constructs to define time properties. As mentioned, in the literature, machine-like drawings are annotated with time information when relevant. With RoboChart, we can model timed aspects of robotic behaviours, and reason about timed properties.

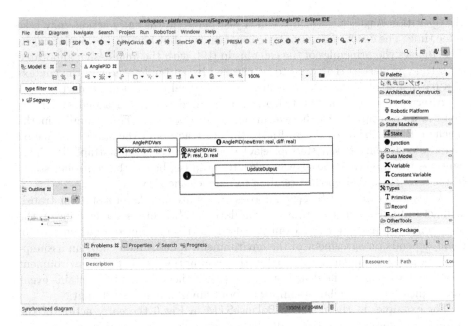

Fig. 7. Creating an operation: AnglePID. In the graphical area, we have the definition of an interface AnglePIDVars, declaring just the variable angleOutput. We also have an operation block, defining an operation AnglePID, with parameters newError and diff, both of type real. In the machine for AnglePIDVars, we show here just the initial junction and the state UpdateOutput.

We can capture in RoboChart time budgets, timeouts, and deadlines. The main principle is that passage of time is never implicit, but always explicitly specified in terms of abstract time units. For that, it is defined that operations provided by the platform take 0 time units, that is, the time they take is negligible. If this is not the case, a budget needs to be explicitly specified as illustrated below. Similarly, transitions take place as soon as they are enabled, that is, as soon as their guard, if any, is true, and their (event) trigger, if any, occurs. So, the time in which a transition is taken is predictable, rather than arbitrary.

Passage of time can be explicitly specified using budget constructs: the statement wait(t) pauses the control flow for t time units, and the nondeterministic wait([t1,t2]) pauses for a period between t1 and t2 time units. Use of the nondeterministic construct, which allows discrepancies in different executions, can provide more accurate models if precise timing is not possible or needed.

These wait statements can be used to define a budget for the execution of an operation. In this case, determining whether an implementation is correct with respect to the RoboChart design requires a worst-case execution time analysis. For example, in the machine BalanceSTM shown in Fig. 6, the entry action of the state CalculateAngle includes a statement wait([0,angleBudget]) that uses a constant angleBudget. It captures the fact that the calculation of the angle by the operation AnglePID, which is called just before in the entry action, may take some time. The exact amount of time is not known, but bounded by angleBudget. This follows the principles of the calculus in [19], with the final design annotated with time properties that need to be checked by an implementer in the context of a particular platform with specific computational power and support.

Alternatively, the wait statements can be used to defined a budget for the behaviour, as opposed to the execution, of an operation. For example, in the machine BalanceSTM shown in Fig. 6, the entry action of the state Initialisation includes a statement wait(startupDelay) that uses a constant startupDelay. This captures the time that the segway takes to initialise, before the controller starts in the next state WaitForNextIteration to balance the segway.

A deadline construct S $<\{d\}$ imposes on a statement S (of a state or transition action) a deadline to terminate. Similarly, t $<\{d\}$ imposes a deadline on the occurrence of an event t (for example, used as trigger). Since occurrence of an event depends on agreement of the environment, a deadline records an assumption about environments. Informally, the assumption is that the environment cooperates to achieve the deadline. In S $<\{d\}$, if the statement S contains event communications, a similar assumption about environments is relevant.

For example, in the machine BalanceSTM in Fig. 6 the entry action of the state CalculateAngle imposes a deadline 0 on two event communications. We have, for instance, the statement angle?currAngle$<\{0\}$, which reads an input via the event angle of the platform and assigns it to the variable currAngle. The deadline 0 means that the platform is assumed to be always ready to provide an input. This can be, for example, via a register that can always be read.

A state machine can also declare and use clocks: see the declaration of the clock loopTimer in the machine BalanceSTM in Fig. 6. These clocks can be reset using a statement #C for a clock called C: see the entry action of the state Initialisation of BalanceSTM. Conditions based on their values can be used in transition guards: the expression since(C) refers to the value of C. As an example, we refer to the guard (between square brackets) of the transition from the state WaitForNextIteration to CalculateAngle in BalanceSTM, which compares the value of the clock loopTimer to that of a constant loopTime. As explained in more detail in the next section, the clock is used to control the iterations of execution modelled by BalanceSTM. The clock loopTimer is initialised before entering the loop through state WaitForNextIteration. The next iteration starts after loopTime time units, when the clock is again reset. Timed conditions can also refer to the time in which a state is entered: sinceEntry(S) refers to the number of time units passed since the state S was last entered.

Exercise 1. Using the RoboChart and RoboTool tutorial[a] instructions, install RoboTool, and complete the exercises in Chapters 1 and 2 of that tutorial.

---

[a] robostar.cs.york.ac.uk/robotool/tutorial-16-08-2021/

In the next section, we describe the segway model in more detail. This example provides useful guidance as to how to develop RoboChart models.

3   An Example: Segway

Our example is a RoboChart model of software for the autonomous control of the Osoyoo Segway robot shown in Fig. 8. Its control software is concerned with self-balancing: it attempts to keep the segway upright when switched on, opposing the force of gravity by moving the motors to balance and maintain its position. As a safety feature, the controller stops the motors if the segway tips over past 30°C, so that it does not drive when it has fallen over. (The speed and direction of the segway can be set via a to allow it to move and turn, but the model here does not cover this functionality.)

Fig. 8. Small segway used as a reference for our example

The starting point to define a RoboChart model is the description of the robotic platform. This identifies the services assumed to be available and out of the scope of the model. As mentioned before, these services are abstractions for sensors, actuators, and the embedded API, of the actual platform. It is, of course, possible to write a RoboChart model without having a specific platform in mind. If, however, the platform to be used is known, as it is the case here, it is wise to take its components into account. In this way, we develop a RoboChart model that can be used to generate code and tests that can be used more directly, because the services used by the model (and therefore by the code and tests) are already available. In general, those services need to be made available for deployment (via hardware components or an embedded API.)

The segway contains an MPU6050 inertial measurement unit (IMU) incorporating an accelerometer and a gyroscope, allowing acceleration and angular velocity to be measured for each of the three axes. There is a motor for each of the wheels. Each motor is fitted with a Hall effect sensor, which detects changes in the strength of the magnetic field caused by the rotation of the motor. With that, it can determine the speed at which the motor is spinning.

In the definition of the RoboChart state machines for the segway model, we are guided by the C++ code that comes with the segway. Although it is not necessary to be familiar with that code to understand our RoboChart model, we do make the case here that the model reflects the design of this code. This is an indication that we can capture in RoboChart realistic and useful designs. The relevant elements of the code are explained as needed. These explanations in addition illustrate how a model can be realised in an implementation.

Section 3.1 describes the robotic platform block for our model of the segway and our considerations in defining it based on the Osoyoo Segway. Section 3.2 describes the RoboChart behavioural model: module, controller, machine, and operations. Finally, Sect. 3.3 describes a more abstract version of the model in Sect. 3.2 to illustrate the use parallelism in RoboChart models. Other artefacts developed using RoboStar technology are available[6].

3.1 Robotic Platform

Here, we describe the segway's sensors and actuators, and explain how they are captured in the RoboChart model. Figure 9 shows the complete definition of the platform block SegwayRP and of the associated interfaces used there.

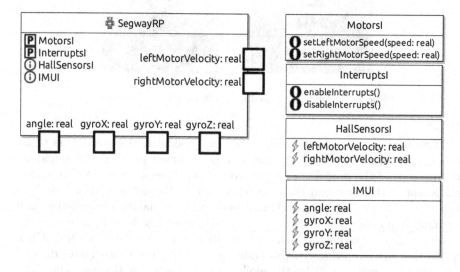

Fig. 9. The robotic platform of the Segway RoboChart model

Inertial Measurement Unit. The values from the IMU are read in the C++ code via the facilities of the MPU6050_6Axis_MotionApps20.h library for communicating with the MPU6050. This declares an MPU6050 class with a method getMotion6() to read the six values from the MPU6050 at the same time: acceleration in the x, y and z axes, and angular velocity around the x, y and z axes corresponding to change in roll, pitch and yaw. These values are passed to a

---

[6] robostar.cs.york.ac.uk/case_studies/segway.

method `Angletest()` of a `kalmanfilter` object along with some constants. This method applies a Kalman filter to smooth out error in the measurements and computes the angle of the segway, storing that angle and angular velocities in fields of `kalmanfilter` named `angle`, `Gyro_x`, `Gyro_y` and `Gyro_z`.

In RoboChart, we abstract the Kalman filter and computation of the angle, so we do not directly model the `getMotion6()` or `Angletest()` methods. Rather, we have a platform event to get the values of each of the fields of `kalmanfilter`. As already indicated, we use an event angle to communicate the computed angle from the vertical, which is the angle about the x-axis for the orientation the MPU is in, and events gyroX, gyroY and gyroZ to communicate the angular velocity around each axis. In Fig. 9, the interface IMUI declares these events.

For a treatment of filters in RoboChart, we refer to [38].

Motors. The motors are controlled in the C++ code by setting analog pins to values that determine the speed of the motors, using the `analogWrite()` Arduino function. The direction in which the motors spin is set separately using a pair of digital pins (using the `digitalWrite()` function) for each motor, with one pin indicating forward motion, and another reverse motion. The desired velocity of the segway is thus set by checking the sign of the velocity, and setting the digital pins accordingly, while the analog pin is set to the absolute value of the velocity.

In RoboChart, we represent the left and right motors by operations, setLeftMotorSpeed and setRightMotorSpeed: see interface MotorsI in Fig. 9. These operations take the desired speed as parameter, with a negative value representing reverse motion. The operations combine the setting of the pins.

Hall Effect Sensors. In the C++ code, the signals from the Hall effect sensors are detected on pin 2 for the left sensor, and 4 for the right sensor. These signals are handled by attaching interrupt handlers, `Code_left()` and `Code_right()`, to them. These handlers increment a count of how many times `Code_left()` and `Code_right()` have been called; these calls represent pulses from the Hall effect sensors. The counts are given a sign based on the velocity set for the motors, and recorded in fields `pulseleft` and `pulseright` of a `balancecar` object.

In RoboChart, we abstract away from interrupt handlers and counting of pulses, and take as input the velocity of the motors measured using the sensors, corresponding to the `pulseleft` and `pulseright` fields. The infrastructure of interrupts is treated as part of the robotic platform. As shown in the interface HallSensorsI in Fig. 9, these velocities are communicated by (input) events leftMotorVelocity and rightMotorVelocity, each with a parameter representing the velocity. The use of interrupts for communication with the platform, however, matches perfectly with the RoboChart paradigm.

Interrupts. Although we abstract away the interrupt handlers for the Hall effect sensors, the C++ code uses a timer implemented by a clock that produces interrupts. The code, therefore, needs to manage the enabling and disabling of interrupts carefully. So, although the timer can be represented by a RoboChart clock, we model the calls to methods of the segway API that provide services for enabling and disabling interrupts: see interface Interruptsl in Fig. 9.

The robotic platform block SegwayRP shown in Fig. 9 declares the interfaces with operations as provided (symbol P in a circle), and the interfaces with events as defined (symbol i in a circle). The events defined by the interfaces are indicated as boxes in the border of the platform block. The same happens with the events defined in the controllers and machines.

In the next section we present the module for the segway.

3.2 Behavioural Model

The RoboChart model presented here is the result of the evolution of an initial model[7]. Taking advantage of reviews by testing experts, and our verification efforts (see Sect. 4), we have changed the structure of the model to match that of the implementation more faithfully and fixed modelling mistakes. In particular, matching the structure of the code makes the characterisation of classes of faults via mutation operators used to generate tests more precise.

The Osoyoo segway has an Arduino Uno microcontroller, which accepts C++ code in a particular format, taking as its entry point a function setup() that is run once when the segway starts, and a function loop() that is run repeatedly while the segway is active. The setup() function for the segway sets up pin modes and initialises communication ports and the IMU. We regard this code as part of the robotic platform configuration and do not model it.

The loop() function attaches interrupt handlers to the Hall effect sensor signals, which is part of the platform configuration, and then accepts Bluetooth input. Like setup(), loop() does not need to be modelled in RoboChart either.

The main balancing control code is instead in a function inter(), bound to a 5ms timer in the setup() function. The behaviour is, therefore, purely sequential, and proceeds iteratively, with iterations controlled by time. For this reason, the RoboChart module for the segway contains a single controller.

The module, called Segway, is shown in Fig. 10. The robotic platform is defined as a reference to that presented in Fig. 9, called SegwayRP. The single controller is called SegwayController. It requires all the operations provided by the platform. This is indicated by the declarations of the interfaces containing these operations following the symbol R in a circle. SegwayController also defines events matching those of the platform (using the relevant interfaces). They are inputs from the platform, as indicated by the connections between the events of the platform and those of the controller, and their directions.

The behaviour of SegwayController is defined by a single machine called BalanceSTM, which is referenced in the SegwayController block. Another three references to machines define operations called AnglePID, SpeedPID, and RotationPID.

The definition of BalanceSTM captures the implementation of the inter() function, which consists of the following steps:

1. enable interrupts,

---

[7] robostar.cs.york.ac.uk/case_studies/segway.

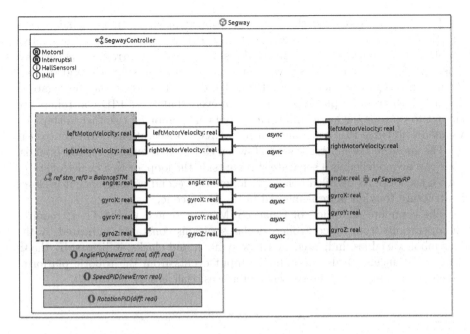

Fig. 10. The module of the segway RoboChart model

2. save the Hall sensor pulse count and compute its sign,
3. get the values from the IMU and pass them through a Kalman filter,
4. compute an angle control value using a PID,
5. compute a speed control value using a PID (but only every 10th iteration, that is, every 50 ms and so every 10th time the function `inter()` is called),
6. compute a rotation control value using a PID (every 5th iteration, that is, every 25 ms), and
7. set the velocities of the motors by combining the three control values output by the PID controllers.

The first step (1) reenables interrupts, since, as mentioned, the timer is implemented using interrupts. So, interrupts are disabled when `inter()` starts because it occurs within an interrupt handler. (We capture this behaviour by calling the platform operation `disableInterrupts()` when the timer triggers, and then `enableInterrupts()` at the start of the model of the behaviour of `inter()`.)

Step (2) is performed in the code of `inter()` via a call to a function that we consider part of the robotic platform provision of the velocities of the segway. The values recorded by this function are obtained via the leftMotorVelocity and rightMotorVelocity events so that they can be passed to the PID controllers.

Similarly, obtaining the IMU values (using the function `getMotion6()`) and the application of a Kalman filter (using the method `Angletest()`), in step (3) above, is part of the robotic platform, as already said. The values computed by the Kalman filter are accessed via the events angle, gyroX, gyroY and gyroZ in the RoboChart model so that they can be passed to the PID controllers.

The PID controller for the angle, mentioned in step (4), is included as a function in the same package as `inter()`. This PID is a central part of the control problem, so it is included as part of the state machine controlling the segway. The PID controllers for the segway's speed and rotation, steps (5) and (6), are defined in a separate package. That might indicate that they may be regarded as part of the robotic platform. Given, however, that these PID controllers are similar to that for the angle and their outputs are combined together in step (7), we model all three PID controllers in RoboChart as operations of the controller.

The speed of the motors is set to 0 when the angle is outside certain bounds. This can be modelled as a separate state outside the loop, or as a choice of states within the loop. As detailed below, we follow the second option, since it is closer in structure to what is implemented in the C++ code.

The complete definition of BalanceSTM is presented in Fig. 11. It requires the operations from its controller, declares various constants, indicated by the π symbol, variables, indicated by the **×** symbol, and clocks, indicated by the ☉ symbol. BalanceSTM also accepts the input events from the robotic platform, which are defined using the relevant interfaces: HallSensorsI and IMUI.

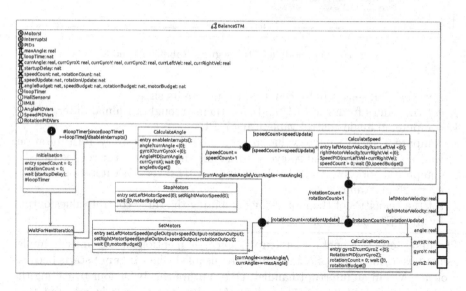

Fig. 11. The state machine of the segway RoboChart model

The first constant maxAngle specifies the angle beyond which the motors should stop trying to balance the segway. As mentioned, this allows the segway to be deactivated when it is lain down and prevents erratic behaviour if it over-balances. The value of maxAngle is 30°C in the C++ code, but we not define a value for maxAngle in BalanceSTM, or for any other constants.

There are a couple of reasons for that. First, the value in the code may be platform-dependent, and we strive to make the RoboChart model platform independent. Second, with the values of the constants open, they become parameters.

We can, therefore, use different values during verification via model checking. This can be essential for scalability. In addition, if using theorem proving, we have the opportunity to prove properties that hold for all values.

We explain the other constants, variables, and clock where they are used.

The initial state of the machine is Initialisation, whose entry action first initialises two variables, speedCount and rotationCount, to 0. They are used to count the number of iterations of the main loop to control when the speed and rotation PID control values are recomputed. (We recall that the speed is only computed on every 10th entry to inter(), and rotation on every 5th entry).

After the variables are initialised, there is a delay of startupDelay time units. This represents a delay in the setup() function, which gives time for the platform to initialise. Next, a clock loopTimer, representing the 5 ms timer, is reset.

Afterwards, BalanceSTM enters a state WaitForNextIteration, in which it waits until loopTimer reaches the value loopTime. This constant defines the number of time units allocated per iteration of the main loop. It corresponds to the 5ms controlling inter() in the C++ code. When that condition, namely, since(loopTimer)>=loopTime, is met, BalanceSTM moves to the state CalculateAngle. In the relevant transition with this guard, loopTimer is reset using #loopTimer. In addition, since the timer operates as a form of interrupt, in the transition action, after the /, the platform operation disableInterrupts() is called so that further interrupts are disabled as the handler begins.

Entering the state CalculateAngle corresponds to the start of the function inter() in the code. This state has an entry action that first calls the operation enableInterrupts() to ensure interrupts are reenabled. Afterwards, the current angle is read via the angle event into a variable currAngle, with a deadline of 0 to indicate the value should always be available. Similarly, an input is taken via gyroX and recorded in the variable currGyroX also with deadline 0. To calculate the new angle, the operation AnglePID of the controller is called. Finally, there is a nondeterministic wait for between 0 and angleBudget time units, representing the time budget for the calculations (in AnglePID) in this state, with angleBudget as a constant recording the maximum time permitted.

As shown in Fig. 11, BalanceSTM requires an interface called PIDs, whose definition, omitted here, declares the three operations AnglePID, SpeedPID, and RotationPID defined in the controller SegwayController. The state machines specifying each of these operations are presented in Figs. 12, 13, and 14.

These operations all provide their results via variables shared with BalanceSTM. For the AnglePID, the shared variable is called angleOutput. It is declared and initialised in an interface AnglePIDVars shown in Fig. 12. This interface is declared as defined in BalanceSTM and required in AnglePID.

A PID controller computes a control value to get an input value to a target. For that, it compares the input and the target value; the difference is the error value. The output is the sum of three components P, I, and D, standing for Proportional, Integral, and Derivative. Proportional is a multiple of the error value. Integral is a multiple of the accumulated error value over time. Finally, derivative is a multiple of the change in error value. These components are used

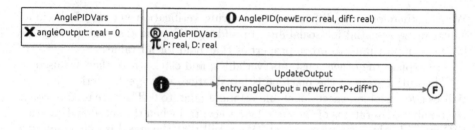

Fig. 12. The AnglePID operation of the segway RoboChart model

to correct the error, ensure convergence, and avoid jitter. The multiplication factors are parameters that are tuned for particular applications.

In the case of the segway, the target values all are 0, and not all components are used. For the angle control, the segway uses a PD controller, because the angle is too unstable to determine a useful integral. For the speed control, the segway uses a PI controller, to allow some jitter for angle control. Finally, the rotation control just uses the derivative, to correct for motor differences.

The parameters to AnglePID are newError, already determining the amount by which the PID value differs from the setpoint, which, as said, AnglePID attempts to get to 0, and diff, which is the change in the error over time. The scaling factors P and D are uninitialised constants, and so they are parameters of the model. In the state CalculateAngle of BalanceSTM, the call to AnglePID provides as arguments the current angle currAngle around the x-axis, and the velocity currGyroX around the x-axis, which defines how currAngle changes over time.

The state machine defining AnglePID starts in a state UpdateOutput, whose entry action records the output of the PID in angleOutput. The value stored is the sum of the two PID components, proportional and differential. The proportional component is the product of the input error value newError and the proportional scaling constant P. The differential component is diff multiplied by the differential scaling constant D. Afterwards, AnglePID terminates.

Going back to BalanceSTM, after the CalculateAngle state is exited, the action of its only outgoing transition increments the speedCount variable. It is then compared to the speedUpdate constant, representing the number of iterations of the loop that should occur before the speed PID is updated (10 in the C++ code). If speedCount is greater than or equal to speedUpdate, BalanceSTM enters the state CalculateSpeed, whose entry action is similar to that of CalculateAngle.

In CalculateSpeed, input values are read using the events leftMotorVelocity and rightMotorVelocity and stored into the variables currLeftVel and currRightVel, with a deadline of 0 as for angle. The operation SpeedPID is then called with the sum of currLeftVel and currRightVel as argument. The speedCount is then set to 0 to restart the count for the next iteration. As with CalculateAngle, the entry action of CalculateSpeed ends with a nondeterministic delay, with the maximum time the calculations can take set by a constant speedBudget.

The definition of SpeedPID is shown in Fig. 13. Similarly to AnglePID, this requires an interface SpeedPIDVars declaring shared variables. In this case, we have the variable speedOutput, which records the output, and an extra variable speedIntegral, which records the running integral over the errors SpeedPID and, therefore, needs to persist between calls. These variables are both initialised to 0. Like AnglePID, SpeedPID takes as input newError with the amount by which the PID value differs from the setpoint. SpeedPID also declares P and I, the proportional and integral scaling constants. An extra constant, maxIntegral, sets the maximum integral value for speedIntegral.

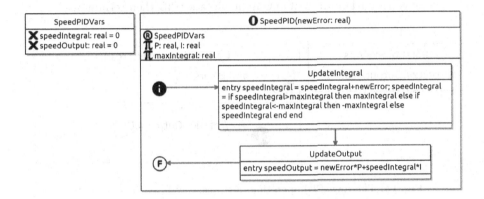

Fig. 13. The SpeedPID operation of the segway RoboChart model

The state machine for the SpeedPID begins in a state UpdateIntegral. In its entry action, speedIntegral is updated to compute the running integral, by adding newError to the existing speedIntegral value. If the absolute value of speedIntegral is greater than maxIntegral, it is set to maxIntegral with the same sign of speed-Integral preserved. This models the clamping of the integral in the C++ code to prevent it from getting too large and having too great an effect on the segway.

After speedIntegral has been updated, SpeedPID enters a state UpdateOutput, in which the output, speedOutput, is computed. This is the sum of the two components, proportional and integral. The proportional component is computed as in AnglePID, multiplying newError by the proportional scaling constant P. The integral component is computed by multiplying the previously calculated integral speedIntegral by the integral scaling constant I. SpeedPID then terminates.

If speedCount is less than speedUpdate, then BalanceSTM skips past Calcu-lateSpeed, rejoining the outgoing transition from CalculateSpeed at a junction. At that point, whether CalculateSpeed was entered or not, rotationCount is incre-mented and compared to a constant rotationUpdate (corresponding to the value of 5 for the iteration when the rotation PID is updated in the C++ code), similarly to speedCount. When rotationCount is equal to or greater than rotationUpdate, BalanceSTM enters the state CalculateRotation.

In CalculateRotation, the rotation around the z-axis is read via the gyroZ event into the currGyroZ variable, with a deadline of zero. The RotationPID is then called with currGyroZ as argument, and the rotationCount is zeroed. Afterwards, there is a nondeterministic delay of between 0 and rotationBudget time units.

The RotationPID is the simplest of them all. Its required interface, which is called RotationPIDVars, declares a single variable rotationOutput that stores the output and is initialised to 0. RotationPID takes in a parameter diff, which represents the derivative of the rotation, and declares the scaling constant D. The machine for RotationPID has a single transition from the initial junction to the final state. The action of this transition simply stores the product of diff and the scaling constant D into rotationOutput. RotationPID then terminates.

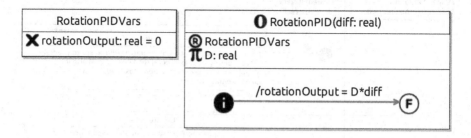

Fig. 14. The AnglePID operation of the segway RoboChart model

In BalanceSTM, if the value of rotationCount is less than rotationUpdate, the state CalculateRotation is skipped. In any case, next, the value of currAngle is checked against the constant maxAngle. If the absolute value of currAngle is greater than maxAngle, then the state StopMotors is entered. There, the speed of both motors is set to 0 using the platform operations setLeftMotorSpeed() and setRightMotorSpeed(). There is then a nondeterministic delay of between 0 and motorBudget time units to account for the communication with the motors.

If the absolute value of currAngle is less than or equal to maxAngle, the machine BalanceSTM enters the state SetMotors. This state sets the speed of the motors similarly to StopMotors, but sets the left motor speed to the sum of the outputs of anglePID and speedPID, minus the output of rotationPID, and the right motor speed to the sum of all three outputs of anglePID, speedPID and rotationPID. Thus, the speeds of both motors are set relative to the outputs of the PID controllers, but the rotation component is applied in opposite directions for each of the two motors so that the segway does not rotate. SetMotors then has the same nondeterministic delay as StopMotors, since communicating with the motors takes the same amount of time in both cases.

After either StopMotors and SetMotors, BalanceSTM returns to the state WaitForNextIteration to await the start of the next loop iteration. All the time budgets (angleBudget, speedBudget, rotationBudget and motorBudget) must add up to less than loopTime, so that each iteration does not overlap with the next.

Restrictions on the values of constants is an aspect of the model that needs to be captured in its documentation, as it may be important for verification.

The structure of the RoboChart model for the segway, including that of the state machines, closely reflects that of the C++ code. An earlier version of the model used a general function computePID to specify the general behaviour of a PID controller. Arguably, this results in a more elegant model, which avoids the somewhat repetitive definitions in AnglePID, SpeedPID, and RotationPID. In addition, computePID is a reusable function that can be useful for other models.

If, however, we use the RoboChart model for automatic test generation, it is useful to have a structure close to that of the code. In this way, coverage of the model can be reflected in coverage of the code. In particular, RoboStar has support for mutation testing based on RoboChart. With mutation of an individual PID, we can capture faults where one of the PID calculations, but not all, has a problem. Additionally, as it turns out, the more concrete model that we present here is more amenable to verification via model checking.

We have used the Segway model to generate automatically 93 tests for the control software. We have also verified 600 properties of the model automatically. Next, we describe a parallel version of the model.

3.3   Parallel Behavioural Model

In this section, we present a different model of the segway, to illustrate the use of parallel machines in a controller. In this version, we define each PID by a state machine that accepts its inputs through events communicating with BalanceSTM. Figure 15 presents the module for this new model. It uses the same robotic-platform block, but has a different controller also called SegwayController. In this controller, besides BalanceSTM, we have three machines AnglePID, Speed-PID and RotationPID connected to BalanceSTM via events.

The events used as inputs to the PID machines are named after the parameters of the corresponding operations presented in the previous section, but have a prefix character indicating to which PID they connect: the inputs of AnglePID are anewError and adiff, the input of SpeedPID is snewError, and the input of RotationPID is rdiff. The output events have the same name as the required variables used to record the outputs of the operations with the suffix E.

Figure 16 presents our version of the BalanceSTM state machine for the parallel model. Besides the variables, constants, and interfaces declared in its previous version, BalanceSTM declares four extra variables: speedSent, angleSent, rotation-Sent and angleReceived, used to track whether BalanceSTM has sent input events to the PID state machines, and angleReceived used to prevent multiple readings of the result from AnglePID in a loop iteration, because AnglePID is not timed in the same way as the rotation and speed PIDs.

As before, BalanceSTM starts in a state Initialisation; its entry action, in addition to what it executes in the original sequential model, sets speedSent, angleSent and rotationSent to false. The transition to WaitForNextIteration and this state itself are unchanged. The state Setup into which BalanceSTM transitions after-

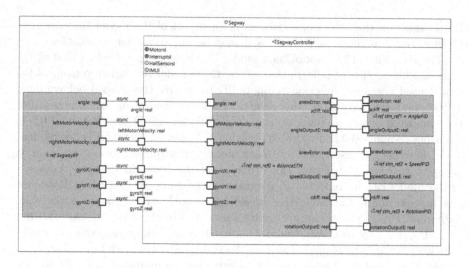

Fig. 15. A parallel version of the Segway model

wards, however, is new. Its purpose is twofold: incrementing the rotationCount and the speedCount, and setting angleReceived to false.

BalanceSTM then moves to ReceiveInput, where most of its behaviour is defined. Unlike in the original model, where each PID calculation is carried out in a set order, BalanceSTM allows for these calculations to occur in any order.

There are seven transitions from ReceiveInput: three to states whose entry actions send data and trigger a PID, three self transitions for receiving data from a PID, and one transition to a junction where a decision is made to define the final part of the iteration. Sending data is handled by the states SendAngle, SendSpeed, and SendRotation. Transitions to these states are guarded by conditions on angleSent, rotationSent, and speedSent. This is to prevent consecutive redundant input events being sent to a PID in the same iteration.

The transition to SendAngle requires both angleSent and angleReceived to be false, to prevent multiple uses of the calculations carried out by AnglePID in an iteration. The variables angleSent and angleReceived are both false at the start of the iteration. Although angleSent is set to true after the AnglePID is triggered, it is then set back to false, once its result is received. The extra variable angleReceived records whether the output of the PID has already been received in the current iteration. In this case, the AnglePID is not used again.

The entry action of SendAngle reads in, with deadline 0, currAngle and currGyroX via the events angle and gyroX. It then sends these values through the new events anewError and adiff events to the AnglePID state machine. The action of the transition from SendAngle back to ReceiveInput sets angleSent to true.

The transition to SendSpeed is also guarded by the condition that speedCount must be greater than or equal to speedUpdate. This means that, as speedCount is only incremented once every iteration, the speed PID is only executed every speedUpdate iterations. In SendSpeed, the entry action reads in the data needed

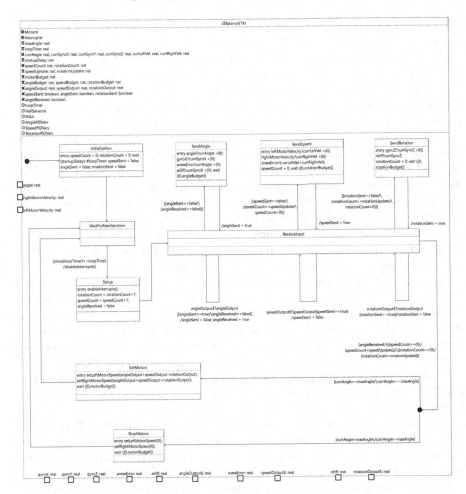

Fig. 16. A parallel version of the BalanceSTM state machine

for SpeedPID (currLeftVel and currRightVel) then communicates their sum to SpeedPID via the event snewError. Next, speedCount is set to 0, to keep the speed PID operating on the correct iterations. Finally, speedSent is set to true in the action of the transition back to ReceiveInput.

SendRotation is similar to SendSpeed. Instead of speedCount and speedUpdate, rotationCount and rotationUpdate are used, and instead of speedSent, rotationSent is set to true. RotationPID only requires one input to be read from the robotic platform, gyroZ, and this value is sent to RotationPID using the rdiff event.

Receiving data is handled in the self transitions of ReceiveInput. The triggers are inputs via the output events of the PID machines: angleOutputE, speed-OutputE, and rotationOutputE. The inputs are recorded in the corresponding variables angleOutput, speedOutput, and rotationOutput. The guards of the self transitions require that each relevant sent variable is true, as BalanceSTM should not accept an output from a PID until it has sent data to start it first.

In the transition whose trigger is angleOutputE?angleOutput, an additional condition requires that angleReceived is false. This prevents multiple inputs of the angle PID being received in a single iteration. This cannot occur for the SpeedPID and RotationPID state machines as they cannot send input data twice in the same iteration due to the speed and rotation counts.

The actions of the self transitions reset the sent variables: angleSent, speedSent, and rotationSent are set to false, to indicate that the output has been received and new data can be sent. In the transition with trigger angleOutputtE?angleOutput, angleReceived is also set to true, indicating that angleOutput cannot be updated again. We note that angleReceived is only set to false in the proceeding iteration in the entry action of the state Setup.

In the entry actions of SendAngle, SendSpeed, and SendRotation, there are nondeterministic wait actions to represent the time spent on the PID calculations. The times are the same assumed in the original model.

BalanceSTM transitions from ReceiveInput to a junction when all required PID results are received. This is ensured by three conditions. The first is that angleReceived is true, since the AnglePID is executed in every iteration. The second is that either speedCount is 0, that is, SpeedPID has been executed, or speedCount is less than speedUpdate, and so SpeedPID should not be executed. The next condition is identical but for rotationCount and rotationUpdate.

The junction, and the proceeding states, StopMotors and SetMotors of BalanceSTM, are identical to those in the original model. BalanceSTM then proceeds to WaitForNextIteration and repeats the iteration as before.

The definitions of the state machines for AnglePID, SpeedPID, RotationPID are similar to those in the previous section, where they are defined as operations. For illustration, we have the AnglePID machine in Fig. 17; it starts in the extra Read state, where inputs anewError?currNewError and adiff?currDiff are accepted. When both inputs are received, the machine transitions to UpdateOutput, where currAngleOut is calculated as before. AnglePID then transitions back to Read; in the transition action, currAngleOut is output via the event angleOutputE.

The parallel model for the segway just presented is more abstract than the sequential model in Sect. 3.2. Formally, the sequential model is a refinement of the parallel model. Intuitively, we observe that the parallel model engages in the same events and call the same operations of the platform SegwayRP as the sequential model at each iteration, but these events and operations may be occur and be called in a different order. Because the parallel model is nondeterministic, it is not a refinement of the sequential model. These facts have been proved using the formal semantics of RoboChart automatically generated by RoboTool.

Next, we describe how we can carry out verification using RoboTool.

4   Application: Verification of Properties

RoboTool can generate automatically mathematical models that capture the meaning, that is, semantics, of a RoboChart model. One such semantics is

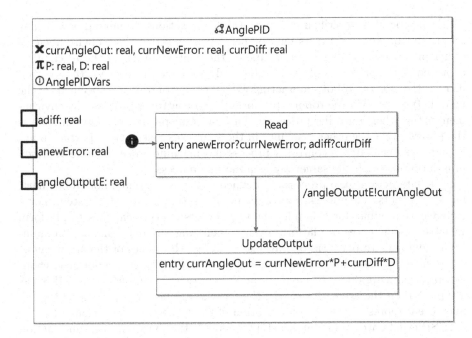

Fig. 17. AnglePID defined as a state machine

described using an algebra called tock-CSP [4, 33]. It captures the reactive visible behaviour of a RoboChart model in terms of the variables, events, and operations of the robotic platform. It also captures the possibility of deadlocks and the passage of time. Section 4.1 gives an overview of tock-CSP. A tutorial on CSP, which is the algebra used as a basis for tock-CSP, can be found in [14].

With such model, we can prove properties of RoboChart components. In particular, we can analyse RoboChart models using the facilities provided by RoboTool via its integration with the CSP model checker FDR [18]. Using the segway example, we describe in detail a typical verification workflow supported by RoboTool. Section 4.2 focuses on the verification of core behavioural properties, such as checking that a model is deadlock free. Next, in Sect. 4.3 we illustrate how application-specific properties can be modelled and verified.

4.1 CSP and Tock-CSP

CSP is a process algebra; it is a language for the description of observable (visible) behaviour. In CSP, as well as in tock-CSP, processes are used to describe the behaviour of systems or components, and properties. So, the tock-CSP specification of a RoboChart model defines a process that describes the behaviour of the module. That module process is defined using other processes that describe the behaviour of the controllers and machines. The controller and machine processes are combined using algebraic process operators of CSP (and tock-CSP).

Each process is described as a pattern of interactions explaining how it may affect, and be affected by, its environment. In this setting, the environment is either processes for other components, or the context in which the mechanism captured by the process is placed. So, basically, for a module process, the environment is that for the robot, interacting with the control software specified by the module (process) via the robotic platform. For a controller process, the environment is the other controller processes. For a machine process, the environment is the processes for the other machines in the same controller. An important point is that, as shown later, a controller process or a machine process can be analysed in isolation in much the same way as a module process.

The interactions of a process are defined in terms of events: not RoboChart, but CSP events. They mark important points in the history of a system. For a RoboChart module, for example, the CSP events capture changes to platform variables, occurrences of platform events, including any data that is communicated, and calls to platform operations, including the values of the arguments.

To facilitate modelling of data communication, CSP embeds a notion of channel. If a channel c does not have a type, it represents a simple event c. If it has a type T, then the events for c take the form c.v, where v is a value of type T. Such event represents the communication of the value v over the channel c.

CSP events are atomic and instantaneous. If the duration of an interaction is important, then it is modelled by two CSP events: one marks the start and the other the end of the interaction. These points become the interactions in the CSP model. In the context of CSP, an interaction is a synchronisation on events, happening at the same time for two or more components. Asynchronous communications, which are available in RoboChart, can be modelled using a process that specifies a buffer. For synchronous communications, various implementation strategies can be used to enforce atomicity and synchronicity.

To capture time properties, the dialect of CSP called tock-CSP uses a special event tock to mark passage of time. In this algebra, the notion of time is discrete and defined in terms of abstract time units, like in RoboChart. The occurrence of the event tock marks the passage of one time unit.

Since time is represented using an event, a concept already present in CSP, we can use CSP tools when dealing with tock-CSP processes. The special interpretation of tock, however, has impact on the expected behaviour of some CSP process operators. FDR has support for modelling and verification of tock-CSP processes that deals with these peculiarities. In particular, we can configure FDR to take the RoboChart view that events take no time, and that we have maximal internal progress. With this, we ensure that internal events that are possible happen urgently. This captures, for example, the fact that enabled transitions are urgent, making passage of time predictable.

Although a dialect of CSP, tock-CSP, due to its flexibility in allowing control over the tock event, is very powerful. For example, we can easily model deadlines, a feature that is not available in several process algebras. With tock-CSP, urgency, and therefore, a deadline can be modelled by refusal of tock. For example, if an event e is accepted, but the event tock is refused, it means that time cannot be observed to pass until e takes places. This corresponds to defining that e is urgent. A deadline can be defined by making an event possible before the deadline, and then urgent once the deadline is reached.

In what follows, we provide some examples of tock-CSP processes used to define properties. We explain the notation for describing processes as needed.

4.2   Verification of Core Behavioural Properties

FDR must be installed separately from RoboTool. The latest version available from cocotec.io/fdr/ at the time of writing is 4.2.7. If installed in a non-standard location, FDR's path should be manually set in RoboTool by going to Window ⟩ Preferences selecting RoboChart ⟩ Analysis and then selecting FDR's installation path by clicking on Browse... followed by OK. Next, we describe how RoboTool can be used to perform basic verifications.

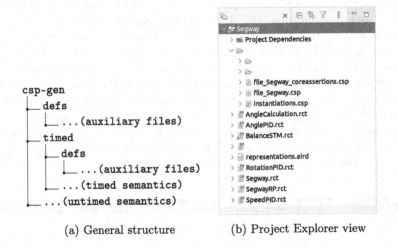

(a) General structure   (b) Project Explorer view

Fig. 18. Filesystem structure of CSP$_M$ semantics as generated by RoboTool

Semantics. Provided a RoboChart model satisfies all well-formedness conditions listed in [24, Chapter 3], then RoboTool automatically calculates and stores under the csp-gen folder the definition of the semantics using CSP$_M$, the machine-readable version of CSP accepted by FDR. This consists of files with the extension csp organised according to the tree structure outlined in Fig. 18a.

RoboChart models can span one or more packages, defined in RoboTool in model files, which have the extension rct. For each such file, a corresponding .csp file is generated by RoboTool under the directory csp-gen: if an rct file defines a **package** named P, then the generated file is named P.csp, and otherwise it takes the name of the .rct file concatenated after a prefix file_. At the root of

csp-gen we have an untimed CSP semantics, with auxiliary .csp files contained within the subfolder **defs**. Since the segway example uses timed primitives (wait statements, a clock, and deadlines), in this section we consider only verification using the tock-CSP semantics, which is generated within the subfolder **csp-gen ▸timed**, that is structured similarly to **csp-gen**.

Within RoboTool, the actual filesystem structure can be seen, for example, using the Project Explorer view. In Fig. 18b we reproduce this view for the segway example, where a subset of the generated .csp files is visible.

Core Assertions Along with the CSP semantics of a model, RoboTool also generates .csp files with the suffix _coreassertions.csp containing CSP_M assertions to check standard properties such as deadlock freedom and determinism. These can be directly loaded into FDR by double-clicking on them. If the .csp file-type has not yet been associated with FDR, such a file can be opened from within RoboTool by right-clicking and selecting Open With 》Other..., then selecting External Programs, and finally pointing at the FDR executable by clicking on Browse... and then clicking OK. It is recommended to make this association permanent by selecting the option Use it for all '*.csp' files before clicking OK.

In the case of the Segway RoboChart project, which contains the sequential RoboChart model presented in Sect. 3.2, loading of the file **csp-gen▸timed▸ file_Segway_coreassertions.csp** in FDR results in the appearance of a window similar to that shown in Fig. 19. It shows FDR's interactive console on the left, and a list of **Assertions** populated on the right. Below there is also an empty list of **Tasks** as no checks have been executed so far. Importantly, the console shows no errors, which indicates FDR has successfully parsed and type-checked the loaded .csp file, and so the analysis can proceed.

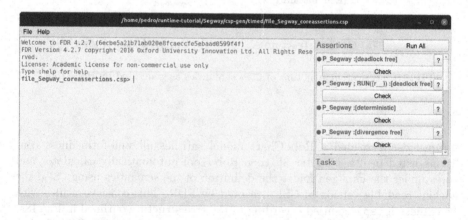

Fig. 19. File **file_Segway_coreassertions.csp** loaded in FDR

The list displayed in Fig. 19 includes several assertions over the automatically calculated CSP semantics of the RoboChart module **Segway**. Assertions in FDR refer to names of CSP processes, so in **P_Segway** :[**deadlock free**], the name **P_Segway**, for example, refers to a CSP process that captures the semantics of the RoboChart module similarly named Segway. Below, we describe informally the meaning of a subset of the assertions visible in Fig. 19.

A.1 **P_Segway** :[**deadlock free**]: checks that the module Segway is deadlock free, that is, it never reaches a configuration in which all observable interactions are refused, including the passage of time. Because in CSP termination is marked by a special event ✓, and afterwards all events are refused, if **P_Segway** may terminate, then this assertion fails.

A.2 **P_Segway** ; **RUN({r__})** :[**deadlock free**]: similarly checks that the sequential composition (;) of **P_Segway** with a process **RUN({r__})**, which offers to synchronise on a dummy fresh event **r__** forever, is deadlock free. Whereas in the previous assertion if **P_Segway** terminates FDR finds a deadlock, here the sequential composition ensures that only genuine deadlocks are found.

A.3 **P_Segway** :[**deterministic**]: checks that the module Segway is deterministic, that is, that it never reaches a configuration where Segway could both perform and refuse an interaction via the platform.

Exercise 2. If Assertion A.1 failed, but Assertion A.2 succeeded, what could be concluded about the behaviour of Segway?

In FDR, assertions can be checked individually by clicking on ⎡Check⎤, or, alternatively, all loaded assertions can be checked at once by clicking on ⎡Run All⎤. To check assertions, FDR constructs Labelled Transition Systems (LTS) using the operational semantics of CSP [33]. While checks are ongoing, the **Tasks** list is populated with information related to the construction of the LTSs, and the progress of verifications, which entail visiting states and transitions of the LTS. This is useful, for instance, to gauge the tractability of ongoing checks.

Successful verification of an assertion is indicated by a green dot ● and the label *Finished: Passed*; for a failing assertion we get a red dot ● and the label *Finished: Failed*. Information about the complexity of an assertion check, in terms of time, visited states and transitions of an LTS, is available by clicking on ⎡?⎤.

Assertions can be negated by adding a **not** in front of them. The automatically generated assertions, however, are all positive, that is, not negated. When a positive assertion fails, a counterexample is produced, and can be viewed and explored by clicking on ⎡Debug⎤. Verification of Assertion A.3 using FDR fails, revealing that the model is not deterministic. Clicking on ⎡Debug⎤ opens a window similar to that reproduced in Fig. 20, where the internal events, τ in the operational semantics of CSP, have been omitted, by unticking **View Taus**, and the panel on the right-hand side has been hidden.

The complete sequence of visible events leading to the nondeterministic behaviour is reproduced below. In this sequence, besides the special event tock, we have events that correspond to calls to operations and occurrence of events of the robotic platform SegwayRP (see Fig. 4) of the Segway module. The event Segway::disableInterruptsCall represents a call to disableInterrupts(). Similarly,

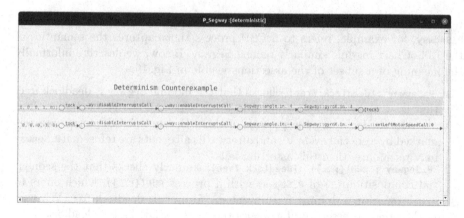

Fig. 20. Analysis of determinism counterexample in FDR (Assertion A.3)

Segway::enableInterruptsCall is a call to enableInterrupts(). In the case of the event Segway::angle.in.-4, we have an input via the platform event angle of the value -4. Similarly, Segway::gyroX.in.-4 is an input of -4 via gyroX. In the CSP$_M$ semantics of RoboChart, events are named according to the RoboChart model hierarchy, where :: is a delimiter, and may have a parameter in or out to indicate whether a CSP event represents a RoboChart input or output, respectively.

```
tock, tock, tock, tock, tock, tock, Segway::disableInterruptsCall,
Segway::enableInterruptsCall, Segway::angle.in.-4, Segway::gyroX.in.-4
```

After this sequence of events, it is possible for **P_Segway** to both: (a) advance time by one unit, by performing the event tock, as indicated by the singleton set shown in red at the end of the top sequence in Fig. 20; or (b) refuse to advance time, and instead offer the event Segway::setLeftMotorSpeedCall.0, shown in abbreviated form at the end of the bottom sequence in Fig. 20.

Here, Segway::setLeftMotorSpeedCall.0 corresponds to calling the robotic platform operation setLeftMotorSpeed with argument 0. Using the counterexample, we can retrace the behaviour of BalanceSTM, as used in Segway, and conclude that the nondeterminism stems from the nondeterministic wait in the entry action of the state CalculateAngle. It is possible for the machine to pause for a longer amount of time, as indicated by tock, or move forward all the way to the state StopMotors and call setLeftMotorSpeed(0) as part of its entry action.

In Sect. 4.3, we discuss the analysis of other counterexamples using FDR.

Exercise 3. Check all core assertions of the Segway module. What do other core assertions, not discussed so far, check for? Information about divergence, for example, can be found, for instance, in [14,33].

Parameters for Model-Checking. Without further user intervention, the core assertions are analysed using default values for constants. In the segway

```
 1  -- generate const_Segway_SegwayController_stm_ref0_loopTime not
 2  const_Segway_SegwayController_stm_ref0_loopTime = 4
 3
 4  -- generate real not
 5   nametype core_real = { -4..4}
 6
 7  -- generate core_clock_type not
 8   nametype core_clock_type = {0..10}
 9
10  -- generate Plus
11  Plus(e1,e2,T) = if member(e1+e2,T)  then e1+e2  else e1
```

Listing 1: Excerpt of an `instantiations.csp` file

example, this means, for instance, that the parameters of the PID controllers are set to defaults by RoboTool. While this provides a starting point for analysis, in practice, it is essential that such values are adjusted to match application requirements. RoboTool generates an `instantiations.csp` file containing defaults for several parameters that can be adjusted for model-checking with FDR:

1. **Constants**: the value of all defined and required constants not initialised in a RoboChart constant declaration can be adjusted. This includes constants at all levels. An excerpt of an `instantiations.csp` file generated from the segway example, and manually adjusted, is shown in Listing 1. The first line is a CSP_M comment, but includes an important keyword not at the end, that prevents RoboTool from overriding the value upon automatic regeneration of the CSP semantics. (The tock-CSP semantics is automatically updated as the model is changed.) On line 2, the value of the constant loopTime as used in the state machine BalanceSTM, which is referenced as stm_ref0 in the controller SegwayController defined in the module Segway, is set to 4.

2. **Data-type bounds**: FDR is an explicit-state model checker, so the domain of RoboChart types, such as real, int and nat must be instantiated as finite discrete sets. By default, RoboTool generates approximate domains that take into account the value of defined constants and literals found in the model. On line 5 of Listing 1, for example, the domain of reals has been manually instantiated as the set of integers between -4 and 4.

3. **Clock bounds**: similarly, clock bounds define the largest number of time units that any clock is expected to count, given their use in transition guards. Currently, RoboTool inserts checks in the generated CSP_M semantics that throw an error in FDR if a clock bound is found to be too small. On line 8 of Listing 1 this is instantiated as the set of integers between 0 and 10.

4. **Arithmetic operations**: because types have finite domains, arithmetic operations need to be mathematically closed. RoboTool generates default definitions for basic arithmetic operations, such as sum and subtraction. A default implementation for addition is shown on line 11 of Listing 1, defined as a CSP_M function. It takes three parameters, the two values being summed as e1 and

e2, and the carrier type T. If the result of adding e1 and e2 is in the set T then the result is their sum, and otherwise it is the value e1.

Exercise 4. Define appropriate data-type bounds for the segway example by overriding the defaults in the csp-gen▸timed▸instantiations.csp file. How do chosen parameter values impact the verification results?

This concludes the basic workflow for verification of core assertions using the model checker FDR. Next we focus on the verification of application-specific properties with the help of RoboTool's domain-specific assertion language.

4.3   Verification of Application-Specific Properties

In the previous section, we have explained how to carry out verification using the _coreassertions.csp file that is automatically generated and includes core assertions. To check additional properties, we can use a domain-specific language (DSL) to specify assertions, including core assertions. This language provides a user-friendly textual frontend for writing simple checks, that allows, for example, values of constants to be set differently for each assertion, instead of relying on the definitions in the file instantiations.csp. With this approach, an HTML report is produced from within RoboTool to record the results of the verification. This route to verification is facilitated by an editor with syntax highlighting, auto-completion, and error feedback, as we explain next.

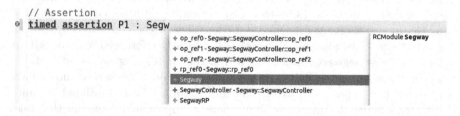

Fig. 21. Typing of a timed assertion while using auto-completion in RoboTool

RoboChart Assertions. Checks written using the built-in DSL are recorded in files with extension assertions. A new file can be created in RoboTool by selecting the current project in the Project Explorer view and after right-clicking, then selecting New⟩File. A new dialog appears, where a unique name with the assertions extension can be filled in, followed by OK. Double-clicking on the newly created file opens the RoboChart assertions textual editor.

An example of a basic assertion is shown in Listing 2. It can be typed with the assistance of auto-completion, available by pressing Ctrl+Spacebar, to find the RoboChart module Segway, as reproduced in Fig. 21. In this example, we

```
1  timed assertion P1 : Segway is deadlock-free
2     with constant P of AnglePID    set to 0,
3          constant D of AnglePID    set to 0,
4          constant P of SpeedPID    set to 0,
5          constant I of SpeedPID    set to 0 and
6          constant D of RotationPID set to 0
7
8  timed assertion P2 : SpeedPID is deadlock-free
```

Listing 2: Excerpt of an .assertions file for the Segway example

define the **timed assertion** P1 with the value of constants P, D and I, used in the operations AnglePID, SpeedPID, and RotationPID, all set to 0. The exact syntax of RoboChart assertions is described in the RoboTool reference manual [35].

> *Exercise 5.* Using the RoboChart assertion language, write assertions that check core behavioural properties of the Segway module.

Besides the analysis of a complete RoboChart module, it is also possible to analyse individual components of a RoboChart model. On line 8 of Listing 2 we have defined the **timed assertion** P2 that checks whether the software operation SpeedPID, on its own, is deadlock free. The ability to analyse components in isolation is useful to identify problems early in a design.

Verification with FDR. After creating a .assertions file, its assertions can be checked with FDR directly from within RoboTool by right-clicking on it, and then selecting RoboTool ⟫ CSP ⟫ Run... . FDR is then run in the background. Upon termination of the verification of all assertions defined in the chosen file, an HTML document is shown containing a table of results. It details, for each assertion, whether it has been successfully verified, or disproved. If FDR cannot be found by RoboTool, or there is an error in a .assertions file, an error is raised when trying to run it. The assertions editor flags any syntactic errors.

> *Exercise 6.* Verify the assertions previously written for Exercise 5 using RoboTool's integration with FDR.

Similarly to how RoboTool calculates the CSP_M semantics of RoboChart components, RoboChart assertions are also compiled to CSP_M. For each file with the extension **assertions**, where no errors are flagged, a corresponding file named with a suffix **_assertions.csp**, is generated under **csp-gen**, and **csp-gen ▸ timed**. The **timed assertion**s are compiled to CSP_M under **csp-gen ▸ timed**. Instead of invoking FDR via RoboTool, we can directly load these generated .csp files in FDR for further inspection of counterexamples as previously described.

Next, we focus on the specification of an application-specific property using CSP_M for verification with FDR. This requires knowledge of CSP.

```
1   timed csp MaxAngleStop csp-begin
2     Timed(OneStep) {
3     -- Top-level tock-CSP process specification, prioritised to ensure correct
4     -- operational semantics is calculated (ie. maximal progress is observed).
5     MaxAngleStop = timed_priority(MSpec)
6
7     -- Accepts CSP events corresponding to the 'interface' defined by the
          robotic
8     -- platform, and after a communication via 'angle?x' if 'x' is outside the
9     -- range {-maxAngle..maxAngle} then behaves as MStop;MSpec, and otherwise
          recurses.
10    MSpec =
11      TCHAOS( diff(SegwayRPEvents,{|Segway::angle.in|}))
12      /\
13      Segway::angle.in?x ->
14        ( if (x > const_BalanceSTM_maxAngle  or x < -const_BalanceSTM_maxAngle)
15          then (MStop ; MSpec)
16          else MSpec)
17
18    -- Other events may happen, but calls to operations 'setLeftMotorSpeed'
19    -- and 'setRightMotorSpeed', both with their only parameter set to 0,
20    -- must happen within 2 time units.
21    MStop =
22      TCHAOS( diff(SegwayRPEvents,
23                  {|Segway::setLeftMotorSpeedCall,Segway::setRightMotorSpeedCall
            |})
24                )
25      /\
26      Deadline(   Segway::setLeftMotorSpeedCall.0  -> SKIP
27                |||  Segway::setRightMotorSpeedCall.0 -> SKIP,2)
28
29    -- CSP events of the Robotic platform, explicitly defined as a channel set.
30    SegwayRPEvents =
31      {| Segway::angle.in, Segway::gyroX.in, Segway::gyroY.in, Segway::gyroZ.in,
32         Segway::leftMotorVelocity.in, Segway::rightMotorVelocity.in,
33         Segway::setLeftMotorSpeedCall, Segway::setRightMotorSpeedCall,
34         Segway::disableInterruptsCall, Segway::enableInterruptsCall |}
35  }
36  csp-end
37
38  timed assertion P3 : Segway refines MaxAngleStop in the traces model
```

Listing 3: Example of a check for a custom property of the Segway

Application-Specific Property. As previously discussed in Sect. 3.2, during normal operation, the segway software monitors the vertical angle, so that if it reaches a value outside a specified range, then the motors are quickly switched off. To check that the software behaves as expected, we first capture this property as a CSP$_M$ specification in Listing 3. This is written in a **timed csp** block named MaxAngleStop (lines 1–36) using RoboTool's assertion language.

Arbitrary CSP$_M$ code can be written between the reserved keywords **csp-begin** and **csp-end**. The precise syntax accepted by FDR is specified in its manual[8].

---

[8] cocotec.io/fdr/manual/.

A report detailing the analysis of other properties of the Segway is available[9]. Next, we explain the CSP specification of MaxAngleStop in more detail.

The property of interest is modelled by the CSP process MaxAngleStop (line 5), defined within a **Timed** section [10] (lines 2–35), where processes are interpreted to be timed: tock events, which mark the passage of time, are automatically inserted to allow time to pass when waiting for interactions with the environment, and the passage of time is uniform across interacting processes. The function OneStep, passed as a parameter, is predefined in RoboTool and ensures that interactions with the environment (CSP events) take no time.

The behaviour of MaxAngleStop (line 5) is defined as MSpec with **timed_priority** applied. This is a function over processes provided by FDR that must be applied to ensure that the operational semantics of tock-CSP is correctly calculated. It should be applied to the main CSP process of every timed specification.

MSpec (line 10) initially engages nondeterministically (TCHAOS on line 11) in events tock and those corresponding to interactions with the platform, specified by a channel set SegwayRPEvents (line 30), with the exception of Segway::angle.in, as defined using the set **diff**erence operator of CSP on line 11.

The process TCHAOS(X) is the least-refined tock-CSP process with events in the set X. The built-in process CHAOS(A) of FDR is defined by the equation CHAOS(X) = ([] e : X @ e -> CHAOS(X)) |~| **STOP**. This allows all events of X to be continuously offered or refused. In the failures model of CSP, an equivalent definition is CHAOS(X) = (|~| e : X @ e -> CHAOS(X)) |~| **STOP**, since any event e can be refused anyway because of the **STOP**. In tock-CSP, however, these processes are not equal. For example, with the second definition for CHAOS(X), given that X includes tock, it is possible for the process to refuse passage of time, that is, the tock event, and then accept another event in X. With the first definition, however, if tock is refused, it is due to the internal choice of **STOP**, after which, no further event is possible. In the failures model, we cannot distinguish behaviour based on prior refusals, and so, as said, the two definitions are the same.

The least refined tock-CSP process can nondeterministically decide to accept or refuse any event, including tock, so that it can nondeterministically decide to accept or refuse passage of time as well. This process is TCHAOS(X) = (|~| e : X @ e -> TCHAOS(X)) |~| **STOP**, given that X includes tock. For convenience, instead of assuming the inclusion of tock in X, we define TCHAOS(X) as follows.

```
1    TCHAOS(X) = let
2                    TC(X) = (|~| e : X @ e -> TC(X)) |~|  USTOP
3                    within
4                        TC( union(X,{tock}))
```

Here **USTOP** is the process that refuses all events, including tock.

This definition, however, is not efficient for model checking with FDR. It has a high-degree of nondeterminism, but mostly importantly, the way in which FDR compiles this process is inefficient. This is a technicality, but instead, we use

[9] robostar.cs.york.ac.uk/case_studies/segway.
[10] cocotec.io/fdr/manual/cspm/definitions.html#timed-sections.

the definition TCHAOS(X) = CHAOS(X) /\ (**USTOP** |~| tock -> TCHAOS(X)), which is equivalent, but more efficient in model checking. Here, the possibility of accepting or refusing passage of time is factored out of the specification of the behaviour in regards to the other events. In this definition of TCHAOS(X), the possibility of a tock event is added explicitly, rather than by inclusion of tock in X.

The nondeterministic behaviour of MSpec can be interrupted (/\ on line 12) by a communication on Segway::angle.in?x, defined using the prefixing operator (->) of CSP and where x subsequently takes the value communicated. The communication Segway::angle.in?x specifies that the interruption can arise from any event Segway::angle.in.v for the channel Segway::angle. If x is outside the range defined by the constants -maxAngle and maxAngle (line 14), then the behaviour is that of MStop sequentially composed (;) with MSpec (line 15), otherwise the behaviour is given by the recursion on MSpec (line 16).

The process MStop (line 21) is defined similarly. Initially it is prepared to engage nondeterministically in events tock and those corresponding to interactions with the robotic platform, except for events representing communications over the channels Segway::setLeftMotorSpeedCall and Segway::setRightMotorSpeedCall, which model the calls to the corresponding operations of the robotic platform, namely, setLeftMotorSpeed and setRightMotorSpeed. This behaviour can be interrupted (/\) by a communication on either of these channels (lines 26–27) with value 0, but this must happen within 2 time units. The order of the communications is irrelevant so their behaviour is specified as the interleaving (|||) of two prefixings that are followed by termination (**SKIP**). In CSP, termination of an interleaving requires termination of both processes, so the Deadline for the interleaving process to terminate is a deadline overall on both communications.

Verification of our property is then stated as a refinement **assertion** called P3 on line 38. It requires that the timed behaviour of the RoboChart module Segway **refines** the CSP$_M$ process MaxAngleStop **in the traces model**, which is adequate to reason about safety, namely to state that a deadline cannot be exceeded. In general, an implementation P **refines** a specification S, if, and only if, every behaviour of P is a behaviour permitted by S [33]. Here, behaviour is characterised by sets of traces, that is, sequences of events, in which a process can engage.

In the case of P3, the verification report indicates that it does not hold: the assertion is false. FDR, therefore, provides a counterexample. In Fig. 22 we show the result of debugging **timed assertion** P3 using FDR. On the left-hand side there is a graph-centric comparison of events that can be performed by the specification, on top, and the implementation, displayed below. With the specification selected, the complete counterexample trace is displayed on the right-hand side as a list under **Trace to Behaviour**.

In the trace shown, we can see that after an input represented by the event Segway::angle.in.-4, where −4 is outside the bounds defined by -maxAngle and MaxAngle, two further tock events take place (as well as other events, namely, Segway::rightMotorVelocity, Segway::leftMotorVelocity, and Segway::gyroZ) before Segway::setLeftMotorSpeedCall and Segway::setRightMotorSpeedCall events take

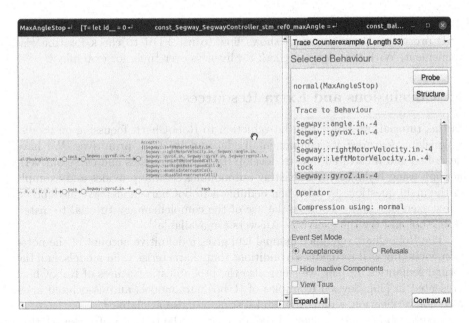

Fig. 22. Counterexample for **timed assertion** P3 under debug in FDR

place. On the left-side, we see that, after the events in this trace, the implementation is then prepared to perform a further tock event, highlighted in red. This is, however, not permitted by the specification as captured by the process MaxAngleStop. On the left-side, a set of channels indicates that several events can be performed by the specification, including Segway::setLeftMotorSpeedCall and Segway::setRightMotorSpeedCall event, but not a tock. Therefore, we can conclude from this analysis that the software can take more than two time units to stop the motors when the vertical angle is out of bounds.

The fact that the deadline 2 is violated could indicate an error in the design. If this were the case, the counterexample is useful to identify the cause of the problem and suggest the required changes to the RoboChart model. RoboTool, as mentioned, automatically (re)generates the semantics for the new model, and the assertions can be checked again. In the case of our example, we do not have a mistake. Our assertion is too strict in its choice of deadline.

> *Exercise 7.* Verify **timed assertion** P3 in FDR while using different values
> for the **Deadline**. Once the angle is outside the accepted bounds, what is
> the maximum time required by the software to set motors' speed to zero?

Using CSP, tock-CSP, and FDR, we can check for other notions of refinement, besides traces refinement. For untimed CSP processes, classical models include the failures and the failures-divergences model. Their refinement relations can be used to check, for instance, liveness properties and absence of livelock (divergence), which happens when a process can engage in an unbounded number of internal events, without ever interacting with its environment again. For tock-CSP processes, the work in [4] shows how to use FDR to check for timewise refinement. With that, we can check for liveness over time, for example.

5   Conclusions and Extra Resources

In this tutorial, we present an introduction to RoboChart, focussing on its distinguishing features: its component model and its time primitives. We have described and illustrated how to develop RoboChart models and carry out verification using RoboTool. An existing autonomous segway provides and example of the main questions to ask when defining a RoboChart model. We have posed a few exercises, and encourage the use of the complementary tutorial to install RoboTool and try the exercises. Answers are available[11].

The RoboChart reference manual [26] gives a definitive account of the notation, including well-formedness conditions that characterise valid models, and the formal semantics. In [26], we cover also the probabilistic features of RoboChart presented in [39]. Several examples of RoboChart models and associated artefacts for verification, simulation, and testing are also available[12].

Figure 23 gives an overview of the notations of the RoboStar framework that complement RoboChart. To cater for the operational requirements, covering assumptions about the platform and environment of the robotic system, we have RoboWorld [8], a controlled-natural language with a formal semantics compatible with that of RoboChart. Namely, the RoboWorld semantics is described in *CyPhyCircus* [27], a hybrid process algebra, based on the works in [20,21]. It is an extension of *Circus* [12], a process algebra that combines CSP [33] with Z [37] for modelling abstract data types and operations.

To describe simulations, we have RoboSim [11]. Like RoboChart, this is a diagrammatic notation, but it provides support to define models of the control software (d-model), and the physical attributes of a robotic platform (p-model) and of a scenario (s-model). Like a RoboChart model, a RoboSim d-model is platform independent, with the robotic platforms described by variables, events, and operations. Control flow is guided by the period of a simulation cycle, as well as by the events, with behaviours defined by state machines like in RoboChart.

A p-model describes the rigid body of the platform (links and joints), and its sensors and actuators [22] using block diagrams. Ongoing work is developing the notation to describe scenarios (as opposed to environments). A scenario determines a particular set of configurations (and evolutions) of the environment, rather than all possible such configurations and evolutions.

Ongoing work is also developing a model-transformation technique to produce RoboSim d-models by translation of a RoboChart model for the same platform. The produced d-models are correct by construction. The notion of correctness takes into account the discrepancies between the interruption-based and cycle-based design and simulation paradigms of RoboChart and RoboSim.

---

[11] robostar.cs.york.ac.uk/notations/.

[12] robostar.cs.york.ac.uk/case-studies.

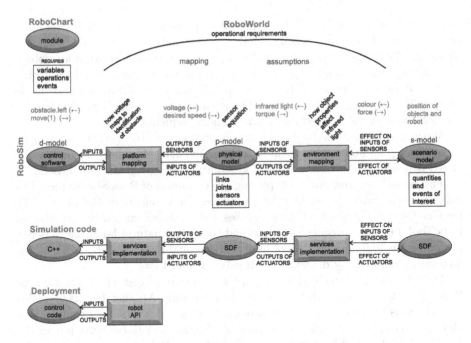

Fig. 23. RoboStar notations

A RoboSim p-model describes the sensors and actuators that can be used to realise the services of the robotic platform described in the d-model. A platform mapping captures this relationship. In Fig. 23, we indicate the example of a p-model that describes an infrared sensor whose output is a voltage. The platform mapping then defines how that voltage is used to define when an event obstacle, defined in the d-model (or RoboChart model), happens.

Similarly, the notation for RoboSim s-models is being designed to support the definition of the quantities and events of interest in a scenario, with an environment mapping defining how those quantities are perceived and affected by the sensors and actuators. In our example, the position of the robot and other objects determine the infrared light that can be perceived by the sensors.

The semantics of RoboSim is given by a combination of tock-CSP, the same process algebra used to defined the semantics of RoboChart, and *CyPhyCircus*. Alternative lines of work are considering the use of UPPAAL instead [40].

At the level of RoboChart and RoboWorld, a mapping is also necessary. As part of a RoboWorld document, as well as describing the assumptions about the environment, we define how the environment is perceived and affected by the services of the robotic platform in the RoboChart model. Future work will relate a RoboWorld model to a combination of a RoboSim p-model and s-model.

Automatic generation of simulation code from RoboSim models covers support for d-models (using C or C++ as a programming language), and for p-models, using an XML-based notation used by robotics simulators, notably,

SDF (Scene Description Format[13]). Importantly, the structure of RoboSim models is preserved in the simulation code that is automatically generated. This is in contrast with hand-written simulations, which are normally monolithic, embedding assumptions about the platform and environment that are undocumented or explicit in any way. In a RoboSim simulation, any assumptions are made explicit by the mappings and the (differential algebraic) equations that govern the behaviour of the platform and environment elements.

With this framework in place, any observations of the reality gap can be more easily pinpointed since assumptions are explicit. Whether the gap can be closed depends on the computational feasibility of more faithful simulations.

Future and ongoing work is exploring the extension of RoboStar to include a diagrammatic language to describe properties for verification: RoboCert. The plan is for a language that encompasses the facilities currently available in RoboTool, but also provides diagrams and controlled natural language to define properties, including properties of hybrid and probabilistic models. Work in this direction using activity diagrams is already advanced [36].

On the pragmatic side, we are exploring another layer of abstraction for RoboChart to capture architectures used in robotics. Another language, called RoboArch, is being designed to incorporate notions of layers, for example. The plan is to enable automatic generation of (sketches of) RoboChart models by transformation of architectural models described in RoboArch.

On the verification side, we plan to continue improvement of theorem proving facilities [15–17]. Experiments with hybrid model checkers are also under way, but require encoding processes using networks of automata. With this semantic framework, we can explore the extension of the testing facilities of RoboStar [9]. Ambitious plans are also considering support for RoboChart models that include neural network components [3], RoboWorld documents that describe user behaviour, and associated system-level verification techniques.

An overview of the workflow supported by the RoboStar notations and approach and extra examples are available in [7].

Acknowledgements. The work reported here is funded by the Royal Academy of Engineering grant CiET1718/45, UK EPSRC grants EP/M025756/1 and EP/R025479/1, and UKRI TAS programme (verifiability and resilience). We are grateful to the ICTAC organisers for the opportunity to present and write this tutorial. We also thank Augusto Sampaio for very helpful and detailed comments. Finally, we are grateful to all members of the RoboStar group, who directly or indirectly contribute to the realisation of the vision described here.

References

1. ISO/IEC 13568:2002. Information technology - Z formal specification notation - syntax, type system and semantics. International Standard
2. Arthan, R., Jones, R.B.: Z in HOL in ProofPower. FACS FACTS **2005**(1), 39–55 (2005). www.bcs.org/upload/pdf/facts200503-compressed.pdf

---

[13] sdformat.org.

3. Attala, Z., Cavalcanti, A.L.C., Woodcock, J.C.P.: A comparison of neural network tools for the verification of linear specifications of ReLU networks. In: Albarghouthi, A., Katz, G., Narodytska, N. (eds.) 3rd Workshop on Formal Methods for ML-Enabled Autonomous System, pp. 22–33 (2020)
4. Baxter, J., Ribeiro, P., Cavalcanti, A.L.C.: Sound reasoning in tock-CSP. Acta Informatica (2021). online April 2021
5. Burdy, L., et al.: An overview of JML tools and applications. Softw. Tools Technol. Transfer **7**(3), 212–232 (2005)
6. Cavalcanti, A.L.C.: RoboStar modelling stack: tackling the reality gap. In: 1st International Workshop on Verification of Autonomous & Robotic Systems, VARS 2021. Association for Computing Machinery (2021)
7. Cavalcanti, A.L.C., et al.: RoboStar Technology: A Roboticist's Toolbox for Combined Proof, Simulation, and Testing, pp. 249–293. Springer (2021)
8. Cavalcanti, A., Baxter, J., Carvalho, G.: RoboWorld: where can my robot work? In: Calinescu, R., Păsăreanu, C.S. (eds.) SEFM 2021. LNCS, vol. 13085, pp. 3–22. Springer, Cham (2021). https://doi.org/10.1007/978-3-030-92124-8_1
9. Cavalcanti, A., Baxter, J., Hierons, R.M., Lefticaru, R.: Testing Robots Using CSP. In: Beyer, D., Keller, C. (eds.) TAP 2019. LNCS, vol. 11823, pp. 21–38. Springer, Cham (2019). https://doi.org/10.1007/978-3-030-31157-5_2
10. Cavalcanti, A.L.C., Dongol, B., Hierons, R., Timmis, J., Woodcock, J.C.P. (eds.) Software Engineering for Robotics. Springer International Publishing (2021)
11. Cavalcanti, A.L.C., et al.: Verified simulation for robotics. Sci. Comput. Programm. **174**, 1–37 (2019)
12. Cavalcanti, A.L.C., Sampaio, A.C.A., Woodcock, J.C.P.: A refinement strategy for Circus. Formal Aspects Comput. **15**(2–3), 146–181 (2003)
13. Chen, J., Gauci, M., Gross, R.: A strategy for transporting tall objects with a swarm of miniature mobile robots. In: 2013 IEEE International Conference on Robotics and Automation, pp. 863–869. IEEE (2013)
14. Davies, J.: Using CSP, pp. 64–122. Springer (2006)
15. Foster, S., Baxter, J., Cavalcanti, A.L.C., Woodcock, J.C.P., Zeyda, F.: Unifying semantic foundations for automated verification tools in Isabelle/UTP. Sci. Comput. Programm. **197** (2020)
16. Foster, S., Cavalcanti, A.L.C., Canham, S., Woodcock, J.C.P., Zeyda, F.: Unifying theories of reactive design contracts. Theoret. Comput. Sci. **802**, 105–140 (2020)
17. Foster, S., Ye, K., Cavalcanti, A.L.C., Woodcock, J.C.P.: Automated verification of reactive and concurrent programs by calculation. J. Logical Algebraic Methods Programm. **121**, 100681 (2021)
18. Gibson-Robinson, T., Armstrong, P., Boulgakov, A., Roscoe, A.W.: FDR3 - a modern refinement checker for CSP. In: Tools and Algorithms for the Construction and Analysis of Systems, pp. 187–201 (2014)
19. Hayes, I.J., Utting, M.: A sequential real-time refinement calculus. Acta Informatica **37**(6), 385–448 (2001)
20. Jifeng, H.: From CSP to Hybrid Systems. In: A Classical Mind, pp. 171–189. Prentice-Hall (1994)
21. Liu, J., Lv, J., Quan, Z., Zhan, N., Zhao, H., Zhou, C., Zou, L.: A calculus for hybrid CSP. In: Ueda, K. (ed.) APLAS 2010. LNCS, vol. 6461, pp. 1–15. Springer, Heidelberg (2010). https://doi.org/10.1007/978-3-642-17164-2_1
22. Miyazawa, A., Cavalcanti, A.L.C., Ahmadi, S., Post, M., Timmis, J.: RoboSim Physical Modelling: Diagrammatic Physical Robot Models. Technical report, University of York, Department of Computer Science, York, UK (2020). robostar.cs.york.ac.uk/notations/

23. Miyazawa, A., Ribeiro, P., Li, W., Cavalcanti, A.L.C., Timmis, J.: Automatic property checking of robotic applications. In: IEEE/RSJ International Conference on Intelligent Robots and Systems, pp. 3869–3876 (2017)

24. Miyazawa, A., Ribeiro, P., Li, W., Cavalcanti, A.L.C., Timmis, J., Woodcock, J.C.P.: RoboChart: a State-Machine Notation for Modelling and Verification of Mobile and Autonomous Robots. Technical report, University of York, Department of Computer Science, York, UK (2016). www.cs.york.ac.uk/circus/publications/techreports/reports/MRLCTW16.pdf

25. Miyazawa, A., Ribeiro, P., Li, W., Cavalcanti, A., Timmis, J., Woodcock, J.: RoboChart: modelling and verification of the functional behaviour of robotic applications. Softw. Syst. Modeling 18(5), 3097–3149 (2019). https://doi.org/10.1007/s10270-018-00710-z

26. Miyazawa, A., et al.: RoboChart: Modelling, Verification and Simulation for Robotics. Technical report, University of York, Department of Computer Science, York, UK (2020). www.cs.york.ac.uk/robostar/notations/

27. Foster, S., Huerta y Munive, J.J., Struth, G.: Differential hoare logics and refinement calculi for hybrid systems with Isabelle/HOL. In: Fahrenberg, U., Jipsen, P., Winter, M. (eds.) RAMiCS 2020. LNCS, vol. 12062, pp. 169–186. Springer, Cham (2020). https://doi.org/10.1007/978-3-030-43520-2_11

28. Naylor, B., Read, M., Timmis, J., Tyrrell, A.: The Relay Chain: A Scalable Dynamic Communication link between an Exploratory Underwater Shoal and a Surface Vehicle (2014)

29. OMG. OMG Systems Modeling Language (OMG SysML), Version 1.3 (2012)

30. OMG. OMG Unified Modeling Language (2015)

31. Park, H.W., Ramezani, A., Grizzle, J.W.: A finite-state machine for accommodating unexpected large ground-height variations in bipedal robot walking. IEEE Trans. Rob. 29(2), 331–345 (2013)

32. Rabbath, C.A.: A finite-state machine for collaborative airlift with a formation of unmanned air vehicles. J. Intell. Robot. Syst. 70(1), 233–253 (2013)

33. Roscoe, A.W.: Understanding Concurrent Systems. Texts in Computer Science. Springer (2011)

34. Tomic, T., Schmid, K., Lutz, P., Domel, A., Kassecker, M., Mair, E., Grixa, I.L., Ruess, F., Suppa, M., Burschka, D.: Toward a fully autonomous UAV: research platform for indoor and outdoor urban search and rescue. IEEE Robot. Autom. Mag. 19(3), 46–56 (2012)

35. University of York. RoboChart Reference Manual. www.cs.york.ac.uk/circus/RoboCalc/robotool/

36. Lindoso, W., Nogueira, S.C., Domingues, R., Lima, L.: Visual specification of properties for robotic designs. In: Campos, S., Minea, M. (eds.) SBMF 2021. LNCS, vol. 13130, pp. 34–52. Springer, Cham (2021). https://doi.org/10.1007/978-3-030-92137-8_3

37. Woodcock, J.C.P., Davies, J.: Using Z - Specification, Refinement, and Proof. Prentice-Hall (1996)

38. Woodcock, J., Foster, S., Mota, A., Ye, K.: RoboStar Technology: Modelling Uncertainty in RoboChart Using Probability. In: Software Engineering for Robotics, pp. 413–465. Springer, Cham (2021). https://doi.org/10.1007/978-3-030-66494-7_13

39. Ye, K., Cavalcanti, A., Foster, S., Miyazawa, A., Woodcock, J.: Probabilistic modelling and verification using RoboChart and PRISM. Softw. Syst. Model. 21(2), 667–716 (2021). https://doi.org/10.1007/s10270-021-00916-8

40. Zhang, M., Du, D., Sampaio, A.C.A., Cavalcanti, A.L.C., Conserva Filho, M., Zhang, M.: Transforming RoboSim Models into UPPAAL. In: 15th International Symposium on Theoretical Aspects of Software Engineering, pp. 71–78. IEEE (2021)

Formal Methods Adoption in Industry: An Experience Report

Benjamin Tyler[✉]

Department of Computer Science, School of Engineering and Digital Sciences,
Nazarbayev University, Astana 010000, Kazakhstan
btyler@nu.edu.kz

Abstract. While formal methods provide powerful means by which designers can show that their systems meet specific requirements, industry has been slow to adopt them. The need for users to learn specialized languages and have a firm grasp of mathematical logic are primary hurdles to such adoption. Even though formal verification tools can make the process less tedious and reduce human error, they generally still require guidance from humans with specialized knowledge.

In this report, the author's experiences working for a small business are presented, which involved the development and promotion of formal methods tools for public and government agencies. It is notable that the end users of these tools were not necessarily specialists, and often had little to no prior experience with formal methods. Here, we specifically look at the general-purpose design language that was used for modeling, the development of intuitive graphics-based tools to make the system design task easier, and how automated model checking was applied to the resulting system models. We discuss the interactions with and feedback from clients regarding these tools, and in the conclusion make some suggestions regarding their adoption.

Keywords: Formal methods in industry · Systems level design languages · Automated model checking · Formal methods adoption

1 Introduction

1.1 Formal Methods: A Reluctance to Adopt

With the increase in complexity of today's software and hardware systems, issues of correctness, reliability, and robustness have posed serious challenges to both designers and developers. Traditionally, testing techniques have been used to find functional errors, as well as to determine system limitations under stress. While testing processes are relatively easy to implement and execute, testing cannot guarantee the absence of errors, since only a finite number of cases can be checked. In systems where bugs can result in critical failure of the system, and it is infeasible or impractical to make fixes after deployment, testing can be complemented by *formal methods* [1]. Formal methods are techniques based on rigorous mathematical analysis that can show that a system under consideration will meet or could potentially violate formally specified requirements. While formal methods are quite powerful, industry has been slow to adopt such technologies given the high overhead and steep learning curve for their proper use [2].

© The author(s), under exclusive licence to Springer Nature Switzerland AG 2023
A. Cerone (Ed.): ICTAC 2021, LNCS 13490, pp. 152–161, 2023.
https://doi.org/10.1007/978-3-031-43678-9_5

One such formal method is the use of automated *model checking* [3]. Model checkers use a finite state model of a system to exhaustively check if given specifications will always hold. Systems that are composed of distributed interacting parts, or interact with external agents, and whose requirements are temporal in nature are often good candidates for model checking. Model checking has the advantage over many other formal methods approaches, such as automated proof assistants, in that the underlying verification process does not require direct guidance from the user.

Model checking, however, has its own challenges. An abstraction of the parts of the system to be verified generally needs to be created, since model checkers require a finite state model. This requires a balance between maintaining fidelity to the original system, while dispensing with details that may not be as relevant to the properties to be verified. Furthermore, even if such an abstraction can be found, the number of possible states could still be too large for an automated tool to process in a reasonable amount of time – the *state space explosion problem* [4].

While some systems do not lend themselves to such abstractions or are relatively deterministic in their execution and use (and thus not well suited for temporal specification), many interesting safety-critical systems *are* good candidates for model checking. Unfortunately, model checking is still not often used in such cases because of the perceived high overhead in adoption of such technologies that have a formal flavor.

1.2 Organization of the Report

This report focuses on the author's experiences in the development and use of formal approaches to system modeling and verification while working in industry. In the following section, the company and its core modeling capabilities will be introduced. Then, the formal design language that the company helped develop, Rosetta, will be described in some detail. We will then discuss the approach that was used in implementing Rosetta and its simulation-based system evaluation capabilities. Then, we will look at the three separate iterations of model checking capabilities that were developed for the company's design tools – two for Rosetta, and one for a heavily constrained subset of Java.

Throughout the report, we will highlight the practical aspects of actually using these tools, both through the eyes of the company's engineers and through the eyes of its customers. At the conclusion of the report, suggestions for promoting the practical adoption of formal methods in industry are provided following these experiences.

2 Company Background

From 2007 to 2011, the author worked for a small business in the United States whose main customers were local and U.S. federal agencies, including departments of the military. Many of the company's contracts were through the Small Business Innovative Research (SBIR) program of the U.S. government, which supports small businesses involved in research and development activities. The company would answer proposal calls from these agencies, and if awarded a project, the customer's primary investment would be in R&D activities that would lead to a prototype. If the customer deemed that the given solution was promising, then significant follow-on funding could be awarded, with the final goal being commercialization of the developed product.

2.1 System Modeling and Simulation Framework

One of the flagship products that the company developed was a generic design framework that allows users to create hierarchical models of systems using a block-diagram editor, and then evaluate them via simulations or performing some other analyses on the models. The design editor of the framework allows users to define structural relationships between components of the system through a graphical, drag-and-drop, user interface, shown in Fig. 1.

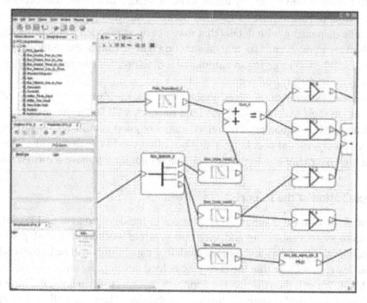

Fig. 1. Screenshot of the framework

In the framework, high-level components can be constructed from interconnected lower-level component blocks, and the user can easily navigate between the levels. Behaviors of the individual components can also be attached to the blocks using a variety of supported languages, such as Java.

Users of the framework would generally create models of systems on which they could perform standard validation and analysis. For a given design project, a user would often create a library of low-level "atomic" components that can be used and reused throughout the system design. Such an approach allows for rapid prototyping and trade-off analysis. Several different modes of simulation were developed, including single simulations with playback capability, and randomized Monte Carlo Simulation. Additional features include animations of the system components during simulation and graphical visualizations of results.

In this report, however, we will focus on how we extended these analysis capabilities to also include model checking. Before this was possible, though, we needed a more formal language to define our component behaviors in the framework. For this, we chose Rosetta.

3   Our Use of Formal Methods

3.1   The Rosetta Modeling Language

The modeling language that we used was the Rosetta System-Level Design Language [5]. Development of Rosetta started in 1997, primarily from the hardware design community, who were looking to generalize hardware description languages such as VHDL [6] into a form that could be used to model a wide variety of systems. Such a language would not only be able to model hardware and software, but should be generic enough to model conceptual systems like human organizations, supply chains, and decision processes. Furthermore, the language should allow for different, but potentially interrelated aspects to be modeled for the same system.

The primary building-block in Rosetta is the `facet` construct, which is similar to the idea of classes or modules in other languages in that they have internal state that generally changes over time [7]. A `facet` definition includes how this state may change using logical assertions which are written in a constraint language that uses a Hindley-Milner type system and unification. However, for practical purposes, these constraints were generally written in a way similar to assignments in imperative languages. In addition, different `facets` of a system can interact with one another directly through input and output connections, and `facets` can contain other `facets` as part of their internal structure.

To facilitate the use of Rosetta across many different modeling domains, the language also includes `domain` constructs, which can be used to define the underlying semantics of a given `facet` in your model [7]. In practice, the main `domains` that are used define how the passage of time is viewed within your model, the most common being the

```
facet oneBitAdder(input1::in bit; input2::in bit;
                  carryIn::in bit; output::out bit;
                  carryOut::out bit) is static
      sum::bit is input1 xor input2;
  begin
    term1: output = sum xor carryIn;
    term2: carryOut = (sum and carryIn) or (input1 and input2);
  end oneBitAdder;

facet fourBitAdder(input1::in bitvector[4];
                   input2::in bitvector[4];
                   output::out bitvector[4]) is cycle_based
      cr::bitvector[3];
  begin
    a1: oneBitAdder(input1[0], input2[0],   0  , cr[0], output'[0]);
    a2: oneBitAdder(input1[1], input2[1], cr[0], cr[1], output'[1]);
    a3: oneBitAdder(input1[2], input2[2], cr[1], cr[2], output'[2]);
    a4: oneBitAdder(input1[3], input2[3], cr[2], cr[3], output'[3]);
  end fourBitAdder;
```

Fig. 2. Ripple-carry adder example in Rosetta

static, cycle_based, event_based, and continuous domains. A simple example of a model written in Rosetta is shown in Fig. 2.

What is perhaps the most interesting feature of Rosetta, however, is that you can combine different aspects (modeled by facets) of the same conceptual component, using the Rosetta component construct, even if the facets are from different domains. This is a critical feature of the language because real-world systems tend to be heterogeneous in nature. Furthermore, the interrelationships between these different facets could be directly specified in Rosetta using the interaction construct, which essentially provides the "glue" between them [7]. A conceptual diagram illustrating these related concepts is pictured in Fig. 3 below.

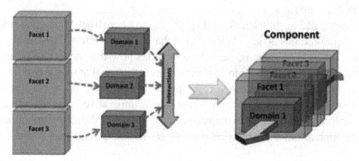

Fig. 3. Component modeled as a collection of interacting facets

3.2 Implementing Rosetta

During this time, there were two available implementations for the Rosetta Language: one developed by the System-Level Design Group (SLDG) led by Prof. Perry Alexander at the University of Kansas, and the other developed in-house at our company. Both toolsets supported the kernel language syntax which was well established at that time, which included facets, components, and domains. In addition to syntactic and static semantic checking, the tools supported model *evaluation* – a validity check on the assertions within the facets against a given internal state, as well as *execution* – essentially simulation of the models. The Rosetta tools also supported *elaboration* – the process by which user-created domains syntactically transform facets into behaviorally equivalent facets which are of built-in domains. User-created domain definitions are essentially reflective in nature, in that they allow for direct access to the syntactic structure of the facets that use them in the form of abstract syntax trees.

At that time, however, there were still discussions between the SLDG and our group about how to best approach interactions from both a syntactic and elaboration standpoint. From our own experiences, we had found that although the approach used for implementing domain elaboration was very powerful, it was very difficult to implement domains that did significantly more than what was provided in the built-in domains.

This left us with the issue of interactions, which were an order-of-magnitude more complex than domains. Using the same approach as with domains was problematic, and so both groups tried slightly different approaches. The SLDG group took a pragmatic approach, where the domain and interaction constructs allowed for embedded Haskell code to be used instead of pure Rosetta, as their underlying toolset was implemented in Haskell. We took a different approach, since we were a commercial and not an academic enterprise and wanted to focus on usability for our customers. We did not want to require our customers to learn a secondary language (e.g., Haskell) to use Rosetta in the first place, so while we kept the same reflective approach of allowing for the modification of abstract syntax trees in interactions, any new domains or interactions that would be needed by our customers were simply implemented as part of the built-in libraries. This had the additional benefit of being much more efficient and easier to debug when it came time to simulate the models.

3.3   Rosetta Modeling in Practice

While those within the company understood the benefits of the use of formal modeling languages such as Rosetta and their associated tools, many of our potential customers were not so familiar. While a few people we interacted with knew about such technologies (notably those who were involved in hardware design), most others were not. Whether or not they had a technical background, they generally approached such things from a business standpoint. The main thing we needed to do is to establish how our solutions were preferable to existing solutions – not only that they were more effective, but that the cost of adoption would not outweigh the benefits. In practice, what this generally meant is that visits to potential customers should not be completely undertaken by technical persons, but also have those who are more business-minded and can see the "big picture" of how formal methods can be beneficial to the customer.

To get an idea about how Rosetta was primarily used at the outset, here are three exemplars that demonstrate the range of the language:

Computer Hardware Systems. Rosetta largely was conceived and initially developed by those from the hardware community, and as such, many of the first large-scale Rosetta models were of parts of microprocessors, some spanning over a thousand lines of modeling code. It was not uncommon for someone to convert an already-existing VHDL (Very High-Speed Integrated Circuit Hardware Description Language) [6] model into Rosetta. For these models, we always used the cycle_based domain. We primarily used these models to simulate the hardware, but also added capabilities to monitor state coverage (essentially through logging) for coverage testing.

Because the customers were very knowledgeable of hardware design and languages such as VHDL, they had very little problem in understanding Rosetta. They saw that the tool and GUI-based modeling support that was provided was very useful. We did not try at this point to model orthogonal properties of such systems (e.g., thermal properties, energy draw, etc.), though the customers understood the benefits of doing so.

Physical Systems and Devices. Beyond low-level hardware systems, we also modeled a variety of physical things, most notably a wide range of military vehicles (including land, sea, and air vehicles), as well as hardware devices ranging from radios and avionics systems. A very common application would be to model something that could be built using a variety of different components and subcomponents, and then create a library of said components so that the user could try out different configurations. The use of different components would result in different capabilities and attributes of the system (including cost and weight), and then a cost-benefit analysis could be done.

What was interesting about our use of Rosetta here is that we could easily provide the individual models of the components to the customer, and they could simply use the graphical block-diagram editor to create and evaluate different configurations. Customers really liked this capability and found the whole framework we were providing beneficial, and they did not really have to understand Rosetta. However, after some saw the possibilities, they became more interested in creating and customizing at the Rosetta level.

Human-based Systems. Perhaps one of the most interesting applications of Rosetta is when we started investigating its use in modeling human systems, such as business organizations, business processes, and human networks of information and influence. As before, we had found that features such as the more GUI-based, block-diagram editor was much more attractive than trying to market the Rosetta technology that was essentially embedded in the models, but not directly visible to the user. This was fine when we used standard graphical modeling notations, such as BPMN (Business Process Model and Notation) [8], as there was little need for customer customization of the individual component blocks, where we would do analysis based on features such as cost, throughput and time. However, we would often have to add custom attributes in the Rosetta code across many of the component blocks in the component library to see the impact of other factors, such as reliability or likelihood of failure at a given point. Here, we also made use of the `event_based domain`, and would sometimes run Monte Carlo simulations on the systems.

3.4 Model Checking – Rosetta and Java

The next step that we wanted to take with our toolset was to add the capability of verifying the correctness of Rosetta models against specifications. Such a capability was very desirable to customers who dealt with mission critical systems. While most of them were initially unfamiliar with model checking, we characterized it as an automated approach that could give the same assurances as exhaustive testing, which is often not feasible in practice.

While the Rosetta assertion language could express temporal properties, Rosetta models and the simulator were based on a deterministic view of execution. Checking adherence to such a property for a single simulation run was simple, but how could we show correctness across all possible inputs and initial model configurations? Furthermore, how could we model different actions that might take place *during* the simulation? To address these issues, we did two things; (1) added nondeterministic ranged value assignment to Rosetta, and (2) developed a model checking capability for `cycle_based` models that had a finite possible number of states. Since Rosetta allows for the use of finite sets as types, creating good model-checkable models was not so difficult. We discuss in more detail how to go about modeling fairly complex systems in Rosetta for facilitating model checking in [9].

We did not create our own back-end model checking engine, however, but utilized the popular SPIN model checker [10]. Our tools would automatically translate our Rosetta models into equivalent Promela (the modeling language used by SPIN), and then run SPIN on the translated models. We chose SPIN primarily because we had developed prior capabilities around the language and knew that SPIN was quite robust.

After performing some proof-of-concept experiments with simple models – essentially discrete pursuer-evader problems, we then applied our Rosetta model checker on models of missile defense strategies. Without going into detail, such problems can be characterized as scheduling and resource allocation problems. Our approach gave acceptable results, but it required manually slicing/partitioning our models so that the model checker would not run out of memory before rendering a result. The primary problem could be seen when we inspected the underlying translation, which had to add a layer of complexity to the resulting Promela models which caused an explosion of the state space, especially when having to deal with nondeterminism.

Due to these issues, we then proceeded to create a second Rosetta model checker, this one using the nuSMV model checker [11] for the back end. One major advantage is that the syntax and semantic of nuSMV is much more like Rosetta, as its models are composed of interconnected components, state change actions within the components are stated declaratively, and time is modeled as discrete steps. The underlying translation was much cleaner using this approach, and the resulting missile defense models were checkable, and so we went forward with this solution.

When trying to convince potential customers about using our toolset for system verification purposes, there was still some unease about the need for them to learn Rosetta in the first place to do their own modeling. If all they were concerned about is system verification, why not learn a much more established language such as Promela or nuSMV? The main value added for using our tools was that many other different features were available via the block-diagram editor, including a variety of simulation and visualization options.

This led us to our third model checking development effort, where we translated component behaviors encoded in Java instead of Rosetta, into nuSMV. Our company already had the capability to create simulation models using the block-diagram editor, where the individual components' state and behavior were encoded in Java, so this did not require major changes in our available tools. Limitations had to be placed on what could be used as types in the Java models – basically booleans, enumerations and annotated integers which would have to state a limited range. We realized that the results may not be as good as those achieved using nuSMV, but most of our customers were familiar with Java, and were not as intimidated as they were with Rosetta.

The primary models that we created and checked using this approach were on-board UAV sensor systems which could detect stabilization problems and try to recover if one of the sensors failed. Our constrained Java model checker did very well for this task, but what was interesting to us is that the customers were most intrigued by the visualization capability that was provided that could show a color-coded representation of the model's state as it executed, which could be used to represent a potential execution path leading to failure of a constraint. (In our case, total loss of control of the UAV.)

After experimenting more with this model checker, we made some small additions to allow Java modelers to annotate state fields in the components so that they would be ignored by the model checker, thus giving us a way to abstract away certain details that we may consider irrelevant during verification, but not simulation.

4   Conclusions

In trying to get potential customers to initially "buy in" to formal methods, it is key that they understand their overall benefits in comparison to more empirical validation techniques such as testing. To overcome this, it is much more expedient and effective to compare formal methods to other approaches and technologies that they may be familiar with, instead of getting overly technical about what they do, and how they do it.

Another hurdle in adoption is that it can be difficult to effectively and accurately represent a system to be developed in a form that is usable by the formal software tools. There are numerous such domain-specific modeling languages that have been developed, but which are not appropriate for other domains. General purpose modeling languages such as Rosetta can be used for this, but they may either lack the needed expressiveness, or may be difficult to learn for non-specialists (Rosetta falls into the latter category.)

We found that potential users gravitate more towards solutions that do not require a lot of time to initially learn and use basic capabilities. This can be greatly facilitated by GUI-based tools that allow users to model systems through a drag-and-drop interface, where they can either use already provided components (which is feasible for particular domain areas), or easily create their own. Once their value is quickly established, users are then encouraged to dig deeper, and possibly learn more about the underlying modeling formalisms. In this same vein, if formal verification is part of your solution, then automation in some form is extremely helpful, such as with model checkers.

References

1. Bowen, J.P., Hinchey, M.G.: Formal Methods. In: Tucker, A.B., Jr. (eds.), Computer Science Handbook, 2nd edn, Section XI, Software Engineering, Chapter 106, pp. 106-1–106-25, Chapman & Hall / CRC Press, ACM (2004)
2. Davis, J.A., Clark, M., Cofer, D., Fifarek, A., Hinchman, J., Hoffman, J., Hulbert, B., Miller, S.P., Wagner, L.: Study on the Barriers to the Industrial Adoption of Formal Methods. In: Pecheur, C., Dierkes, M. (eds.) FMICS 2013. LNCS, vol. 8187, pp. 63–77. Springer, Heidelberg (2013). https://doi.org/10.1007/978-3-642-41010-9_5
3. Emerson, E.A.: The Beginning of Model Checking: A Personal Perspective. In: Grumberg, O., Veith, H. (eds.) 25 Years of Model Checking. LNCS, vol. 5000, pp. 27–45. Springer, Heidelberg (2008). https://doi.org/10.1007/978-3-540-69850-0_2
4. Clarke, E.M., Klieber, W., Nováček, M., Zuliani, P.: Model checking and the state explosion problem. In: Meyer, B., Nordio, M. (eds.) LASER 2011. LNCS, vol. 7682, pp. 1–30. Springer, Heidelberg (2012). https://doi.org/10.1007/978-3-642-35746-6_1
5. Alexander, P., Kamath, R., Barton, D.: System specification in Rosetta. ECBS **2000**, 299–307 (2000)
6. Barker, D.: Requirements modeling technology: a vision for better, faster, and cheaper systems. In: VHDL International Users Forum (VIUF '00), pp. 3–6 (2000)
7. Alexander, P.: System Level Design with Rosetta. Morgan Kaufmann Publishers (2006)
8. White, S.A.: Process modeling notations and workflow patterns. Workflow Handb. **2004**, 265–294 (2004)

9. Tyler, B., Langdon, A., Chawla, P.: Formal verification of layered sensing architectures. In: 2010 IEEE National Aerospace & Electronics Conference (NAECON), pp. 41–44 (2010)
10. Holzmann, G.J.: The Spin Model Checker: Primer and Reference Manual, Addison-Wesley (2004)
11. Cimatti, A., Clarke, E.M., Giunchiglia, F., Roveri, M.: NUSMV: a new symbolic model verifier. In: CAV '99 Proceedings of the 11th International Conference on Computer Aided Verification, pp. 495–499 (1999)

Security Research: Program Analysis Meets Security

Padmanabhan Krishnan[(✉)]

Oracle Labs, Brisbane, QLD 4000, Australia
paddy.krishnan@oracle.com

Abstract. In this paper we present the key features of some of the security analysis tools developed at Oracle, Labs. These include Parfait, a static analyser, Affogato a dynamic analysis based on run-time instrumentation of Node.js applications and Gelato a dynamic analysis tool that inspects only the client-side code written in JavaScript. We show the how these tools can be integrated at different phases of the software development life-cycle. This paper is based on the presentation at the ICTAC school in 2021.

1 Motivation

Cloud-based execution of large applications enables consumers to buy services as-and-when it is required without investing in expensive infrastructure. The challenge of ensuring that such services are always secure and available is shifted to the provider of the cloud services. There is no doubt that the attack surface associated with cloud-based services is larger than that for on-premise based execution. Cloud services can be sub-divided into infrastructure as a service (IaaS), platform as a service (PaaS), and software as a service (SaaS).

From a SaaS or application security perspective, security breaches aim to steal data. That is, the customers' data (e.g., credit card information, health records) is valuable. It is the cloud provider's responsibility to protect customer's data. So information security is one of the main guarantees that the customer is looking for. Secure information flow is one way to ensure that the customer's data-protection requirements are satisfied. Software security provides a variety of mechanisms to ensure proper information flow is enforced. One can detect improper information flows at different levels of the infrastructure and software stack. For instance, firewalls can be used to detect and prevent improper flows at the network level while RASP solutions can provide application specific protection.

The research questions our group addresses are as follows.

- What are the security issues that matter? Can we identify vulnerabilities that when exploited have high impact? Can we detect and prevent 0-day attacks?
- How can one leverage different program analysis concepts to detect security vulnerabilities?

A. Cerone (Ed.): ICTAC 2021, LNCS 13490, pp. 162–168, 2023.
https://doi.org/10.1007/978-3-031-43678-9_6

– What are the tradeoffs when handling industrial scale systems? For instance, how can a single application that uses different technologies be analysed?

In this paper we discuss some of the solutions and challenges towards ensuring applications are secure. That is, we describe techniques that check the applications have the correct behaviour. This has to be linked with the desired information-flow security. We focus only on *integrity* (i.e., is data coming from untrusted sources deemed to be safe) and *confidentiality* (i.e., is data released only to the proper entities) [9]. The analysis of other properties such as non-repudiation, and availability is beyond the scope of this paper.

Ideally, we would like to mitigate all risks. Hence a defense-in-depth approach is adopted. We check for a wide variety of potential security vulnerabilities (e.g., OWASP Top 10). We do not restrict our attention to only exploitable vulnerabilities. For instance, SQL injection can be used to violate both integrity (by inserting malicious values) and confidentiality (by exfiltrating sensitive values) requirements. To prevent potential attacks, we check if user-controllable data is sanitised and if any value returned by security-sensitive states is declassified.

In the next section we describe our tools based on a decomposition of the structure of applications and the software development life-cycle.

2   Approach

All modern applications can be abstracted into client-side (i.e., behaviour seen via the browser) and server-side (i.e., behaviour executed by servers which are not directly accessible to the client) sub-systems. Most client-side behaviour is written in JavaScript and executed by the browser. There is diversity in server-side code and such code includes Java, Python, C, and C++. Towards deploying our tool, we adopt a simplified software development process which is shown in Fig. 1.

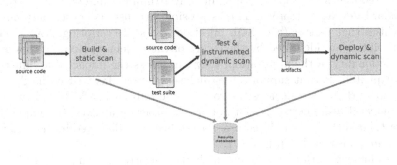

Fig. 1. Simplified Software Development Process

Given the complexity of these systems, we support two main strategies to detect potential security vulnerabilities. These are as follows.

- Static analysis (also called SAST or static application software testing) where the source code is analysed. Here we do not need the entire working system as the source code is not executed. Our approach also supports the analysis of partial code; i.e., the entire codebase is not required.
- Dynamic analysis (also called DAST or dynamic application software testing). If the source code is available, we can instrument it at a high-level while if the source code is not available where we can perform low-level instrumentation. In both cases we can have monitors that can observe the behaviour.

Various tools have been developed at Oracle Labs to improve automated detection of security vulnerabilities. These include Parfait, Affogato and Gelato and the key aspects of each of these tools is described below.

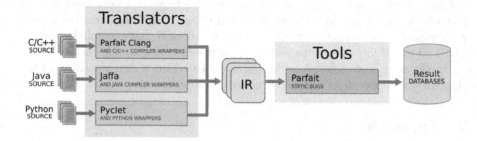

Fig. 2. High-level Architecture of Parfait

3 Parfait

Parfait [2,6] is a static analysis tool that focuses on high precision (90% true positive reports) and scalable (approximately 10 min per million lines of code on a standard developer laptop). This is possible because it focuses only on vulnerabilities that matter (e.g., SQL injection, cross-site scripting, XXE). These vulnerabilities are identified by the owner of the codebase. Because they know the functionality of the application, they can assess the impact if a vulnerability is exploited. Parfait supports the analysis of programs written in C, C++, Java and Python. It translates the source code into an LLVM IR [11] which is then analysed using customisations of classic program analysis techniques [12]. Figure 2 shows Parfait's architecture. Parfait has been deployed in the *Build and static scan* phase as shown in Fig. 1.

In summary, Parfait has a very high true positive rate and thus identifies actionable items. Parfait thus minimises developer effort in fixing issues reported by Parfait. Being a static analysis tool it can handle incomplete code. The usual challenges of static analysis (e.g., how to summarise the use of frameworks and reflection) remain. We are also working on incremental (e.g., commit time) analysis which will improve the scalability [10].

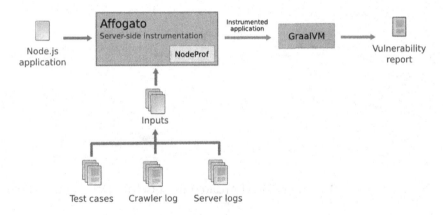

Fig. 3. High-level Architecture of Affogato

4 Affogato

Affogato [4] is an instrumentation-based dynamic analysis tool for Node.js. Affogato uses taint tracking and inference mechanisms to detect vulnerabilities. The precision and overheads can be tuned by controlling the exact behaviour of the taint analysis. As with any instrumentation-based analysis the overhead amortises for long runs but is high for short running tests. The high-level architecture of Affogato is shown in Fig. 3. Affogato can detect the usual injection attacks (such as SQL injection) and other specific vulnerabilities such information leakage. Affogato has been used in the *Test and instrumented dynamic scan* phase as shown in Fig. 1.

In summary, Affogato works on an running instance of the application. It relies on test cases to exercise the behaviour. The runtime overheads for long-running tests are acceptable. The main challenge is related to the effect of instrumentation. We need to ensure that the original semantics are preserved after instrumentation. As with any dynamic analysis, we have to reduce the runtime overheads introduced by extra code that has been introduced.

5 Gelato

Gelato [7] is a client-side analysis tool that does not rely on the availability of the server-side source code. The client-side JavaScript code is analysed and used to detect end-points exposed by the server. It also uses taint tracking and hence can detect DOM-XSS and reflected XSS. Figure 4 shows the high-level architecture of Gelato. Gelato is a state-aware crawler that uses a man-in-the-middle proxy to intercept traffic between the browser and server. This traffic is both instrumented and analysed to detect security issues. Gelato has been used in the *Deploy and dynamic scan* phase as shown in Fig. 1.

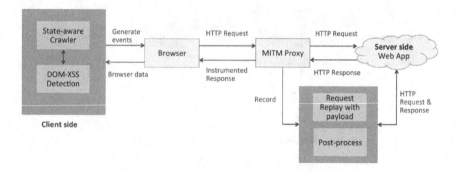

Fig. 4. High-level Architecture of Gelato

Gelato, like Affogato, works on a running instance. But unlike Affogato, Gelato does not require test-cases. By analysing the client-side code, Gelato mimics an external, real-world attacker. A key challenge is how to detect if Gelato is making progress without access to the server code. Without such knowledge, it is hard to estimate the coverage, say the percentage of endpoints that are actually detected, of the analysis. While integrating fuzzers might help, it is still difficult to get precise information.

6   Safe-PDF

Safe-PDF [8] uses the SAFE abstract-interpretation framework [13] to detect malicious JavaScript code in PDF documents. While abstract-interpretation can, in general, be expensive, it takes less than four seconds per document which is acceptable, say when scanning e-mail attachments. While Safe-PDF uses a static analysis technique, it can also be used when the application (say the mail system) is executing. The delay introduced by the analysis is not noticeable in a mail-delivery system.

Using abstract-interpretation allows Safe-PDF to go beyond detecting syntactic patterns. By using the semantics of the JavaScript code, Safe-PDF has very low false-positives. The main challenge is how to generalise this approach. For instance, what techniques are needed for other types of documents, e.g., MS-Office documents.

7   Future Work

Thus far our research has focused on preventing security vulnerabilities being introduced (at the coding level), check for potential violations of information-flow policies at the testing phase, and preventing attacks at run time (at the deployment and operations phases). Currently, our tools are run independent of each other.

But security analysis is like a game where the attacker has to find only one exploit while the defenders (e.g., the cloud service providers) have to protect against all possible attacks.

Real systems consist of different technologies including the use of many third party libraries. It is unrealistic to expect that a single tool that can handle all these technologies. Tools that focus on specific aspects are more effective in practice. Therefore, different tools are required to cover all security aspects. These tools generate different signals and it is important to combine them to have a single security view. This is what we call the Intelligent Application Security (IAS) [1]. It is our vision for the future. We envisage IAS as providing the necessary infrastructure that enables different security-analysis tools to share information and refine their analyses based on the input received from other tools. An initial step in this vision is described in [5] which combines the features of Affogato, Gelato and a fuzzing tool.

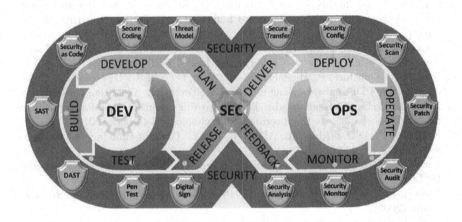

Fig. 5. DevSecOps Cycle

Our future research will address the tools needed to address all aspects within the DevSecOps [3] (see Fig. 5) process. DevSecOps is a continuous process designed to overcome silos in the development of large systems [14]. The challenge is that security needs to be considered at every stage. The role of various tools is shown in Fig. 5. While the tools presented in this paper address some of these phases (e.g., develop, build, test), we need to develop tools and techniques for other aspects such as security configuration, patching, audit etc.

Acknowledgements. This paper is reporting the work done by the entire team at Oracle Labs, Australia over many years. The author is thankful for their support in developing this paper.

References

1. Cifuentes, C.: Towards intelligent application security (invited talk). In: SOAP (2021)
2. Cifuentes, C., Keynes, N., Li, L., Hawes, N., Valdiviezo, M.: Transitioning Parfait into a development tool. IEEE Secur. Privacy **10**(3), 16–23 (2012)
3. Officer, D.D.C.I.: DoD enterprise devsecops reference design. Tech. rep, Department of Defense (2019)
4. Gauthier, F., Hassanshahi, B., Jordan, A.: AFFOGATO: runtime detection of injection attacks for node.js. In: Companion Proceedings for the ISSTA/ECOOP Workshops, pp. 94–99. ACM (2018)
5. Gauthier, F., Hassanshahi, B., Selwyn-Smith, B., Mai, T.N., Schlüter, M., Williams, M.: Experience: Model-Based, Feedback-Driven, Greybox Web Fuzzing with BackREST. In: European Conference on Object-Oriented Programming, ECOOP. LIPIcs, vol. 222, pp. 29:1–29:30. Schloss Dagstuhl - Leibniz-Zentrum für Informatik (2022)
6. Gauthier, F., Keynes, N., Allen, N., Corney, D., Krishnan, P.: Scalable static analysis to detect security vulnerabilities: Challenges and solutions. In: IEEE SecDev (2018)
7. Hassanshahi, B., Lee, H., Krishnan, P.: Gelato: Feedback-driven and guided security analysis of client-side web applications. In: SANER (2022)
8. Jordan, A., Gauthier, F., Hassanshahi, B., Zhao, D.: SAFE-PDF: robust detection of javascript PDF malware using abstract interpretation. Tech. rep, CoRR (2018)
9. Krishnan, P., Lu, Y., Raghavendra, K.R.: Detecting unauthorised information flows using points-to analysis. Engineering and Technology Reference (2016)
10. Krishnan, P., O'Donoghue, R., Allen, N., Lu, Y.: Commit-time incremental analysis. In: SOAP. ACM (2019)
11. Lattner, C., Adve, V.: The LLVM compiler framework and infrastructure tutorial. In: LCPC: Mini Workshop on Compiler Research Infrastructures (2004)
12. Nielson, F., Nielson, H.R., Hankin, C.: Principles of Program Analysis. Springer, 2 edn. (2005)
13. Park, J., Ryou, Y., Park, J., Ryu, S.: Analysis of Javascript web applications using SAFE 2.0. In: ICSE, pp. 59–62. IEEE Computer Society (2017)
14. Rajapakse, R.N., Zahedi, M., Babar, M.A., Shen, H.: Challenges and solutions when adopting devsecops: A systematic review. Information and Software Technology 141 (2022)

Author Index

© The Editor(s) (if applicable) and The Author(s), under exclusive license
to Springer Nature Switzerland AG 2023
A. Cerone (Ed.): ICTAC 2021, LNCS 13490, p. 169, 2023.
https://doi.org/10.1007/978-3-031-43678-9

Printed in the United States
by Baker & Taylor Publisher Services